17 Italian Greats in Sports and Italian Insights

By Al Bruno

NFB Publishing
Buffalo, New York

Copyright © 2020, 2022, 2023 Al Bruno

Printed in the United States of America

17 Italian Greats in Sports and Italian Insights/ Bruno— 3rd Edition

ISBN: 978-1-953610-60-7

    1. Title.
    2. Sports.
    3. Italian Heritage/History.
    4. Sports (Italian) Commentary.
    5. Bruno.

No part of this book may be reproduced or transmitted in any form by any means, electronic or mechanical, including photocopying, recording, or by any information storage and retrieval system without permission in writing by the author.

All pictures and images are used with permission. All rights reserved.

NFB
NFB Publishing/Amelia Press
119 Dorchester Road
Buffalo, New York 14213

For more information visit Nfbpublishing.com

DEDICATION

This book is dedicated to Danielle Bruno, my only child, for her professional achievements in the legal field and her sustained interest in writing for research and publication, as imparted by her Dad, since childhood. Danielle is my treasure.

ACKNOWLEDGEMENTS

A special thanks to Dennis DiPaolo, owner of Ilio DiPaolo's Restaurant and Banquet Facility, for inspiring me to write this book,
17 Italian Greats in Sports and Italian Insights.

CONTENTS

FOREWORD
11

PART ONE
17 ITALIAN GREATS IN SPORTS AND ITALIAN INSIGHTS
17

COACH VINCE LOMBARDI'S WINNING
WAYS STILL RESONATE IN BUSINESS AND ACADEMIA
19

COACH VINCE LOMBARDI: MEMORABLE
AXIOMS ON WINNING AND LEADERSHIP
25

COACH VINCE LOMBARDI: RECORDS AND HONORS
33

COACH VINCE LOMBARDI: THE EARLY YEARS
35

A TRIBUTE TO ILIO DIPAOLO,
WRESTLER AND COMMUNITY BENEFACTOR
41

BUFFALO'S ILIO DIPAOLO AND HIS REMARKABLE STORY
45

OPPORTUNITY MOTIVATED ITALIAN
ILIO DIPAOLO TO COME TO AMERICA
49

ITALIAN GREAT ROCKY MARCIANO
LIVED THE AMERICAN DREAM
53

ROCKY MARCIANO'S TRAINING ROUTINE DEFINES HIS
UNBEATEN BOXING LEGACY (PART 1)
57

ROCKY MARCIANO'S INCREDIBLE DETERMINATION WAS
HALLMARK OF HIS UNBEATEN BOXING LEGACY (PART 2)
61

HOW THE SON OF AN ITALIAN FISHERMAN
BECAME THE SYMBOL OF AMERICAN BASEBALL
65

DOM DIMAGGIO:
BELOVED BOSTON RED SOX HALL OF FAMER
69

THE LORENZO PIETRO "YOGI" BERRA
BASEBALL STORY
71

YOGI BERRA AND FAMOUS YOGISMS
75

ITALIAN GREAT BRUNO SAMMARTINO BECOMES A
WRESTLING HALL OF FAMER CHAMPION IN AMERICA
79

MARIO ANDRETTI:
THE ITALIAN DRIVER OF THE CENTURY
83

IMMIGRANT ITALIAN LEO NOMELLINI ACHIEVED
TWO HALLS OF FAME IN FOOTBALL AND WRESTLING
87

COACH GENO AURIEMMA:
FROM MONTELLA TO UCONN
89

REMEMBERING A FRIEND: PHIL SCAFFIDI
93

QUARTERBACK RICK CASSATA REALIZES AN INDUCTION
INTO GREATER BUFFALO SPORTS HALL OF FAME
97

RICK CASSATA PASSED ON YANKEES' BASEBALL OFFER
103

BUFFALO'S TONY MASIELLO: COLLEGE BASKETBALL AND
MAYORAL HALL OF FAMER (PART 1)
107

TONY MASIELLO'S POLITICAL CAREER IN BUFFALO KICKED
OFF IN 1971: 35 YEARS OF SERVICE (PART 2)
111

COACH DICK VITALE: "I AM LIVING THE AMERICAN DREAM"
115

LEGENDARY COACH JIM VALVANO: NEVER QUIT CAMPAIGN
AND THE V FOUNDATION
119

DIANA TAURASI'S BASKETBALL STARDOM SHOWCASED AT
2020 TOKYO OLYMPICS
123

REMEMBERING JAKE LAMOTTA:
BOXING MIDDLEWEIGHT CHAMPION AND HALL OF FAMER
127

CFL HALL OF FAMER ANGELO MOSCA WON
5 GREY CUP CHAMPIONSHIPS (PART 1)
131

ANGELO 'KING KONG' MOSCA BECOMES
LEGENDARY IN CANADIAN WRESTLING (PART 2)
135

GIOVANNI "NINO" BENVENUTI: AMERICA'S, MOST
BELOVED ITALIAN BOXER DURING THE 1960s
139

BASEBALL HALL OF FAMER TOMMY LASORDA
EMBODIED "DODGER BLUE" FOR EIGHT DECADES
141

CHARLIE TRIPPI: THE PRIDE OF PITTSDON
145

REMEMBERING CARMEN BASILIO: FROM ONION
PICKER TO CHAMPION TO BOXING HALL OF FAME
149

THE CATCH
155

**PART TWO
ITALIAN IMMIGRATION ISSUES
159**

HOW IT USED TO BE:
EARLY ITALIANS ARRIVE AT ELLIS ISLAND
161

THE GREAT ARRIVAL AND THE
DAWN OF ITALIAN AMERICA
163

EARLY ITALIAN IMMIGRANTS
WERE SECOND-CLASS CITIZENS
169

EARLY ITALIANS AND IRISH CLASH IN NEW YORK
173

ITALIAN AMERICANS IN U.S.
WERE TARGETED DURING WORLD WAR II
177

FIRST GENERATION ITALIAN GREATS REFUSED TO
FOLLOW THEIR FATHERS' FOOTSTEPS
181

FIRST GENERATION ITALIAN AMERICANS
TRAILBLAZE PATHS OF OPPORTUNITIES
FOR THE PROFESSIONS
185

THE MEMORABLE 1960 ROME OLYMPICS
CATAPULTED ATHLETIC COMPETITION WORLDWIDE
LIKE NEVER BEFORE
199

**PART THREE
GREAT BUFFALO ITALIANS, IMAGES,
AND LESSONS LEARNED
205**

BUFFALO WRESTLING HALL OF FAMER
ILIO DIPAOLO HONORED IN ITALY
207

BELOVED BUFFALONIAN JOEY GIAMBRA
SUCCUMBS TO COVID-19
211

RESTAURATEUR RUSSELL J. SALVATORE HAS GENEROUSLY
GIFTED MILLIONS TO BUFFALO AND WNY PROJECTS
215

MY FATHER, JOSEPH SALVATORE
219

FROM SKIPPING CLASS TO FIRST CLASS
223

BUFFALO'S SAM NOTO:
A WORLD-CLASS JAZZ TRUMPET VIRTUOSO
227

REMEMBERING FRANK A. SEDITA:
SOJOURNING FROM "SHOESHINE BOY"
TO ATTORNEY TO BUFFALO MAYOR
231

REMEMBERING DR. THOMAS LOMBARDO:
BELOVED, BUFFALO WEST SIDE PEDIATRICIAN AND WORLD WAR II HERO
235

REMEMBERING MARIO G. DICRISTOFARO, ITALIAN-BORN
COLLISION SHOP OWNER WHO COULD FIX ANYTHING
239

THE IMPORTANCE OF ITALIAN WINEMAKING
243

WINEMAKING IS A BRUNO FAMILY TRADITION
245

THE CONNECTICUT STREET ITALIAN FESTIVAL OF THE
LATE 1970S: CULTURAL IMAGES THAT NO LONGER EXIST
249

BUFFALO'S OLD WEST SIDE OF THE MID-1960S
251

LESSONS LEARNED FROM MAMA BRUNO
253

IMMEDIATELY REMOVE CARL PALADINO
257

FBI ARRESTS ITALIAN IMMIGRANT SUSPECT IN
EXTORTION LETTER TO BRUNO FAMILY
259

ABOUT THE AUTHOR AND TEACHER
263

Foreword

By Al Bruno

Al Bruno is a teacher and writer and has been reporting on sports events and personalities since his college reporting days at Canisius College in the late 1970s. His passion and insights in sports is fueled by his experiences as a published sportswriter, high school coach, and football player.

17 Italian Greats in Sports and Italian Insights (2023) by Al Bruno is an Italian sports and culture publication, an anthology, presenting 58 of his best Italian sports stories and Italian cultural insights about early Italian immigration issues, great first-generation, Italian Americans, images, traditions (St. Anthony's Day Festival in Buffalo and winemaking), and lessons (good and painful), and the unexpected succumbing of Buffalo's Italian icon and ambassador, Joey Giambra, to covid-19.

Al Bruno's insights reveal Italian events and cultural experiences he lived and observed along the way as a first-generation, Italian American and the only child of Italian immigrants (from Pratola Peligna from the Abruzzi region of Italy), perilously arriving at Ellis Island, alone and startled; they survived, making Buffalo, New York, their permanent home for the past 67 years.

Importantly, it primarily focuses on the inspiring insights and successes of the Italian sporting greats by traveling through a time tunnel, remembering and honoring Italian sports heroes from the 1940s to the present day.

What makes them special, great, and worthy of their accomplishments? They were Italians that paid the price for American success beyond their most hopeful dreams: They became the Italian sporting greats and headliners, and they earned it by capitalizing on opportunity with hard work and determination. In fact, Italian sporting greats often achieved the unimaginable, beating the steep odds against them and becoming American champions, mostly beloved by all.

They won, fairly and squarely, to the crowd's delight and enthusiasm: Winning necessarily defines the Italian sporting greats, and they stand out, in front of the rest, the best, and are included in many American city annals for honor and posterity; some deservingly arrive for induction into the football, basketball, baseball, boxing, wrestling, and auto racing sports halls of fame in America.

When a discussion intensely ensues about Italian sporting greats, at the top of the list for most is the venerable, Coach Vince Lombardi of the Green Bay Packers of the 1960s; yes, he is the best football coach of all-time and four articles are presented to clearly distinguish how he is remembered from his early days on, Lombardi winning, and his leadership model, a classic. Lombardi is still appreciated and his winning ways continue to resonate in America 50 years after his death in 1970.

Respectfully, many have called Lombardi the patron saint of the NFL. Lombardi has become synonymous with winning in America, earning him rightful recognition as "Coach of the Century" by ESPN in 2000.

Winning makes the Italian sporting greats memorable, entertaining, and ultimately sports heroes, our Italian icons, like Greater Buffalo Sports Hall of Fame Wrestler Ilio DiPaolo did for me as a thrilled youngster in the early 1960s. We cheered on DiPaolo at the top of our lungs, our version of the "Italian Hercules," while we anxiously awaited his much-anticipated, twirling, signature move, "the airplane spin" on Saturday nights, in front of a packed house at the old Memorial Auditorium in downtown Buffalo.

Then there are the great performers in Buffalo's sports history that will always be remembered and respected for what they do after they retire from competition: That Buffalo and Italian great is wrestler Ilio DiPaolo, a member of the Buffalo and Wrestling Halls of Fame.

What distinguishes DiPaolo apart from all the rest, the best, is his 'giving back' and involvement as a civic leader and Buffalo's, greatest community benefactor, providing food donations, charities, and millions of dollars in college scholarships to outstanding, local athletes. The DiPaolo tradition carries on at Ilio DiPaolo's Restaurant and Banquet Facility in Blasdell.

Undefeated at 49 and 0 as a boxer, heavyweight champion Rocky Marciano must be included in any discussion about Italian sporting greats and hall of famers. The Rocky Marciano story is an amazing trail of achievements every step of the way, including honorable Army service in Europe during World War II.

He returned home a war hero and almost made the Chicago Cubs as a promising young catcher with great hitting ability. Marciano shifted his focus to boxing, an undersized heavyweight at 186 pounds, and determined to become a heavyweight champion, outpunching, outworking and outlasting all his opponents. The son of an Italian shoemaker achieved the American dream for himself and his family.

Presenting Italian baseball great Joe DiMaggio, the Yankee Clipper, is a pleasure. DiMaggio is etched deep into America's, all-time, sports consciousness: DiMaggio achieved nine World Series championships, named American League MVP three times, selected a 13-time all-star, and garnered an astounding, 56-game, hitting streak with the New York Yankees: one of the greatest achievements in baseball history.

On the day of DiMaggio's passing in 1999, President Bill Clinton voiced these defining, memorable words to honor the venerable Joe DiMaggio: "This son of Italian immigrants gave every American something to believe in. He became the very symbol of American grace, power, and skill."

Dominic "Dom" Paul DiMaggio was a former, all-star center fielder in Major League Baseball who played his entire career for the Boston Red Sox from 1940 to 1953. An effective leadoff hitter, batted .300 four times and led the American League in runs twice (1950 and 1951) and in triples and stolen bases once each. His 1338 games in center field ranked him eighth in AL history when he retired. His 34-game hitting streak in 1949 remains a Boston club record. He also had a 27-game hitting streak in 1951. DiMaggio was inducted into the Boston Red Sox Hall of Fame in 1995.

He was the youngest of three DiMaggio baseball brothers who became major league center fielders as well: Joe DiMaggio was a star with the rival New York Yankees and Vince DiMaggio played for five different National League teams.

New York Yankee baseball greats are abundant in number for good reasons, but none is more colorful and more memorable than the great Yogi Berra. Yogi was an all-star for 15 seasons, won the American League MVP three times, was named a member of Baseball's All-Century Team, won 10 World Series championships as a Yankee great, and had his number "8," retired by the NY Yankees.

Yogi was the talented Italian kid from "The Hill" in St. Louis and transcended the world of sports to become an American icon. In fact, Yogi was a child of Italian immigrants, a World War II gunner who served at D-Day, record-breaking athlete, a major league coach and manager, a husband and a father, a son, a community member, and a friend to many – he had done it all and more.

Italian wrestling great Bruno Sammartino was truly a throwback gladiator in the 1960s, 70s, and 80s, and even today is considered by virtually all as one of the most honorable and great athletes in wrestling history.

For more than 11 years combined, during two reigns, Sammartino was the World Wide Wrestling Federation Champion between 1963–71 and 1973–77 (4040 days). Sammartino headlined New York's famous Madison Square Garden 211 times, including 187 sell-outs, a record that still endures today.

Courageously as truthful accounts confirm, Sammartino and his family had endured treacherous times, hiding in the hills of Abruzzi, Italy, from ensuing German soldiers in their Italian occupation during World War II. Sammartino and his family fortunately survived through all the near-death atrocities and were then consequently blessed in America as Sammartino earned passage for himself and his family as a wrestling legacy, "The Living Legend," for all to honor and appreciate and against-all-odds: a miracle story for the ages for retelling and posterity.

Italian-born Mario Andretti is presented as an Italian sports great who came to America in 1955, with his twin brother, Aldo, and became the greatest race car driver of the 20th century. After World War II, Andretti and his family were faced into a treacherous, Yugoslavic refugee camp in Montola for eight years, 1948 to 1955, wondering whether they would ever get their visa to America. Andretti's passion for race car driving would flourish for him and his family in the 1960s and 1970s, winning the Indy 500 in 1970.

Andretti's winning ensued, efficiently and magically at times, and he took the checkered flag 111 times during career, a career that stretched five decades; he was named Driver of the Year in three different decades (the 60s, 70s, and 80s), Driver of the Quarter Century (in the 1990s).

Leo "The Lion" Nomellini, a star tackle for the San Francisco 49ers from 1950 – 63 and a member of both the Pro Football and NWA Wrestling Halls of Fame, is forever remembered as that tough-and-gritty, football Italian kid and all-around athlete: He was born on June 19, 1924, in his native town of Lucca, Italy.

Nomellini immigrated to Chicago, Illinois, as an infant with his family. Because he had to help support his family, he dropped out of high school early on, working in a foundry as a young adolescent.

Sometimes Nomellini played both ways, garnering him incredible respect among his NFL peers and pro football insiders. Nomellini was one of the few players ever to win All-NFL recognition on both offense and defense. In 1979, Nomellini was also inducted into the National Italian American Sports Halls of Fame; his sports versatility made him even more of a unique Italian sports great.

This Italian sporting great from Montella, Italy, came to America with his family in 1961, at age seven, not knowing how to speak English, not knowing the American customs, and feeling out of place. That is the incredible story of a soon-to-be hall of fame basketball coach Geno Auriemma of the University of Connecticut Women's Basketball Team, arriving in 1985 and chronicling the greatest women's basketball program in American sports history.

The UConn women's basketball team has won 41 regular season tournament titles, advanced to 17 Final Fours, posted six perfect seasons, and won 11 national championships. Auriemma is an eight-time, AP College Basketball Coach of the Year, seven-time Naismith Coach of the Year, and three-time American Athletic Coach of the Year; his cumulative record at UConn remains the best-winning percentage in the history of the sport.

Auriemma was the head coach of the United States women national basketball teams 2009 through 2016, during which time his team won the 2010 and 2014 World Championships; he garnered gold medals at the 2012 and 2016 Summer Olympics, going undefeated in all four tournaments.

Greater Buffalo, Tonawanda, and Ottawa Sports Halls of Fame quarterback Rick Cassata was named in 2016 as one of the 11, three-sport best hall of fame athletes ever produced in the Buffalo area. In 1973, Cassata led the Ottawa Rough Riders to a Grey Cup, and he was named MVP, the Italian kid from Buffalo's West Side, moving with his family to Tonawanda in the 9th grade and excelling in three sports.

Cassata led his Tonawanda HS Warriors in 1965 to an undefeated season and was an All American in football and baseball; as a result, Cassata was presented with 20 football scholarship offers, including Notre Dame and Miami, but he chose Syracuse University, staying close to WNY and joining future, NFL hall of fame running backs Floyd Little and Larry Csonka.

Unknown to most, Cassata passed on a major league opportunity presented to him to be the future, franchise shortstop with the New York Yankees to follow his quarterbacking passion at Syracuse, instead.

No one who lived in Western New York in the late 1970s and early 80s will ever forget the competitiveness of the great Phil Scaffidi, an uncommon, four-sport phenom and a member of the Greater Buffalo Sports Hall of Fame, excelling as an all-star in football, basketball, baseball, and track at St. Joseph's Collegiate Institute and Niagara University. Sadly, Scaffidi was taken tragically due to cancer at only age 23.

Buffalo's Tony Masiello is remembered for his achievements in college basketball and as a three-term mayor for the city of Buffalo. Few hall of famers are recognized honorees in two professions, and former Buffalo Mayor Tony Masiello accomplished that and much more in his celebrated life Canisius College basketball history, and more recently, in public for 35 years: In those years, has served as a Buffalo common councilman, state senator, and mayor of Buffalo. Masiello was inducted into the Greater Buffalo Sports Hall of Fame in 2007 and in the Canisius College Hall of Fame in 1982.

In 1973, few knew of Dick Vitale outside of those residing in the tri-state region; he is a first-generation Italian American, who was born in 1939 in Passaic, New Jersey, to John and Mae, Vitale, Italian immigrants, both working tirelessly in the clothing industry to give him a better life in America, indeed.

Now in 2021, Vitale is known almost everywhere in "Sports America" where he enjoys his legendary status as a hall of fame basketball coach and active ESPN broadcaster: all in one storied, ambitious life. "I am living the American dreams," Vitale passionately emphasizes to this day.

First-generation, Italian American Jimmy Valvano closely followed on the Italian pioneering trial that Dick Vitale did in the 1970s for men's college basketball.

Valvano demonstrated his remarkable winning ways at NC State from 1980 to 1990. He led the Wolfpack in one of greatest Cinderella stories in college basketball history, culminating as winners of the 1983 NCAA Division I Championship. Most importantly, he succumbed to cancer in the prime of his career and is remembered for his "never quit campaign," inspiring the creation of the V Foundation for Cancer Research.

First-generation, Italian American Diana Taurasi's basketball stardom shined brightest and was showcased for all to witness worldwide this past summer's 2020 Tokyo Olympics where she amazingly garnered her fifth gold medal (in 2004, 2008, 2012, 2016, and 2020) with the USA women's basketball team.

Powerful, all-encompassing words like <u>winner,</u> <u>legendary,</u> and <u>immortality</u> meritoriously describe Taurasi's unprecedented contributions in professional, college, and Olympic competition in the history of women's basketball.

First-generation, Italian American Jake LaMotta is remembered for hall of fame boxing career, winning the middleweight championship in spectacular fashion at Madison Square Garden in New York City on June 16, 1949. LaMotta experienced a rough, seedy, and even criminal early life as a teenager and beyond, and it is well documented, but his boxing tenacity, toughness, and slugging power made him a dangerous fighter in the ring and respected by all and feared by opponents.

Ring Magazine, a respected authority on boxing, ranks LaMotta as one of the 10 greatest middleweights of all-time. In 106 total fights, La Motta garnered 83 wins (30 by knock-out), 19 losses, and four draws.

The 1960s, 70s, and 80s were great football and wrestling times for first-generation, Italian American Angelo Valentine Mosca, growing up in Waltham, Massachusetts, never imagining that he would someday develop into a sports celebrity and legacy in Canada and North America.

Mosca's physical gifts would eventually empower him to become an international sports celebrity for his exploits on the gridiron and in the wrestling ring: A rags-to-riches story of an incredibly-determined and physically-gifted Italian American kid who over the near impossible to achieve both the American and Canadian Dreams in one lifetime.

These 17 Italian sports greats were very special and were encouraged to be the trailblazers in competitive, physically-demanding sports like football, baseball, boxing, wrestling, weightlifting, and even car racing. They intuitively knew that they possessed the physical skills for sports but lacked the academic abilities to go farther in life in the white-collar professions.

In sum, these 17 Italian American sports greats wanted very much to forge their own distinct identity, helping their families see, experience, and benefit from the "American Dream" and making their parents proud of their resilient efforts, most of all. And they succeeded in unimaginable ways for all to appreciate and retell for years to come.

PART ONE

17 Italian Greats in Sports and Italian Insights

Coach Vince Lombardi's Winning Ways Still Resonate in Business and Academia

Green Bay Packers Coach Vince Lombardi is carried off, after beating the Oakland Raiders, 33 to 14, in Super Bowl II in 1968. (Permission from Vince Lombardi, Jr).

By Al Bruno,
American Football Monthly,
Spring 2018

Prelude

Coach Vince Lombardi is regarded by most as the greatest NFL Coach of all time. His winning record and five championships (including the first two Super Bowls) with the Green Bay Packers are still unmatched and unparalleled 50 years after his untimely death in 1970, earning him recognition as "Coach of the Century" by ESPN in 2000.

Lombardi helped the men he coached succeed in getting the most of their God-given abilities better than any other coach in NFL history. He brought them pride and victory, and his legacy of perseverance, hard work, and dedication remain the staples of success for any worthwhile human endeavor to this very day. Lombardi was more than a football coach; he was a great leader in any forum for all-time, and that is why he is still remembered and quoted so much so that the NFL's most coveted, team award, that is the Super Bowl trophy, bears his name (i.e. The Vince Lombardi Trophy).

Many herald Vince Lombardi as the patron saint of the NFL: what reverence for a great coach and leader. Lombardi is now the classic, winning model from which other coaches and leaders are and will be measured against in effectively assessing successful coaching and leadership in any goal-oriented, forward-thinking organization.

Lombardi's Memorable Words and Spirit are Still Felt in 2020

In 2020, Lombardi's spirit still resonates throughout the American landscape like a shepherd gathering his flock, moving purposefully to their next destination. The football flock organizes and huddles together, recognizing one and only one, distinct voice that leads them to grassy fields where replenishment is a staple of life. That intense voice, the forceful voice of Lombardi, commands a certain respect that few have been able to wield in those football fields of opportunity.

Respectfully, many have called Lombardi the patron saint of the NFL: Lombardi has become the embodiment of everything that was once good about sports and the eternal values of competition. The mere mention of his name brings to mind and celebrates such qualities as character, courage, and sacrifice in schools and colleges, corporations, and sporting organizations (from Pop Warner Football Programs through the professional ranks). Lombardi has influenced and touched virtually every sector of the American society, instilling confidence and demanding excellence from its participants in the quest for winning.

The Lombardi name is a summoning, a call-to-arms, and a call for discipline, effort, and most of all – winning. Lombardi has become synonymous with winning in America. That is why Lombardi remains a symbol of what was once great about the NFL and, perhaps, is no longer; but, he still keeps appearing in education, sports, and in business and corporate formulas for success and winning.

Lombardi is exemplary because he was ahead of his time with his approach to winning and leadership. To realize those ends, he instilled character-building in his players, and character-building meant working hard on the basics by drilling through repetitions, chasing perfection and settling for excellence in the process. Emphasis on the basics certainly applies today in almost everything; many are calling for a return-to-the-basics, even in retail technology. Dan Scheraga, in Chain Store Age (2004), credits Lombardi about the importance of the basics:

"Lombardi's lesson is applicable to IT, too…I'm telling you again, because Lombardi was right: The basics are crucial, and too often, they aren't emphasized enough."

Observably, Lombardi's leadership model is present in today's, retail technology industry as portrayed by the points made by Dan Scheraga (2004). In the corporate world, as well, Lombardi is often mentioned in the same sentence with excellence; Ben Rothke in eWeek (2003), writes:

"If Lombardi were a chief information security officer today, he would be relentless in pursuing quality; excellence; the understanding of risk. Chief security officers today cannot find a better role model."

The Lombardi legacy centers on a commitment to excellence and character-building in leaders and organizations. Chasing perfection was an everyday practice for Lombardi in search of excellence: Lombardi was relentless and pushed the winning agenda on his players; that was first and the Lombardi way. Kenny Rathledge, in Coach and Athletic Director (2001), writes in detail:

"The term that suited him best was perfectionist. He made harsh demands on his players to prepare them for the harsher demands of the game. He felt that every fiber in your body should be used in pursuit of excellence. Lombardi would not tolerate excuses or compromises. He was interested only in results. He taught his players that success and winning are habits. To play for him, you had to be mentally tough."

Lombardi's emphasis on teaching the basics to near, perfect execution meant excellence, and excellence cultivates a winning attitude and winning teams. He was a great motivator, too; Andrew Singer, in Across the Board (2000), writes:

"Regarding motivation, Lombardi was a master, and here again his example is relevant to business. All things being equal, a manager who can engender trust and loyalty from subordinates will reap a higher performance over time."

Lombardi accomplished the arduous task of motivating his players by actively demonstrating motivation and commitment to his players with his tremendous energy and preparation during practices and meetings. He paid the price, and as a matter of fact, Lombardi, too, dealt with adversity and hostility among his players. He was discerning and fair, and, then, he made the necessary adjustments. Porter Crow, in Vital Speeches of the Day (1972), recalls:

"How do you think a hater could be used in football? As a linebacker! That's right; so Lombardi made that kind of assignment for hostile men. Jesus, too, used hostility... Hostility can be used in a positive way. Lombardi turned haters into linebackers and he turned lovers into split ends and quarterbacks."

Lombardi knew football, but more importantly, Lombardi knew how to use individual talents for the greater good of the team, harnessing the players strengths while directing a winning project; however, there are the Lombardi detractors out there still condemning the man for placing winning first, above all. Pete Hammill, in Literary Cavalcade (2000), writes:

"Winning isn't everything," Lombardi declared. "It's the only thing." Winning isn't the only thing in love, art, marriage, commerce, or politics; it is not even the only in sports... The true athlete teaches us that winning isn't everything, but struggle is – the struggle to simply get up in the morning or to see hope through mine fields of despair."

It is true that Lombardi believed in winning, first and foremost, but there was a compassionate side of him, even for the loser. Lombardi speaks to losing: "In great attempts, it is glorious even to fail" (vincelombardi.com). Although remembered and revered most for winning, Lombardi had a sense of balance and realized that every game could not be won.

It has been nearly 50 years since his untimely death, and Lombardi still exudes an exemplary character-in-action by emphasizing the basics, insisting on hard-working team members, and winning with consistency on the battlefield. Success has a price, and Lombardi understood that clearly. Looking at Lombardi objectively, James Bowman in National Review (1999), writes:

"It was the real Lombardi, the very essence of the man and the means by which he transformed himself into the myth. Like the rest of us, Lombardi had his faults, but unlike the rest of us, his faults were also his virtues, and the reasons we remember and admire him so long after his death."

The reality is that Lombardi has withstood the test of time with most, who remember him, admiring and still emulating his winning ways. One such person is Dr. Linda Casser, optometrist and associate dean for academic programs at the Pacific University College, in Forest Grove, Oregon. Jane Haseldine, in Review of Optometry (2003), writes about Dr. Casser, the academician, who lives by Lombardi:

"The quality of a person's life is in direct proportion to their commitment to excellence, regardless of their chosen field of endeavor. Appropriate words for this Wisconsin native to have framed in her office at Pacific University College... Throughout her 25-year career in academic life, Casser has committed her life to the pursuit of that philosophy."

Living and striving in the Lombardi way is a noble undertaking, and Dr. Casser is a great example of how the enduring, Lombardi philosophy for leading and winning continues to positively affect people he has touched in some way. The Lombardi legacy seems to be mentioned every time someone discusses great leadership. Weingardt (2000) emphasizes that creating a strong lasting legacy as a strong leaders can help make the world a better place; Richard Weingardt, in Journal of Management in Engineering (2000), specifically writes about Lombardi's greatness as a leader:

"Look at Vince Lombardi's astonishing turnaround of the Green Bay Packers in the early 1960s. He took unmotivated, undisciplined, and underperformers, got them fit physically and mentally, and turned them into world champions in less than three years...Effective leaders identify opportunities; they have a vision that others will embrace and rally around."

Great leaders are visionaries, and Lombardi was certainly a visionary, a leader, a winner, a remarkable character, and much, much more. Lombardi was right about the importance of building character from within among the players and, then, tying it to the team vision for winning. The Lombardi leadership model still shows today's leaders that leading is embedded in visions for success; therefore, following the Lombardi line of thinking, cultivating character from within the organization enlists member commitment to those visions. Leadership without vision is leadership not at all, according to Lombardi logic.

Lombardi's emphasis on character building was complemented by a strong senseof integrity; he was a square shooter, fair, and a moral leader as well. Donald Phillips, in his 2001 book, Run To Win, sums up Lombardi and his contributions to leadership and society:

"He was able to combine a caring and compassionate nature with an enviableability to get things done. Lombardi had heart – and he had goals that went beyond the game of football. "Integrity is the most priceless thing you possess," he lectured his players. Vince Lombardi's principles, his style, and the way he lived his life can be employed as a sterling model for effective leadership in any organization – football, business, and beyond."

Football was Lombardi's laboratory, but he was concerned about moral growth, national leadership, and the challenges ahead; Donald Phillips (2001) writes:

"The test of this century will be whether man mistakes the growth of wealth and power with the growth of spirit and character...Our country needs people will keep their heads in emergencies; in other words, leaders who will meet the intricate problems with wisdom and courage."

Relevantly, Lombardi was speaking to a calling for great leaders for a society, he hoped, not to be overtaken by greed and wealth. Lombardi was a character man, and greed and excesses were deeply disturbing to him, especially in the late 1960s; understandably, he was liberal on issues concerning the needy and on issue of social justice, and he was taking an opportunity through his celebrity to comment on the social issues of the day, specifically the youth countermovement and their rebellious, anti-establishment agenda, as he saw it.

Lombardi's plea for better leadership and for a better society suddenly ended when he was admitted to Georgetown Hospital in June 1970 and died (way before his time) of colon cancer on September 3, 1970, at age 57: A battle even the great Lombardi could not win. Lombardi did not lose; he simply ran out of time. The ones Lombardi was closest, his immediate family and the Green Bay family of players, spoke of the loss of Lombardi; Donald Phillips (2001) writes:

"He's the greatest coach I ever played under," said Paul Horning. "I would have gone through a wall for that guy." Most players immediately realized what they had lost – and despaired of ever seeing the likes of it again…To some, Lombardi was a father teaching his sons. Bart Starr said of Lombardi, "I owe my life to that man."

Lombardi nurtured something special in the lives he touched. Certainly, he demanded character people committed to excellence; that is as basic and as dedicated a leader must be in creating a winning organization like Lombardi did in Green Bay. Nowadays in 2020, Lombardi remains special, and so many leaders, coaches, and teachers try to live a vibrant, Lombardi-like life by giving it their best in the things that mean the most. The Lombardi legacy still compels people to be hard working and disciplined in achieving worthwhile goals in life. That is so Lombardi.

Undeniably, the spirit of Lombardi seems to be everywhere? When there is a special call for decisive action, Lombardi is there, but could Lombardi make it now? David Maraniss sheds some light about Lombardi in the modern context, almost 50 years after his death. David Maraniss, in his 1997 book, When Pride Still Mattered, insightfully writes about what Lombardi would be like in today's NFL:

"Some go searching for the Old Man (Lombardi) out of a sense of longing for something they believe has been irretrievably lost. What would Lombardi do about this? Why isn't there anyone like the Old Man out there anymore? Lombardi's football philosophy relied on adaptability above all else, reacting to conditions quickly enough to bend things his way."

Along the same lines, poignantly, then, what would Lombardi think of the outlandish and excessive showboating by NFL players during games? David Maraniss (1997) further writes about Lombardi's response: "When Travis Williams, the exhilarating kickoff return man on his 1967 team, danced a jig after scoring a touchdown that year, a modest ancestor of the elaborate celebrations so common now, the Old Man called him over and appealed to Williams's pride. "Travis," he said, "try to act like you've been there before." That was all he had to say. It reinforced the message he gave to his players at the beginning of training camp: You are the Packers, you are professionals, you are above the rest."

Lombardi handled the matter in a direct yet appropriate manner, and he sent the message about unnecessary celebrating and showboating. At the beginning of training camp, Lombardi probably would have given his players a collective talk about the importance of character and professionalism, even after scoring thrilling touchdowns. In addition, he probably would have fined players a substantial amount for celebrating touchdowns and going against Lombardi's policy on proper conduct.

Obediently, like good boy scouts, the players would have exhibited exemplary behavior on-the-field because they are Lombardi's boys; they fear Lombardi's disapproval and, therefore, do not want to fall from his grace, subjecting themselves to the wrath of Lombardi.

Again, the football flock recognized the distinct voice of its shepherd, its leader, its provider, and Lombardi knew the way and naturally led the way to phenomenal winning in Green Bay. While playing with the Packers, Jerry Kramer said of Lombardi: "We knew that the only difference between being a good football team and a great football team was him and only him" (Phillips, 2001). Kramer and the Packer players were right: Lombardi was the way to winning and winning often.

FINAL THOUGHTS ABOUT LOMBARDI'S LEGACY

The lasting legacy of Lombardi is a direct measure of the extraordinary life he lived as a great coach and great leader. Mention the name, Lombardi, and so many hear the calling, the call for the football master of all-time. A call for Lombardi translates into serious readiness for hard work, discipline, and a commitment to excellence. Above all, Lombardi represents the winning formula for any goal-oriented organization, promoting character-building at the very core of its existence.

Just look at the Green Bay Packers of the 1960s, and the evidence is abundantly clear; the Green Bay Packers of Lombardi are the greatest dynasty in NFL history not because they won more consistently than any other team (in NFL history), but because they won with phenomenal success with the same players and the same coach. They were bonded together by their enduring respect for Lombardi and their belief in each other: Their winning ways were Lombardi greatness. No NFL coach has ever experienced such reverence because Lombardi's will, his character-in-action, transformed average players into good men, achievers, and winners.

The Lombardi myth has now become the property of American posterity to appreciate and emulate. From the distance of decades, the spirit of Lombardi as a maker of men continues to flourish in today's, competitive world. The name, Lombardi, is exhorted as an inspirational force in untold corporate board rooms, in sales meetings, in political rallies, and even at an occasional, Sunday sermon. A symbol for character, courage, and sacrifice, Lombardi remains, even with his passing, the sports ego, the will to win, of American consciousness.

Celebrating Lombardi is to celebrate winning and achievement in America. Therefore, remembering the Lombardi legacy is really an act of instilling confidence and faith in doing our best with what God gave us: Who could ask for more? That is why Lombardi was recently revered as "The ESPN Coach of the Century."

Coach Vince Lombardi: Memorable Axioms on Winning and Leadership

Coach Vince Lombardi was a fierce, football virtuoso with a commanding presence on the Green Bay Packer sideline. He is simply the best head coach in NFL history: That is why the Super Bowl Trophy was renamed in his honor as the Vince Lombardi Trophy.
(Permission from Vince Lombardi, Jr.)

By Al Bruno,
La Gazzetta Italiana
January and February 2019

Editor's Note in Italian (italicized):
Vince Lombardi nacque a Brooklyn nel 1913 da figli di immigrati dall'Italia meridionale e divento un mitico allenatore di football americano per essere stato negli anni '60 il coach dei Green Bay Packers, con i quali vinse cinque campionati e due Super Bowl consecutive nel 1966 e nel 1967. Lombardi cominciò la sua carriera da assistente alla Fordham University e nei New York Giants prima di diventare allenatore dei Green Bay Packers dal 1959 al 1967 e poi dei Washing-

ton Redskins nel 1969. Nella sua leggendaria carriera non ebbe mai una stagione perdente: in 202 partite ottenne 147 vittorie, 47 sconfitte e 6 pareggi. In suo onore, il trofeo del Super Bowl fu rinominato il Vince Lombardi Trophy.

COACH VINCE LOMBARDI ON WINNING

No head coach in NFL history has been quoted more on winning and leadership axioms than Lombardi; Lombardi was really ahead of his time in the 1960s, creating a winning system as a classic model of leadership for all professions and occupations to emulate. Nowadays, mention "Lombardi" and a certain magic still lingers in the name.

When speaking about winning and character-building in organizations, Lombardi comes to mind. If business people speak about the importance of punctuality and preparedness, they are reminded about "Lombardi time" (i.e. 10 minutes earlier than the scheduled time) and a "commitment to excellence," sacrificing for the greater good, the organizational goal, to insure enhanced quality of a person's life, for example. It does not stop there; Lombardisms, they almost could be called, have permeated every sector of society, instilling confidence and achievement efforts among employees in organizations throughout America. Lombardisms invoke a call for action, a call for winning at all cost.

There will probably never be a coach and leader with a better ability to organize, rally the troops, and win. In many school, sporting, and corporate structures, Lombardi contributions are revived every time there is a call for team improvement and winning. What a tremendous accolade for a deserving and great coach, but it was not without plenty of sacrifice and hard work on his part.

Lombardi learned from his parents, his religion (Catholicism), the Jesuits at Fordham, and great coaches like Fordham's Jim "Sleepy" Crowley, a disciple of Notre Dame's Knute Rockne; Earl "Colonel Red" Blaik, West Point's best ever; and Jim Lee Howell of the New York Giants; observably, history certainly chronicles this, Lombardi's work was remarkable: He was the attentive and engaging student of the game who embellished the work of coaching notables to a new height of coaching genius and sport leadership.

According to Lombardi, hard work and the will to win, a character-in-action, is what makes people and organizations thrive and succeed. Therefore, learning from Lombardi should be encouraged as an ongoing process of promoting character-in-action for today's leaders when improved, team performance and winning are the company goals. What follows are Lombardi's renditions on winning and leadership.

Everything that Lombardi speaks about, that is leadership, character, commitment, and discipline, naturally lead to winning like free-flowing tributaries merging into the main river, swiftly, and upstream with impetus. The name, Lombardi, in America has become associated and synonymous with winning. After all, "Winning isn't everything; it's the only thing" (vincelombardi.com). That celebrated axiom is probably recalled more often than anything else Lombardi has profoundly stated in his great coaching tenure.

However, it should be noted, it was first uttered by UCLA Coach Henry Sanders in the 1940s, but it is attributed to Lombardi time and time again. Afterwards, Lombardi regretted making that statement; he retorted with this explanation: "I wish to hell I'd never said the damned thing. I meant the effort. I meant having a goal...I sure as hell didn't mean for people to crush human values and morality" (Lombardi, 2001).

Verifiably, like it or not, Lombardi did say it, and history has recorded it as his property on winning philosophies, although evidence points to Coach Sanders saying it first. Poignantly, that hard-hitting axiom has concisely framed the very essence of the Lombardi legacy for most. Insightfully, Vince Lombardi, Jr. (2001), in his book, What It Takes To Be #1, summarizes:

"I'm constantly amazed at the number of people who know nothing about my father except that (1) he was a football coach and (2) he uttered (or endorsed or seemed to have endorsed) that truly memorable sentence. Some people take the saying on face value and agree with it. Other people are a little uncomfortable with the aggressive little statement. A third group of people are deeply offended by it. They take it as the distillation of everything that's wrong with football, American culture, capitalism, or mankind."

The intensity of such an enormous statement on winning is received differently by people as is evident, but its impact is surely felt by most. Along the same lines, Coach Lombardi also writes: "The will to excel and the will to win – they endure" (Lombardi, 2001). This statement really reflects what Lombardi wanted to say originally because Lombardi was always focusing on the will: The will to win is what fuels the run to win.

The goal for Team Lombardi was winning. Winning was the company mission. The company business for Lombardi was football and his organization was the Green Bay Packers. Lombardi (2001) spoke about the rigors of the football organization and its objective on winning:

"Being part of a football team is no different than being a part of any other organization – an army, a political party. The objective is to win, to beat the other guy. You think that is hard or cruel – I don't think it is. I do think it is the reality of life that men are competitive, and the more competitive the business, the more competitive the men. They know the rules, and they know the objective, and they get in the game. And the objective is to win – fairly, squarely, decently, by the rules, but to win."

As a result, Lombardi was criticized for making winning the most important goal in a game of brutality among men. Lombardi's critics accused him of callousness and insensitivity.

In defense of his strong emphasis on winning, Lombardi fired back, repeatedly saying: "If it doesn't matter who wins or loses, then why do they keep score?" (vincelombardi.com). They keep score because the winners need to be recognized and rewarded for their commendable efforts. Lombardi affirms the grace of winning:

"I firmly believe that any man's finest hour, the greatest fulfillment of all that he holds dear, is the moment when he was worked his heart out in a good cause andlies exhausted on the field of battle – victorious" (vincelombardi.com).

Winning places the victor on the highest rung of success; conversely, according to Lombardi, losing is never laughable, and it is the time when men need to examine themselves, a soul-searching experience if you will, and make that firm resolution to battle back more competitively than before. Players did not want to be around Lombardi after a Green Bay loss, and son, Vince Lombardi, Jr., too, admitted his family did not want to be around him after a losing effort by the Packers, especially if the Packers played poorly.

Lombardi would eventually accept a loss on the field because "after all, we are not perfect," he would say, but the effort had to be a solid one – a close game to the end. However, Lombardi was discerning and consoled his players about losing, saying: "In great attempts, it is glorious even to fail" (vincelombardi.com). Losing was not a habit or practice for the Green Bay Packers, and it did not happen often during Lombardi's winning reign in the NFL.

Lombardi also spoke to the importance

of discipline and consistency as the necessary cogs of the winning formula; he writes:

"Winning is not a something thing: it's an all the time thing. You don't win once in a while; you don't do the right thing once in a while; you do them right all the time. Winning is a habit. Unfortunately, so is losing" (vincelombardi.com). Disciplining oneself by sacrificing, being consistent, and being committed all lead to winning, according to Lombardi. Ultimately, a person's character is shaped by discipline, and Lombardi constantly reminded his players of that. In particular, Lombardi wrote this about discipline:

"It's easy to have faith in yourself and have discipline when you're a winner, when you're number one. What you've got is faith and discipline when you're not yet a winner" (vincelombardi.com).

Lombardi spoke to the importance of faith along with discipline toward achieving the winning formula. He was right: Faith is the belief system within the individual and discipline is the orderliness and the rightful actions that the individual performs to become a winner. Lombardi speaks to the importance of the grinds, the efforts, in life:

"And in truth, I've never known a man worth his salt who in the long run, deep-down in his heart, didn't appreciate the grind, the discipline. There is something in good men that really yearns for discipline and the harsh reality of head to head combat" (vincelombardi.com).

Lombardi believed that the grinds, the knocks, and the repetitions are the building blocks of outstanding efforts and building a winning team.

With sound religious and military-like training, Lombardi understood the importance of discipline and communicated it frequently to his players in building a winning organization; in essence, Lombardi understood that there could be no winning without discipline. Discipline is the key.

No one in football has been able to duplicate the winning ways of the Green Bay Packers of the 1960s. History proves Lombardi right on winning. Winning is Lombardi.

Coach Vince Lombardi on Leadership

Building a winning organization like Lombardi did at Green Bay made Lombardi a household name in the 1960s and a leader to be revered because his winning ways and charisma had transcended him beyond football into business, education, and even politics.

As a matter of fact, President Richard Nixon had considered asking Lombardi to join him as his vice presidential, running mate in 1968, until he learned that Lombardi was a Kennedy democrat. Lombardi was approached as a candidate for the U.S. Senate and was talked about for a gubernatorial run in Wisconsin as well. His public stock was soaring due to all the recognition he reaped for establishing a winning tradition in Green Bay, but he declined the political offers.

Lombardi was strictly a football coach, a great one, indeed, and politics was not his passion; football was his love, and he knew it. The Packers were winning, and Lombardi's leadership in coaching reigned over the NFL.

Winning organizations do not just become victorious, winners, and heralded without a character person leading the way. Lombardi believed that "Character is the perfectly disciplined will," (Lombardi, 2001). Character is built on truth and faith as well. Lombardi was that remarkable character that would successfully lead the Packers into football immortality. Relevantly, Lombardi (2001) states:

"Leadership rests not only upon ability, not only upon capacity; having the capacity to lead is not enough. The leader must be willing to use his authority. His leadership is then based on truth and character. There must be truth in the purpose and will power in the character" (vincelombardi.com).

Winning made the sports world take notice that winning is realized because of exceptional leadership, clamoring for Lombardi leadership techniques in sports programs in schools and colleges throughout the land. Lombardi's public appearances were increasing, and he was a hot commodity and celebrity on the rise.

As a result, Lombardi began writing down his thoughts about leadership, creating speeches and axioms that would define his leadership style for all-time. Winning for Lombardi prompted others to ask Lombardi to define what leadership meant to him, that is what good leaders do to inspire their teams and organizations. Relevantly, Vince Lombardi, Jr. (2001) recalls his father's speeches:

"Like all great speakers, he left his audience asking for more. In fact, many organizations asked him to come back repeatedly. Nobody seemed to mind that Lombardi gave it to them. Inspiration is essential, like air and food. But I think there is even more to be gotten out of my father's words and deeds."

Lombardi was certainly hard-working, but coaching and winning were what made Lombardi. His writing and speech-giving on winning and leadership came later in his career because his winning record, just on face value, spoke volumes about his credibility. He wrote about leadership axioms and goals but did not leave much of road map on how to achieve what he had truly experienced and achieved as a great coach and leader because Mother Time would take him from us early like so many great leaders in history.

Lombardi believed that "Leadership is based on a spiritual quality; the power to inspire, the power to inspire others to follow" (vincelombardi.com). He believed that leadership was special and God-sponsored, so leaders must excel. He very much wanted good leaders to be recognized and rewarded for their achievements; Lombardi (2001) writes:

"Our society, at the present time, seems to have sympathy only for the misfit, themaladjusted, the criminal, the loser. Assist them – absolutely. But I think it is hightime that we stand up for the doer, the achiever, the winner, and the leader, the one who sets out to do something and does it...The one who is constantly looking to do. The one who carries the work of the world on his shoulders. We will never create a good society, much less a great one, until individual excellence is respected and encouraged".

Lombardi was on-the-mark with recognizing individual excellence because a great society is measured by the achievements of its citizens. A commitment to excellence was very much what Lombardi believed and preached to his players, saying,

"Perfection is not attainable. But if we chase perfection, we can catch excellence" (vincelombardi.com). And who can ever forget that Lombardi was strongly driven by commitment to doing his best and committed to the Green Bay Packer family. Lombardi (2001) writes: "The quality of a person's life is in direct proportion to their commitment to excellence, regardless of their field of endeavor."

Commitment to excellence was the foundation of the Lombardi leadership model: It was the rock that the Green Bay Packers built their football dynasty on for generations to admire.

Winning bestowed Lombardi with great respect as a leader because great deeds usually require great directions to accomplish worthwhile outcomes. What qualifies a leader to lead? Excellence was materialized with the creation of a Lombardi leadership model (2001); naturally, it was outlined by his son, Vince Lombardi, Jr. The Lombardi leadership model is built on four, major tenets: 1) knowing self, 2) building character, 3) earning competence, and 4) building vision.

Everyone, it seemed, marveled at the winning success that Lombardi achieved at Green Bay and had people wondering what was exemplary about his leadership. Everyone loves a winner, at least most of the time. When asked about what are the qualities or characteristics of great leadership, Lombardi responded:

"What is needed, too, is people who will keep their head in an emergency, no matter what the field. Leaders, in other words, who meet intricate problems with wisdom and with courage. Leadership is not just one quality, but rather a blend of many qualities. Contrary to the opinion of many leaders, they are not born; they are made. And they are made by hard effort, which is the price we pay for success" (Lombardi, 2001).

Leaders are not selected to lead simply by their birthright; they need to be trained and molded into leaders, and it does not come easily. Hard work is always part of leader success as they (leaders) embellish their skills and resourcefulness and strive for competence, getting results as Lombardi did with his winning ways at Green Bay.

According to Lombardi, self-knowledge is the central building block for character: Identifying leader strengths as well as weaknesses and shortcomings is crucial to leading more effectively; Lombardi writes: "If I had to do things all over again, I think I would pray for more patience maybe, and more understanding" (Lombardi, 2001). Self-knowledge of leader strengths and areas needing improvement allows leaders to plan and execute more successfully, of course.

Seemingly, everything Lombardi professed about centered in some way on hard work, discipline, and character as the necessary ingredients of successful leadership; Lombardi (2001) writes about mental toughness and a leader's will:

"Mental toughness is many things. It is humility. It is simple. The leader always remembers that simplicity is the sign of true greatness and meekness, the sign of true strength. Mental toughness is Spartanism, with all its qualities of self-denial, sacrifice, dedication, fearlessness, and love. Mental toughness is also the perfectly disciplined will. The strength of your group is in your will – in the will of the leader. The difference between a successful man and others is not in the lack of strength, nor in the lack of knowledge, but rather, in the lack of will."

Lombardi calls for a character leader that builds character among its members. Character, Lombardi points out, cannot be wished for; it does not magically appear. It must be developed from within (introspection): A process that only the individual can make that happen for himself or herself, the hard way, through hard work and life's lessons. That is the Lombardi model on leading by exuding character and building character among team members. Lombardi (2001) writes:

"Remember that the will is character in motion...Character is more than intellect. Character is the direct result of mental attitude. A man cannot dream himself into character; he must hammer out and forge one for himself." Leadership without character is eventually leadership not at all. Character builds and promotes successful leadership in organizations per Lombardi, and he is right, again.

Self-knowledge, character development, and competence are three of the four tenets of the Lombardi leadership model; their relevance to leadership success has been discussed in this presentation. That leaves the big picture, that is a vision for success, to discuss. Lombardi (2001) writes:

"The difference between a good coach and an average coach is knowing what you-want, and knowing what the end is supposed to look like. If a coach doesn't know what the end is supposed to look like, he won't know when he sees it."

Building a vision for organizational success is crucial in leadership. A comprehensive vision is much like the main river with its tributaries (i.e. self-knowledge, character development, and competence), merging there at the main to form one, powerful rush moving toward the mouth of the river.

Verifiably, a comprehensive, clear vision unifies the whole organization under one robust purpose, one mission. Lombardi (2001) writes about the importance of enlisting support for the vision:

"The key to my father's success was his extraordinary ability to get people to gobeyond themselves – to give more to the cause than they ever believed they were capable of giving. He did this through his personal example of enormous energy and unflagging commitment. He did this by embodying the high standards that he wanted to see in others. He did this by bestowing or withholding his approval."

It was not easy to get Coach Lombardi's approval and favor: A player had to demonstrate it on the field and in practice through hard work and the display of sacrifice. He was hard to please, but his approval would come for good reasons. Lombardi (2001) writes:

"When you got that smile, that pat on the back, that "Attaboy," made all the sacrifice and the hardship seem worthwhile. And the next day, you'd start all over again, working to win his approval and avoid his disapproval. I know this is what motivated his players, and it's certainly what motivated me."

The troops, through the character-building program in the Green Bay organization, believed in their leader, Lombardi; because of that belief and trust, skillfully and remarkably on the world stage, Lombardi rallied-the-troops under the team's vision for winning and succeeded in an enormous way so much so that Lombardi will always be remembered for leading a winning team into the NFL Hall of Fame.

The Lombardi leadership model is a great one because it is based on such qualities as self-knowledge, competence, character, and vision in organizations. "As a manager, wouldn't your job be infinitely easier if the people working with you embodied these qualities?" asks Vince Lombardi, Jr. (2001, p. 48). The Lombardi leadership model remains a classic for leaders to emulate nearly 48 years after the death of its inventor. After all, Lombardi is great leadership.

For modern-day leaders, Lombardi's tenets of self-knowledge and competence more times than not are accomplished by individual sacrifice and determination. A dedicated leader can assess his or her knowledge base through skill inventories, tests, and experiences. Competence is usually acquired by hard work, repetitions, and experiences, too, mostly through individual effort. However, most modern-day leaders seem to fall short at promoting Lombardi's tenets of character-building and vision-building within organizations because they are less individualistic and require more cooperation and collaboration among the team members to become realized.

Cooperation and collaboration are nebulous factors and often require exceptional, interpersonal skills to successfully build character and build vision in organizations: Variables that are more difficult to control and oversee. That is where successful leadership bogs down.

Getting personnel on the same page for character and vision building in organizations is a frustration shared by leaders, garnering support for improvement initiatives. Character and vision building seem to be more boundless and elastic in the equation aimed at achieving leadership success; contrarily, self-knowledge and competence are more specific, more visible, and can be isolated and improved with better regularity.

The beauty of the Lombardi leadership model is that he harnessed all four tenets masterfully and gracefully into a winning wonderland for the Green Bay Packers of the

1960s. Proudly before games in the Green Bay Locker Room, Lombardi reminded his players, saying: "Remember this: You are the Green Bay Packers, and you are the world champions of football. Make me proud" (vincelombardi.com). It must have been a memorable, uplifting experience to be a Green Bay player on game day and be inspired by the Coach of the Century (as voted by ESPN).

References

Lombardi, V. (2001). What It Takes To Be #1. New York:, NY: McGraw-Hill.

Maraniss, D. (1999). When Pride Still Mattered. New York: Simon & Schuster Paperbacks.

Maraniss, D. (1997). When football mattered. Esquire, 128 (2).

www.vince lombardi.com. The Official Website of Vince Lombardi.

Coach Vince Lombardi: Records and Honors

Coach Vince Lombardi and quarterback Bart Starr are pictured here during the early 1960s Green Bay Packer dynasty. (Permission from Vince Lombardi, Jr.)

By Al Bruno
La Gazzetta Italiana
January 2019

In the 1960s, the Green Bay Packers ruled the NFL with 5 NFL Championships (i.e. three in a row - 1965, 1966, and 1967). Their coach was Vince Lombardi, the venerable one, who led the Green Bay dynasty and was voted by ESPN in 2000 as the Coach of the Century. Their championship record still stands: No NFL team since Lombardi's Packers has ever won three in a row.

It was Lombardi's tremendous leadership to motivate and inspire players to play their best that transformed NFL coaching. Observably, Lombardi was the conduit and responsible for turning the losing Packers into a championship team in just three years.

The Packers only won one game the year before Lombardi became head coach. With team development, Lombardi harnessed togetherness and nurtured a belief in each other that allowed players to perform collectively beyond their perceived physical and mental abilities, chasing perfection and achieving excellence in the process.

Lombardi coached the likes of quarterbacks Bart Starr, Zeke Bratkownski, running backs Jimmy Taylor and Paul Hornung, receivers Boyd Dowler, Max McGee, and Carroll Dale, offensive linemen Jerry Kramer and Forrest Gregg, defensive lineman Willie Davis, linebacker Ray Nitschke, and safeties Herb Aderley and Willie Wood.

Under Lombardi's direction, the Packers clinched six division titles, five NFL Championships (i.e. 1961, 1962, 1965, 1966, and 1967), two Super Bowls victories, I and II, achieving an overall record of 98-30-4 and compiling a winning percentage of .758, the highest in NFL history.

In 1967, after nine phenomenal winning seasons with the Packers, Lombardi decided to retire as head coach and continue on as the general manager. After a year away from the sideline, Lombardi yearned to coach again and was recruited by other teams.

The offers to coach again were irresistible to Lombardi, and he decided to accept a head coach position with ownership with the Washington Redskins. Lombardi kept the winning reputation alive by leading the Redskins to a winning record of seven and five in his only season: This was the first winning season for the Redskins in 14 years.

In January of 1970, Lombardi's coaching career tallied an impressive 105-35-6 overall record with no losing seasons in his remarkable, 10-year watch as the greatest of all time in the NFL. Deservingly, the NFL named Lombardi, "Man of the Decade" and ESPN named Lombardi, "Coach of the Century." Lombardi was inducted into the NFL Hall of Fame in 1971, following his untimely and tragic death in 1970.

References

Lombardi, V. (2001). What It Takes To Be #1. New York:, NY: McGraw-Hill.

Phillips, D. (2001). Run To Win. New York, NY: St. Martin's Griffin Publishers

www.vince lombardi.com. The Official Website of Coach Vince Lombardi.

Coach Vince Lombardi: The Early Years

Young Vince Lombardi as a football player at Fordham University. (Permission from Vince Lombardi, Jr.)

By Al Bruno
La Gazzetta Italiana
March and April 2019

Most modern-day, sports enthusiasts would probably acknowledge that Vince Lombardi is the greatest or certainly one of the greatest football coaches of all-time. An impressively-qualified and forward-thinking Lombardi, a virtual unknown from Brooklyn in 1948, could have indelibly etched his football legacy into Buffalo's, sports annals as the new football coach at Canisius College. Unfortunately for Lombardi, Canisius passed on him, and his head coaching quest would be foiled and crushed, sending him reeling and even doubting himself, privately; he was only 35. Most believed Lombardi was politically snubbed by the Canisius decision-making process. This is a true story that Canisius College has never commented on. If Lombardi were hired back in 1948, can you futuristically imagine how Canisius College would have flourished and transformed its football program into a division one powerhouse like Notre Dame or Boston College? This Canisius alumnus ('79) can certainly envision it.

The long and arduous journey to coaching greatness for Lombardi would begin humbly in the New York City borough of Brooklyn. Vincent Thomas Lombardi was born on June 11, 1913, in Brooklyn, to Neopolitan-born father Enrico "Harry" Lombardi (emigrated at age two), a butcher and meat distributor, and Brooklyn-born Matilda Izzo, the daughter of a barber (from east of Salerno in southern Italy).

Harry Lombardi was a strong, domineering father while his mother, Matilda was soft and caring, providing a strong religious-oriented, stable Catholic household. Italian mothers were usually the nurturers while the Italian fathers were the hard-driving enforcers of the household.

Young Vince Lombardi and his brothers were very much influenced by the strong will of their father, Harry. Phillips (2001), a Lombardi biographer, vividly describes Harry Lombardi:

"At the age of eleven, he quit school to help support his family and became a well-respected and successful butcher. Short, stocky, and strong, Vince's father was hot-tempered and overbearing. He had an intimidating style about him that allowed no back talk from his children...

"Harry was honest, straightforward, and a pure perfectionist. Those around him had to do things right or not at all. He constantly lectured his three sons that they'd be successful only if they worked harder than everybody else."

Lombardi was raised in the Sheepshead Bay area of southern Brooklyn and attended public schools through eighth grade. After eighth grade, young Lombardi faced the first critical decision of his young life: Where should he continue his education? In 1928, at age 15, he entered the Cathedral College of the Immaculate Conception, a diocesan preparatory seminary and a six year secondary program to become a Catholic priest. Why did Lombardi choose the preparatory seminary? David Maraniss (1999), an award-winning Lombardi biographer, explains in detail:

"The Trinity of Vince Lombardi's early years was religion, family, and sports. They seemed intertwined, as inseparable to him as Father, Son, and Holy Ghost. The church was not some distant institution to be visited once a week, but part of the rhythm of daily life...

"When his mother baked bread, it was one for the Lombardis, one for the priests, with Vince shuttling down the block between his house and the St. Mark's Rectory delivering food and tendering invitations."

Following his faith, young Vince was devoted and followed his mother's lead in worship:

"From an early age, her son Vince revealed an equally strong affinity to Catholicism's routine. He accompanied his mother in prayers to St. Jude and St. Anthony, the family's patron saints, and toted his own prayer book to church for seven o'clock mass. As an altar boy, he never wanted to be just another candle bearer, but up front in the procession, bearing the cross."

After four years of a six-year, preparatory seminary program, Lombardi decided not to pursue this vocational and spiritual path toward priesthood. He was a good athlete and a solid high school football player; he loved the physicality and camaraderie of sports and continued playing sports in spite of the discouraging views of sports by his seminary priests and teachers.

Maraniss (1999) describes Lombardi, the student and adolescent, at Cathedral College, the seminary, this way:

"He was remembered at Cathedral for three characteristics: his smile, a sudden, wide flash of teeth that heated the room; occasional eruptions of anger; and his physical maturity. He had the body of an adult at age fifteen. He is five eight and 175 pounds...

"They knew that he played football on a sandlot team on Sunday afternoon. Every now and then he arrived at school with a black eye, which he earned boxing in a Golden Gloves program under a pseudonym. The Cathedral priests disapproved of violent sports; the only thing worse was going out with girls. Boys found to be dating faced suspension."

The love for football, in particular, and sports, in general, won out over the calling for priesthood; consequently, he transferred to the St. Francis Preparatory High School, where he was a standout on the football team, making the All-City team as a fullback.

In 1933, Lombardi accepted a football scholarship to Fordham University in the Bronx to play for Sleepy Jim Crowley, the new head coach who was one of the Four Horsemen of Notre Dame under Coach Knute Rockne in the 1920s.

During the early 1930s, Fordham was recognized as the largest Catholic university in the nation; Fordham was nationally heralded for stressing character and the development of social morality. Relevantly, Phillips (2001) recalls Lombardi's impact at Fordham:

"At Fordham, Lombardi gained a reputation for being extremely tough – playing all-out, even when seriously hurt. At one practice, after suffering a separation of his small intestine, he was carried off the field writhing in pain. Severe internal bleeding landed him in the hospital...

"On another occasion, Lombardi continued to play a regular-season game even though several teeth had been knocked out. In later years, Lombardi was fond of retelling the story – saying that his father had often ignored the small injuries; that hurt is in the mind."

Lombardi was converted from fullback to offensive guard. Lombardi was an undersized offensive guard at 5'8" and 185 lbs., but his hustle and toughness won him a starting position at guard on Fordham's offensive line. He and the offensive line gained football notoriety and were acclaimed as the Seven Blocks of Granite for their staunch, tough play on the line.

In the classroom, Lombardi was, at best, a slightly above average student. He earned his Bachelor's degree from Fordham in June 1937; he was 24 years old.

The importance of Fordham in Lombardi's life went beyond football. It was Lombardi's understanding of the Jesuit tradition and philosophy at Fordham that would forever fuel his methodologies in coaching, leadership, and in life. Maraniss (1999) explains:

"There is a direct line in thinking from the Jesuits to football to what would become the philosophy of Vince Lombardi. They also maintained a hierarchical order inwhich the inferior submits willingly to the superior...

"This willingness to accept a rightful order required believing that the chief – God, the general, the coach – loved each member of the group with the same love."

The devotion to Catholicism and a deep understanding and practice of Jesuit philosophy would provide Lombardi with the spiritual direction and balance necessary in his life as coach, father, and spouse. Lombardi's daily attendance to early morning mass as a child became a staple in his life – something he would continue to observe the rest of his life.

In 1939, after two years of unfulfilling jobs, semi-professional football with the Brooklyn Eagles (bulking up to 205 lbs.) and Wilmington Clippers, and a semester of Fordham's law school at night, Lombardi gladly accepted an assistant coaching job at St. Cecilia's, a Catholic high school in Englewood, New Jersey.

He was hired by its new coach, a Fordham teammate, former quarterback "Handy" Andy Palau. In addition to coaching, Lombardi, age 26, also taught Latin, chemistry, and physics for an annual salary of under $1800 at the high school. He and Palau shared a boarding house room across the street for $1.50 each per week.

In 1940, Lombardi married Marie Planitz, a cousin of another Fordham teammate, Jim Lawlor. In 1942, Palau left for Fordham, and Lombardi became the head coach at St. Cecilia.

At St. Cecilia, Lombardi was given his first opportunities as head coach for football and basketball, and he turned out to be extraordinarily successful at both; Lombardi stayed on for a total of eight years (five as head coach). Phillips (2001) recalls the stellar debut and overall record of Coach Lombardi at St. Cecilia's:

"Under his direction, the high school won six state championships in the two sports. In football, Lombardi's teams ran off a thirty-two-game unbeaten streak. And, at one point, his teams won twenty-three games in a row…

"Part of the reason that Lombardi's players were willing to work with him was that he nurtured and cared for them like a father. When Lombardi succeeded, so did they. Twenty-two of St. Cecilia's players were named to All-County and All-State teams while he was coach."

Lombardi left for Fordham in 1947 to coach the freshman teams in football and basketball. The following year he served as an assistant coach for Fordham's varsity football team. His coaching stay at Fordham would be a brief one.

In 1948, Lombardi fathered his only daughter, Susan Lombardi. Vince Jr. was now six years old. Susan would be the second and last child born to Vince and Marie Lombardi.

Lombardi believed he was motivated and prepared to take on the responsibilities of becoming a head coach at the college level. One such opportunity presented itself in 1948 at Canisius College of Buffalo, NY. A Jesuit-school grad from Fordham, Lombardi felt certain that he was the most qualified and best candidate for the Canisius job.

Larry Felser (2008), an award-winning sportswriter for the Buffalo News, recalls how Lombardi ruefully responded: "Canisius was the disappointment of my career. In 1947, their coach, Earl Brown was hired by Auburn as its new head coach, and I wanted that Canisius job. I came to Buffalo, interviewed, and thought that I had it. Instead, they hired some local lawyer (Jimmy Wilson), from years before."

Following the 1948 football season, Lombardi accepted another assistant's job, at the United States Military Academy, a position that would greatly influence his future coaching style. As offensive line coach under legendary head coach Colonel Red Blaik, Lombardi worked long hours and refined his leadership skills.

Blaik's emphasis on execution would become a hallmark of Lombardi's NFL teams. Phillips (2001) writes about Blaik's influence on Lombardi:

"Coach Earl Blaik was an important person for Vince Lombardi to have adopted as a mentor. His practice sessions were precise, efficient, and highly organized. Blaik was conscientious, honest, and fair, though also a hardworking taskmaster. Vince savored every moment and appreciated all that he had learned from his mentor."

Lombardi coached at West Point for five seasons with varying results. The 1949, 1950, and 1953 seasons were very successful, but the 1951 and 1952 seasons were poor and mediocre, respectively, due to the aftermath of the cadet cribbing scandal in the spring of 1951, severely depleting the talent on the football team.

Coaches Vince Lombardi and Tom Landry work on plays at New York Giants training camp. (Permission from Vince Lombardi, Jr.).

To cite, Lombardi applied for head coaching jobs at West Point and Notre Dame, and he was rejected for both positions because of his Italian ethnicity; it was troubling and perplexing for Lombardi. David Claerbout (2004), a biographer, reflects on the hiring dilemma and obstacles that oppressively faced Lombardi in his coaching search; he writes:

"Lombardi watched helplessly as the other less competent coaches were elevated for political and ethnic reasons. He once applied for the head coach job at Wake Forest; Lombardi was confident he was the most qualified for the job...

"When the school did not call, Lombardi called an insider friend who told him Wake Forest will never hire a coach whose last name ends in a vowel. This is something Lombardi said himself when he was removed from consideration for the Army head coaching position when the renowned Earl Red Blaik - on whose staff he served - resigned, also after the '58 season...

"Lombardi was an Italian Catholic in an era of Waspish (and, in some parts of the gridiron world, Irish and Polish Catholic) dominance."

Following these five seasons at Army, Lombardi accepted an assistant coaching position with the NFL's New York Giants. Lombardi was even successful as the offensive coordinator for the New York Giants from 1954 to 1958, under head coach Lee Howell; in fact, Lombardi coached side-by-side with defensive coordinator Tom Landry, who later coached the Dallas cowboysand is an inducted member of the NFL Hall of Fame.

The year before Lombardi joined the staff, the Giants suffered through a three and nine record and scored the least amount of points in the NFL. Within three years of Lombardi's arrival, the Giants won the NFL Championship and three division titles. Including the five years as the Giants' offensive coordinator, Lombardi never experienced a losing season in football on any level.

References

Claerbaut, D. (2004). Bart Starr: When Leadership Mattered, Lanham, MD: Taylor Trade Company.

Felser, Larry (2008). The Birth of the NFL. Gullford, CT: The Lyons Press.

Lombardi, V. (2001). What It Takes To Be #1. New York:, NY: McGraw-Hill.

Maraniss, D. (1999). When Pride Still Mattered. New York: Simon & Schuster Paperbacks.

Maraniss, D. (1997). When football mattered. Esquire, 128 (2).

Phillips, D. (2001). Run To Win. New York, NY: St. Martin's Griffin Publishers

www.vince lombardi.com. The Official Website of Coach Vince Lombardi.

A Tribute to Ilio DiPaolo:
Wrestler and Community Benefactor

Ilio DiPaolo is a Buffalo sports great and the most generous, hall of famer community benefactor.

By Al Bruno,
La Gazzetta Italiana
October 2018

Editor's Note in Italian (italicized):
Ilio DiPaolo e stato un wrestler ed un ristoratore italiano premiato nel 2003 con il New York State Award conferitogli dal Professional Wrestling Hall of Fame and Museum. Nato in Abruzzo, emigrò prima in Venezuela (dove un agente vide in lui un potenziale campione) e poi nel 1951 a Buffalo. Nel 1965, si ritirò dall'attività agonistica. Ilio DiPaolo fu ucciso in un tragico incidente automobilistico enfrente di un ristorante popolare in Hamburg, New York, nel 1995. La sua famiglia fu premiata con l'inclusione nel New York Chapter of the National Wrestling Hall of Fame per la creazione della fondazione Ilio DiPaolo Scholarship che sostiene le scuole di wrestling.

Great athletic achievements are rare, recorded, and remembered for the ages in the city's annals for all to reflect, recite, and even relive those precious moments and events.

How, then, do you accurately measure the greatness of local athletes, long after their days of competition and glory are over? Who is the greatest, locally? What is your criteria?

Is it their exceptional physical abilities, number of competitive wins, individual records, public consensus, or induction into the Greater Buffalo Sports Hall of Fame?

Clearly, athletic greatness encompasses all these criteria.

What stands alone and sets the greatest ones apart, the best-of-the-best, and distinguishes them from all-the-rest is what they give back to the community as a civic leader and community benefactor, long after their passing.

Purposefully driven as a positive outcome, their civic leadership-in-action, a spiritual quality, is internally activated and somehow it is magically transformed into inspired civic participation, promoting and benefiting community groups and members through their support, generosity, and commendable work for charities, scholarships, memorials, and even foundations.

In the history of Buffalo sports, no hall of fame athlete has given back more to the community as a benefactor than professional wrestler, Ilio DiPaolo. Born and raised in Abruzzi, Italy, and known as Hercules in his small town of Introdacqua, DiPaolo immigrated and arrived in Buffalo in 1951.

It was love at first sight, and he married Ethel in 1952, looking for opportunity and chasing after the "American dream" and "gold in the streets" he had heard so much of and hoped for when he was growing up and working in the vineyards and farmlands of Introdacqua.

DiPaolo, a 6'2" and 260 lb. agile strongman, came to Buffalo with a fury, full of confidence, and fiercely determined to become a welcomed, professional wrestler from Italy. He had his own doubts, privately, because he realized he and Ethel were poor, challenged, and still uncertain how he would be received by the fans, locally, in Buffalo.

Much to DiPaolo's heartfelt delight, "When he came to Buffalo, people embraced him and brought young Ilio into their homes. This was something he never forgot,"

remembers Dennis DiPaolo, Ilio's oldest son. "Dad was very popular in Buffalo. Toronto and Hamilton, which also had large Italian communities, so he had two other major cities where he could go and he could draw well from too."

DiPaolo became a huge wrestling sensation and spectacle in the Buffalo area, winning the tag team world championship twice among other honors, until a bad ankle injury forced him to retire in 1965 and focus on starting an Italian restaurant. This was a goal and vision young DiPaolo had for him and his family. He never wanted to be hungry again like he was in Italy during World War II. Ilio and Ethel built a restaurant in Blasdell, NY after a "handshake agreement" was made with George Taylor, a local businessman, and M & T Bank. After Ilio's death in 1995, the entire family continued to take part in running the restaurant which has now become one of the most popular dining spots in Western New York. The restaurant has expanded to a Banquet Facility that can hold up to 250 people, a Courtyard Dining Area, and also expanded our Ringside Lounge, and Takeout Area. In 2020, Ilio's opened Solé at Woodlawn Beach State Park and the Lodge Banquet Facility. Ilio and Ethel's four children, Dennis, Barbara, Michael, and Lisa, grew up in the midst of a busy restaurant environment and, as a result, gained valuable insight and experience with regards to the hospitality industry. The third generation is led by Ilio, Dennis's son, along with the many nieces and nephews and long-time, loyal employees. Through Divine blessing, along with many loyal employees, the staff has grown through the years from four employees to over 100.

The wrestler-turned-community benefactor firmly believed that education, athletics, and community involvement were the essential ingredients to success. "He believed in giving back to the community as much as you could. He knew there always had to be an end game, and that he couldn't wrestle forever," recalls Dennis.

Pictured (left to right) are Michael DiPaolo, Dennis DiPaolo, and Bud Carpenter (former Buffalo Bills Trainer), next to a portrait of the late, great Ilio DiPaolo. (Permission from Dennis DiPaolo).

In fact, DiPaolo had a special connection with children, especially those with disabilities; they were close to his heart. "When those kids close their eyes, you are their hero. Even though they are in a wheelchair, they know their heroes," the wrestling giant would explain to the younger Dennis. DiPaolo was sensitive to those children because he, too, had experienced and remarkably overcame polio, a disability, as a young child in Italy.

"He signed autographs before the matches and even after the matches. He would get dressed, and all the people would be waiting outside the locker room. He would sign all the autographs. It was one of the ways he gave back to the people," said Dennis.

DiPaolo was the patriarch of an extended family that included thousands of Western New Yorkers and a long list of Buffalo Bills. DiPaolo's pleasant demeanor and warm hospitality is what brought people in from all parts of the country.

"Even on the busiest nights, Ilio found time to stop at each table to shake hands and say hello, especially if there were children at the table. His son, Dennis, has carried on this tradition," recalls Tony Giardina, of Hamburg, and longtime friend of the DiPaolo family.

DiPaolo had a special relationship with NFL Hall of Famer Jim Kelly during his playing days with the Buffalo Bills. "My dad was like a second father to Jim. Jim would love listening to my dad about his wrestling matches in the early days," said Dennis.

Although DiPaolo's restaurant became a gathering place for celebrities and Buffalo Bill players, the owner's generosity equally extended to the less famous and less fortunate. To note, DiPaolo campaigned vigorously for a variety of causes including the Leukemia Society, Children's Hospital, Cystic Fibrosis, People Incorporated, and Camp Good Days and Special Times. Hunter's Hope was added after DiPaolo's passing.

DiPaolo's community involvement was recognized by outstanding citizen's awards from many community organizations, including Hilbert College, Southtowns Rotary Club, Lions Club of Blasdell, Boys Town of Italy, St. Francis High School, and Western New York Italian-American Association.

To honor his wrestling championships and accomplishments, DiPaolo was inducted into the Greater Buffalo Sports Hall of Fame, Professional Wrestling Hall of Fame and Museum, and Canadian Wrestling Hall of Fame. He is a member of the Worldwide Wrestling Association, Midwest Wrestling Association, and Stampede Wrestling Association as well.

After DiPaolo's, unforeseen tragic passing in 1995, friends and family organized a scholarship fund in DiPaolo's named led by Bud Carpenter, Jim Kelly, and Randy Ribbeck of the Buffalo Bills. Today the fund has awarded close to $1.2 million in scholarships and donations for the less fortunate in the community. The Ilio DiPaolo Scholarship Fund has been honored by the NYS Section VI Hall of Fame, Buffalo News Prep Hall of Fame, WNY Wrestling Coaches Hall of Fame, and numerous other organizations, thanking them for their contributions.

DiPaolo's civic leadership produced fruitful community gains for all to appreciate and share in their own lives, establishing himself as the greatest benefactor among all the great athletes in Buffalo's sports history; he is the gift that keeps giving back to young athletes and charities. That kind of philanthropy is so very special and truly uncommon: DiPaolo's generosity lives on and continues to be promoted by his son, Dennis, and grandson, Ilio, owners of Ilio DiPaolo's Restaurant and Banquet Facility in Blasdell.

Buffalo's Ilio DiPaolo and His Remarkable Story

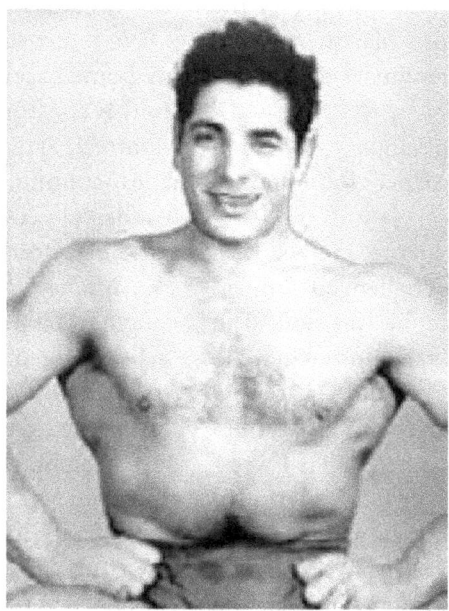

Ilio DiPaolo in his heyday.

By Ilio DiPaolo

Editor's Note: During a long and remarkable journey from his native Introdacqua, Italy (Abruzzi region) to Caracus, Venezuela, in 1949 to begin his great wrestling career. He arrived in Buffalo, New York, in 1951 to become a legendary figure and hall of famer in the world of professional wrestling.

In the early 1960s, DiPaolo battled Pat O'Connor to a draw for the World Wrestling Championship in Toronto and did the same against Lou Thesz for the Wrestling World Title in Winnipeg. He has also won the Canadian Championship, teaming with Italian-born great, Leo Nomellini, a member of the Pro Football and Wrestling Halls of Fame: one of the most remarkable, Italian-born athletes of all time for sure.

Before a chronic ankle injury forced him to retire in 1965, he would travel the globe, enjoying a considerable amount of success and popularity at almost every step. DiPaolo was tragically taken early from us in 1995 in a motor vehicle accident; he was 67. Deservingly, he is now enshrined in the Buffalo Sports Hall of Fame. DiPaolo is remembered best for his most generous, community giving in scholarship and his popular restaurant in Blasdell, New York, where his sons, Dennis and Michael, and grandson Illio DiPaolo are carrying on the restaurant tradition of the great Ilio DiPaolo.

Ilio DiPaolo: In His Own Words…

"Born in Introdacqua (Aruzzi) Italy on November 8, 1926. I left Italy in 1949 for Venezuela. While I was wrestling in Caracas, I met Tutz Mondt, promoter of the wrestling alliance and the Madison Square Garden Arena. I signed a contact at this time to wrestle in the United States, while waiting for the document and visa. I wrestled in the Dominican Republic and Cuba.

In August 1951, I arrived in New York with my working visa. Within a few, I met Pedro Martine; he was the promoter of the New York territory. At this time, I met my lovely wife, Ethel; she was working in the office for her father Pedro Martinez. It was love at first sight. We were married on May 22, 1952.

I left the country in January 1953 and traveled to Haiti to get papers for a permanent visa.

While in the Port of Prince, I talked with a local promoter and challenged Omelio Agromonte, at that time, he was ranked in the top 10 in Ring Magazine in boxing. We had a mixed match, boxing and wrestling. I pinned him in the third round at Stadium Magloire with 17,000 in attendance. I wrestled three more times while there. I wrestled Pontera Negra, defeating him both times and Tarzan De Las Pampas from Argentina, defeating him in 27 minutes. On May 23, 1953, I received my visa and traveled back to New York City.

Next, I went to wrestle for Frank Tunney, promoter of the Toronto territory. I had great success in my single matches and also in my tag-team, winning the Canadian Tag-Team Championship with Whipper Billy Watson as my partner. During this time, I wrestled in Montreal, Maple Leaf Garden in Toronto, Quebec City, Ottawa, Hamilton, and many other towns in between.

I went to Minneapolis to wrestle for Steker. He was the promoter at the time we traveled extensively between Toronto and Minneapolis. It is during this period that I made my appearance in Buffalo. Don George was the promoter.

I again left the United States and traveled with my wife, Ethel, and son, Dennis (16 months old), and went to Australia. I was extremely busy and had continued success over the next four months.

Returning back to the United States, we stopped in San Francisco, and I teamed up with the great Leo Nomellini, winning the West Coast Tag-Team Championship at the Cow Palace. My family and I stayed in San Francisco for six months where my daughter, Barbara, was born in 1957.

We returned to Buffalo, and I made this my home base. I continued to travel to Detroit, NYC, Toronto, Pittsburgh, Cleveland, Montreal, Syracuse, Hamilton, and so many cities, continuing my success. I met many wonderful people. My wife and I decided to settle here to raise our family. In 1960, my son, Michael, was born, and in 1962, my daughter, Lisa, was born.

I continued to travel, and in 1963, I went to Japan. It was a tremendous experience for me; I had much success and wrestled 40 days straight. I won the All-Asia Championship from Mr. Togo and Ricki Donzene with my partner, Buddy Hoston.

Returning to Toronto, I wrestled against Pat O'Connor for the World Championship, and it ended in a draw. Also, I had a draw against Lou Thesz in Winnipeg, Canada, for the World Title. Dick Hutton, and I wrestled in Minneapolis: all three matches were a one-hour, time limit.

Back in Buffalo, I had decided to look to start a restaurant. My ankle injury had been giving me trouble, and I realized I needed to start a new career. In 1965, I opened a pizzeria with four employees. We worked hard, made many changes, and eventually our hard work paid off; we enlarged and put much emphasis on good food and friendly service. I retired from wrestling in August of 1965.

I became involved with the Rotary Club of South Shore and Romulus Club, also the Lake Erie Italian Club. Throughout the many years, I have enjoyed the people. I had the opportunity to meet and through these clubs, I am able to reach out and help those who have been less fortunate than myself. I find this very gratifying.

In 1977, my son, Dennis, graduated from

The DiPaolo Family is pictured here. Standing: Ilio DiPaolo, Barbera DiPaolo, Dennis DiPaolo, and Michael DiPaolo. Seated: Ethel DiPaolo, DiPaolo niece Elicia, and her shy son, Talon.

Baldwin Wallace College with a degree in business administration, and he came into the business with me. Four year later, my son, Michael, graduated from the Culinary Institute of America and is now a "Certified Working Chef."

Together with my wife, Ethel, my sons, Dennis and Michael, and my daughters, Barbara and Lisa, my granddaughters-in-law, Dawn and Patti, and my son-in-law, Ken, we built this restaurant over past 25 years into DiPaolo's Restaurant and Banquet facility with almost 100 employees.

As I reflect over my past years, I must say the people in this area are the best I have encountered throughout my travels worldwide. I am very happy and proud to be part of a community who has made me feel as if I am part of its family of fans and friends."

Opportunity Motivated Italian Ilio DiPaolo to Come to America

Ilio and Ethel DiPaolo are pictured here in 1970 at the Atremeus Adelphi Italian Social Club Dinner. (Permission from Dennis DiPaolo).

By Al Bruno,

Wrestling Hall of Famer Ilio DiPaolo was not always a great athlete, as most believe. DiPaolo was, physically, very large for a youngster.

Mama DiPaolo constantly worried about him and his future. When he was 12 years old, he became afflicted with polio. Undaunted by the setback and armed with incredible determination, this brave youngster battled this scourge of mankind in every conceivable way.

The young DiPaolo helped with chores on his family's farm, like the very good son he was, honoring his Italian parents, family first. He and other Abruzzesi sons had heard about the widely-circulated tale told that there was gold in the streets in America.

He relentlessly worked for full-movement therapy, in a constant endeavor to rebuild and defeat polio's debilitating effects.

DiPaolo was a huge, 14-year old with incredible strength, and the small town residents of Introdacqua began to notice his amazing size, stature, and athletic/acrobatic-like skills. Introdacqua's legend says he soon became known as the "Italian Hercules."

DiPaolo's boyhood friends in Introdacqua automatically recruited young DiPaolo, if they believed a confrontation would ensue with eager Italian boys from the nearby Abruzzi towns: DiPaolo became the stopgap measure and their secret weapon of physical domination against local kids.

DiPaolo's rehabilitation efforts worked, and at age 14, DiPaolo had successfully beat polio, his childhood malady. The exhilarating experience of having his limb returned to normal activity made a happy lad of DiPaolo. He continued to exercise and he made incredible, physical strides, becoming a proud athlete from his hometown of Introdacqua in Abruzzi, Italy.

DiPaolo wrestled and began envisioning that it was a natural for him to become a professional wrestler, travelling to Venezuela and Cuba in 1949; then in 1951, he entered the United States to establish his place in wrestling legacy.

DiPaolo was thrilled at the opportunity, but not knowing whether he would be received well and appreciably by the fans. DiPaolo intuitively knew and believed that the immigrant Italian people and first-generation Italians would appreciate him, wondering though whether he would be received well by non-Italian fans as well.

Pleased by the unexpected outpouring of affection by virtually all fans, DiPaolo and Ethel soon learned that Buffalo, and many Italian families on the West Side really wanted their friendship and brought them into their homes. They were bestowed an uncommon appreciation with an abundance of Italian hospitality, food, wartime stories, and forever friendship: "This is something that my dad never forgot," vividly remembers Dennis DiPaolo, Ilio's older son.

Their prayers and hopes from afar were answered in Buffalo. The sincere kindness shown to the DiPaolos convinced them that Buffalo would become their new home in America.

While he is an advocate of the scientific approach, DiPaolo also spent many hours learning the catch-as-catch-can style of wrestling so popular back then that he used so effectively in both Canada and the U.S. However, if an opponent chose unorthodox tactics, he was equal to the occasion.

"Wrestling is an art as well as a sport," affirmed DiPaolo, and he had a wrestling philosophy that he would promote and demonstrate, when possible.

"Wrestling can be compared with dance in its artistic form. Both a well-trained dancer and a wrestler must have perfect balance, excellent leverage, and split-second timing. Each performer must have control of his body at all times and be able to execute the next step, or meet the next onslaught of his opponent, or sump to the attack when an opening appears," explains DiPaolo.

"Another common need to both the wrestler and the dancer is in the control of breathing. It would be bad strategy for a wrestler to run out of breath before a match is finished. His opponent would pin him in seconds, if he did. Unlike a boxer who gets a chance to breathe between rounds, a wrestler must keep in motion until the match is ended," concludes DiPaolo on wrestling techniques.

More confident now because of his superb conditioning, DiPaolo sought bouts from the best opponents this country had to offer. DiPaolo went on to wrestle for Frank Tunney, promoter in the Toronto territory. He had success in single matches and also in his tag team, winning the Canadian Championship with Whipper Billy Watson, his partner.

The incurred many difficult times because Ilio and wife, Ethel, lived on the road when he wrestled in Montreal, Toronto, Quebec City, Ottawa, Hamilton, and many other towns during that time. DiPaolo and Ethel slept on the side of the road, Ethel saying she was not hungry so DiPaolo could eat her dinner to keep up his strength for the next fight.

DiPaolo continued to meet and impress the best the U.S. had to offer and he then went on a world tour, displaying and touting his wrestling skills. Trained in the Greco-Roman style used in Europe, Ilio became a popular figure with the fans on that side of the Atlantic Ocean.

When the bell rang to start a bout, DiPaolo threw aside any gimmicks, fancy hairdos or robes and came up solid, rugged and athletically powerful, battling down the line. He was the master of many holds but specialized in flying drop-kicks and airplane spins, his signature moves in the ring, using them repeatedly and gaining many victories along-the-way.

Dipaolo's wrestling skills would now be in demand on three more continents: South America, North America, Australia and Japan, in addition to his homeland, Italy, in Western Europe. He soon became an international brand of a professional wrestler sought by so many fans around the world.

DiPaolo returned from his world tour and stopped in San Francisco and teamed up with the great Leo Nomellini for the West Coast Tag-Team Championship at the Cow Palace in 1957. Six months later DiPaolo, Ethel, and young Dennis returned to Buffalo, making the "Queen City" his permanent home.

DiPaolo continued to travel and compete in Detroit, NYC, Toronto, Pittsburgh, Cleveland, Montreal, Syracuse, Hamilton, and many other cities, continuing his success on-the-road while fortifying his Buffalo-based, wrestling legacy in the 1960s.

Italian Great Rocky Marciano Lived the American Dream

Rocky Marciano achieved the American Dream and became the Boxing Heavyweight Champion of the World by hard work, an incredible training regimen, and the determination to be the best. Marciano was an astounding 49 and 0, retiring as the only undefeated heavyweight boxing champion of the world in boxing history. He remains the beloved, favorite son of Brockton, Massachusetts (Permission from Rocky Marciano, Jr).

By Al Bruno
La Gazzetta Italiana,
January 2020

SOME HISTORIANS HAVE called the 1950s the greatest period of peace and prosperity in America: The 1950s represented a golden era of achievement, undergirded by an affirming age of simplicity, when homespun, working values and patriotism were at an all-time high for the multitudes of multicultural, multiethnic makeup of its citizenry.

America was a "melting pot" and new economic opportunities were spurred everywhere in industry and education. Nationalism and optimism permeated all segments of society, and most felt the positive effects that were sweeping the national landscape, clamoring chants of America's superiority and greatness in the world.

During WWII and immediately thereafter, Americans came to appreciate their sports heroes like heavyweight boxing champion Joe Louis and Yankee greats Joe DiMaggio and Yogi Berra; all served honorably in the war effort and returned home to garner championships, fame, and enduring respect.

Enter Rocky Marciano, in the early 1950s, the "Brockton (MA) blockbuster," returning from honorably serving in the Army in WWII as well, to defeat former heavyweight

Pasqualina Marciano proudly serves her prize son, Rocky Marciano, a penne pasta dinner and homemade Italian bread in their Brockton home kitchen in 1950 (Courtesy of Boston Globe and permission from Rocky Marciano, Jr.).

champions Joe Louis and Jersey Joe Walcott in knockout fashion to claim the undisputed, heavyweight boxing championship, shocking most in the civilized world.

How could a first-generation, Italian American and the son of a non-union, native Italian shoemaker suddenly rise to become the heavyweight boxing champion of the world? Marciano had achieved the American dream, and almost everyone appreciated him, and some even loved him.

Marciano, originally named Rocco Francis Marchegiano at birth on September 1, 1923, achieved the unthinkable and unimaginable to become the boxing world champion.

"Get out of this factory and be somebody important," Marciano's father, Pierino, would repeatedly urge and remind his oldest son, Rocco, fueling him emotionally to do something "special" and ridding himself of oppressive factory work and imminent poverty. Young Marciano feared poverty most for his parents, and he wasn't going to let that happen, remembers his younger brother, Louis.

Marciano felt pressured to make something special of himself and rescue his family. As the oldest, good son, Marciano felt compelled to honorably lift them from their family's impoverished and limited lifestyle in their modest section of an old and immigrant-filled city of Brockton. He had a burning desire to succeed and make his Italian parents proud: family first, the most important Italian mantra, honorably accepted by the oldest, first-generation son.

Marciano soon realized as an adolescent that academic achievement came with difficulty and even not at all, and he dropped out in the 10th grade, working with his father in a shoe factory and driving a coal truck in Brockton: This was not the end game he wanted for himself and his parents.

Rocky Marciano KO's Jersey Joe Walcott, and becomes the new heavyweight champion. (via sharply Historical Photo Archive and permission from Rocky Marciano, Jr.)

Marciano was stronger than most adolescents and developed a reputation as a "tough Italian kid." He worked hard at baseball and was an outstanding hitter for a catcher, turning heads as he drove baseballs out of James Edgar Park near his house. His hitting display afforded him an eventual tryout with the Chicago Cubs, did well, but he was cut because he lacked right-arm strength in his throws to second base as a catcher.

Marciano was humbled but not discouraged and then shifted his training to become a heavyweight boxer despite being harshly forbidden to not do so by his mother, Pasqualina, a domineering and protective, robust mother of her eldest son and treasure:

"Rocco, figlio mio, cuore di mamma," translating into 'Rocky, my son, and the heart of my life,' she would proudly say to family and friends. Most believed that Marciano's strength and tenacity was from Pasqualina's side, the Napolitano half of Marciano's lineage; the other half of Marciano's lineage was Pierino's side, a native from Abruzzo.

To mask his training efforts, Marciano and best friend and training partner, Allie Columbo, would run the streets of Brockton tossing a football back-and-forth to prepare him for a tryout in professional football, they would always tell Pasqualina; at first, they had her fooled with the football-tossing obsession.

Columbo strictly monitored Marciano's diet as well, regulating Marciano from overeating his favorite Italian pasta dishes prepared in earnest by Pasqualina.

Marciano was on a "no-lose" mission to achieving greatness, and he did so by simply outworking and out-conditioning all fighting foes. For starters, he ran seven miles a day through the streets of Brockton with Colombo, sometimes eating fresh fruit tossed to him from the native Italian grocers, cheering him on in Italian for his next fight that he always won.

In addition to his road work, Marciano's work ethic was nothing short of remarkably consistent and disciplined: hours of gym work, sparring, hundreds of push-ups and sit-ups, countless medicine-ball thumps to the gut, not fun for anyone, but determined, sustained, and highly effective to his training regimen.

His boxing career was almost golden, achieving a 49-0 record with 43 knockouts, and retiring as the only undefeated, heavyweight boxing champion in history; perplexingly, most boxing historians have him ranked number no higher than eighth all-time, citing weak heavyweight competition in his era and his undersized, physical stature at 5'11" and 185 lbs.

Marciano characteristically beat his competition by hitting them more often than other fighters and by relentlessly chasing them around-the-ring, until the fighters got weary usually in the later rounds; then, they (the fighters) would unconsciously drop their hands and get tagged to the jaw with Marciano's, heavy hammers from the floor, dropping foes like old timber with his powerful right hand, famously known as his "Suzie Q."

He is remembered and honored for his class as an individual and being a winner in everybody's book. Ask the Brockton residents for evidence: They always betted on Marciano, and they never lost a bet - Some even paid off mortgages with Marciano winnings, as Brockton sports lore records. Rocky Marciano is deservingly recognized as Brocton's, all-time, favorite son.

Rocky Marciano's Training Routine Defines His Unbeaten Boxing Legacy (Part 1)

Rocky Marciano is pictured here at work with his craft, practicing shadow boxing, at his training camp in Catskills rural region in New York (Wikimedia.com, Google Art Project, and permission from Rocky Marciano, Jr.).

By Al Bruno,
La Gazzetta Italiana
December 2022

Editor's Note in Italian:
L'articolo spiega la routine di allenamento che aveva Rocky Marciano, un pugile Italo – Americano molto famoso che gli permise però di essere in ottima forma negli incontri di boxe. Marciano si allevava su montagna, nelle zone rurali di New York, correndo quasi 10 chilometri ogni giorno su e giù per le montagne. Segui un regime alimentare rigido. Andava a dormire alle 21:30 esatte. Non ebbe tentazioni sessuali. Marciano fu determinante e disciplinato. Marciano non perse mai un incontro e registrò un record di 49-0. Ebbe anche 43 knockout nella sua carriera.

First-generation, Italian American Rocky Marciano's training routine and incredible determination continue to define his unbeaten boxing legacy. Marciano's boxing career was golden and distinguished, achieving a 49-0 unblemished record with 43 knockouts and compiling an 88% knockout rate of his heavyweight opponents.

Marciano achieved the unimaginable as an undersized fighter with bad footwork, overcoming the stacked odds against him and thus making him one of the most celebrated and greatest heavyweight boxers of all-time.

Simply put, Marciano's impressive training routine and incredible determination were the conduits and secrets to his phenomenal success in boxing: Marciano's discipline, the natural ally of determination, and his uncanny willingness to do the real work, the physically-demanding repetitive sacrifices, were the difference-makers that transformed him into an inspiring boxing anomaly whose legend is still alive and often retold by inquiring masses of boxing enthusiasts throughout America's landscape and abroad.

To begin with, Marciano's training regimen and his overall conditioning efforts to one of the most physically-demanding training programs and models were superb, thereby making him one of the fittest professional athletes of all-time, sports history affirms.

His road work was exemplary, running every day for five to six miles, side-by-side, with his beloved trainer and best friend, Alie Colombo, encouraging Marciano every step of the run. Marciano ran uphill at full speed, then back down the hill backward; importantly, he believed in cross-training and would jump into the swimming pool, up to his shoulders in the water, shadow-punching continuously for 45 minutes: exhausting.

Marciano's work ethic was nothing less than remarkably consistent and disciplined. He truly enjoyed his grueling workouts: Religiously working out for the sake of working out, in essence.

In addition to his dedicated, arduous road work and his cross-training in the swimming pool, he tirelessly honed his boxing skills with gym work sessions which included hundreds of hours sparring, continuously hitting the heavy and speed bags, thousands of push-up and sit-ups, countless medicine ball thumps to the gut, not fun for anyone, but determined, sustained, and highly effective to his training regimen and preparation for success in the ring.

Marciano trained in a remote Catskill area in Grossinger, NY, a requirement imposed on Marciano by his trainer, Charley Goldman, and his handlers, relocating their task-directed contingency into virtual isolation by design: In this remote setting, Marciano's focus and dedication to the tasks at hand were remarkably intense.

"He was almost completely cut off from wife and daughter while at camp, with no visits and only nightly telephone calls and occasional letters were allowed. Marciano went training for a fight with vigor and passion," vividly writes Russell Sullivan in his book, Rocky Marciano: The Rock of His Times.

When he was not training vigorously, Marciano was also serious about eating properly and getting to bed at 9:30 pm each night; his diet was strictly monitored by Alie Colombo. Marciano completely refrained from the night life and steadfastly abstained from sexual activity, firmly believing in the adage, "Women weaken legs." However, Marciano's handlers put his ironclad resolve against sexual activity to the test one night: Scheming boys being playful boys, pranksters at their best.

A group of sportswriters verified a true story about a female visitor to Marciano's room while in training camp.

"Some of the people around Marciano sent Hollywood blond bombshell Jane Mansfield into a room where Marciano was alone. The objective of her mission was obvious. Mansfield nevertheless failed, emerging from the room after a while and saying, 'What is he crazy? He didn't want anything to do with me,'" reveals Sullivan.

Marciano's critics have asked how Marciano would have handled modern era, super-sized heavyweights. After all, he possessed the shortest reach in heavyweight boxing history at just 67 inches and he only stood 5 foot and 10 and ½ inches in height and never weighed more than 192 pounds, fighting at 186 and 187 pounds in most of his matches.

Younger brother Peter Marciano adamantly refutes this argument, saying: "Rocky fought a number of guys who were 30 to 40 pounds heavier than he was, and those were his easiest fights. It was guys who were a little smaller, a little quicker, who threw punches in combinations that gave Rocky a more difficult time. Forget size, Rocky was tremendously strong. His strength was that he was almost superhuman. Big guys were made for him. The bigger they were, the easier it was for Rocky to tire them out and then knock them out."

Peter Marciano added: "Rocky lived like a monk. He was always in incredible condition. He was devoted to training, and he could always throw more punches than he faced. He's never been given full credit for his conditioning." Yes, young brother Peter Marciano is absolutely right on-the-mark about Rocky Marciano's exceptional conditioning and not being fully credited for his tireless conditioning efforts.

As the evidence clearly portrays, Marciano was one of the fittest professional athletes of all-time, running five to six miles a day, in particular, all-year-round, including Christmas. This kind of eccentric aerobic conditioning was unheard of at that time among the majority of heavyweight boxers; in fact, most heavyweight boxers would run a mile or two at best.

Marciano's conditioning was superb and a model of commitment and consistent sacrifice. Consider this as a boxer: If you can outmuscle, outwork, and ultimately outpunch the competition, winning will eventually and earnestly happen, yielding positive outcomes in the ring, and it surely did for Marciano in monumental ways and for posterity.

Importantly, let's not ever forget about Marciano's right-hand knockout power, devastating his opponents to succumbing; again, Marciano knocked out 43 out of 49 of his opponents for an 88% knockout rate: That is simply unexplainable and amazing power for an undersized heavyweight boxer at 186 or 187 pounds.

Marciano's training routines in the backwoods of the Catskill region in New York was the perfect backdrop for maintaining focus and building determination: the private secrets of his boxing success and unbeaten boxing legacy. Therefore, clearly, Marciano's training routines continue to define his unbeaten boxing legacy.

Rocky Marciano's Incredible Determination Was Hallmark Of His Unbeaten Boxing Legacy (Part 2)

The referee raises Rocky Marciano's left hand again as the winner and still heavyweight champion of the world, with legendary trainer Charley Goldman on his left (Wikimedia.com, Google Art Project, and permission from Rocky Marciano, Jr.).

By Al Bruno
La Gazzetta Italiana
January 2023

Rocky Marciano's greatest attribute was his incredible determination to succeed and win, and that hallmark characteristic was based in his core beliefs of his abilities in the ring. He truly believed he could not be defeated, and this insatiable will-to-win distinguishes him as the great champion he is.

Important to note, Marciano's mother, Pasqualina, imparted the Catholic faith to Marciano, his two brothers, and three sisters as children. Pasqualina repeatedly reinforced the importance of regularly attending mass, praying the rosary, and trusting in God in tough times. His immediate family still believe that his Catholic faith and prayerfulness strengthened his determination, spiritually transforming his great desire into courage, superhuman energy, and success in the ring.

Mike Silver, eminent boxing historian, concurred: "The key to Marciano's success is that he never gave up. Rocky never threw in the towel. He had the physical and mental attributes of a great fighter: Tremendous heart, tremendous durability, knockout power and the belief that he could not be defeated…

"His volume of punches per round is among the highest of any heavyweight champion. No heavyweight could keep up with the incessant pressure and was either knocked down or worn out by this almost superhuman specimen, (Marciano, was in the ring). A fighter who has the one-punch knockout power to end the fight at any time is very, very dangerous."

Boxing historian Bert Sugar described

Marciano's right hand punch, his "Suzie Q," as "The most devastating weapon ever brought into the ring." New York Times columnist Arthur Daley exalted Marciano's devastating power as a "perpetual motion punching machine."

Dan Cuoco of the International Boxing Research Organization agreed, adding: "What Rocky "Marciano gave up in height and reach he more than made up with one-punch knockout power, extraordinary strength and stamina, an insatiable will-to-win, mental toughness and plenty of guts…

Although he missed on a lot with his punches, his savage body attack would wear his opponents down. What he lacked in speed, he more than made up for by the volume of punches he threw. When he was caught with a good punch, his world class chin would hold up admirably."

Steve Corbo, a well-known boxing announcer, added this about Marciano: "Watching old films, it seems he (Marciano) didn't care how rough things got. He just seemed to know he was going to win. Knock down, cut-off nose, split open eye. It didn't matter because he'd get up and keep coming like a freight train until he rolled over his opponent."

When asked his opinion of Marciano after being knocked out in the ninth round by him, opponent Archie Moore had this to say: "I was impressed by his determination to win."

Floyd Patterson, Marciano's successor as heavyweight champion, emphasized: "He was the most determined heavyweight I have ever seen in my life. That man got in the ring, and there was no way he was going to lose. Determination is based in the mind. How far can you go? What is your limit? With Marciano, there was no limit."

Marciano's incredible determination-in-action was best showcased against Joe Wolcott, behind on the judges' scoring cards, dramatically delivering the greatest knockout of all-time, and winning the heavyweight title.

Later in his second match against Ezzard Charles, Marciano's incredible determination was on display again, as he was in serious danger of losing the heavyweight championship, suffering from a badly split and bleeding nose that almost stopped the contest. Marciano responded with another clutch performance and win for the ages.

"Once his nose was cut, the ring doctor was going to stop the fight, but my father and his corner convinced him to give my father another round in which my father knocked out Ezzard Charles in the 8th round," explains Rocky Marciano, Jr. A spectacular finish was not an uncommon thing for Marciano. What unexplainably happened was almost magical as Marciano summoned up his incredible determination, his hallmark, which manifested itself into one of the most memorable, one-round clutch performances in the annals of boxing history, prevailing Maricano as the heavyweight champion again.

Strangely it seems, Marciano somehow acquired a reputation of being an underdog, and he was never an underdog. His contemporaries expected him to win, and he always won with class, never boasting, bravo. Marciano never disappointed: an enduring Italian American boxing legacy that lives on.

Marciano was voted three times the Ring Magazine Fighter of the Year (1952, 1954, and 1955) and from 1952, the same journal awarded his involvement in the Fight of the Year for three consecutive years. Most boxing experts place Marciano in their top ten, some even higher. In the Ring Magazine 2000 poll, Marciano was voted the ninth greatest fighter of the 20th century among all weight classes. Bert Sugar rated Marciano as the sixth best ever heavyweight boxer.

Marciano is an inducted member of the International Boxing Hall of Fame, World Boxing Hall of Fame, and Italian

American Sports Hall of Fame. Marciano won the Sugar Ray Robinson Award in 1952. In 2006, an ESPN poll voted Marciano's 1952 championship match against Joe Walcott as the greatest knockout ever. Marciano also received the Ray Hickok Belt for the top professional athlete of the year in 1952.

Boxing News author appreciably assessed the great, transcontinental effect of the Marciano boxing legacy, observing: "Marciano's brutal slugfests are still replayed to a savvy social media generation. Sports stadiums and commemorative statues across the United States and in Italy are named after him. Annual boxing shows and sporting festivals are held in tribute to Marciano. Let's not forget his toughness, persistence, and never-say-die combative spirit and triumph over adversity inspired Sylvester Stallone to pay homage to him in iconic Rocky films. His legend continues."

In fact, the unveiling of a bronze statue of Rocky Marciano was held on September, 23, 2012 on the grounds of Brockton High School: the 60th anniversary of Marciano's winning of the world heavyweight title. Across the Atlantic Ocean, a bronze statue of Marciano was also erected in Ripa Teatina, Italy, to celebrate the birthplace of Marciano's father, Peirino Marciano.

Sullivan, a Marciano biographer, assessed Marciano's boxing legacy this way:

"In the final analysis, his contemporaries didn't give Marciano his proper due as a great fighter. Their opinion of him as a fighter was the flip side of their opinion of him as a man. If they overrated him as a man by giving him a larger-than-life, too-good-to-be-true image, they underrated him as a fighter by constantly harping upon his flaws and failing to recognize his many great attributes in the ring. Rocky Marciano was, warts and all, a great heavyweight champion."

Yes, contemporary boxing writers continue to undercut and shortchange Marciano, refusing to give him his rightful due as a top tier, great fighter; however, they constantly clamor about Marciano's quiet class and humility to compensate for their unfairness in assessing Marciano, the legendary boxer.

In any sport, how do the experts determine the greatest performers, the "greatest of all-time (the goats)?" The straightforward answer is by the number of championships and official win-and-loss records in professional games and matches.

In terms of individual performers, for example, that is why Tom Brady (seven super bowl wins) is the "goat" of NFL quarterbacks. Here are six sports icons to credit and honor:

Bill Bellichick (six super bowl wins) and Vince Lombardi (five NFL championships, including super bowls one and two) are the "goats" of NFL coaches. Joe DiMaggio (nine championships and five MVPs) is the "goat" of major league baseball. Bill Russell (11 championships and five MVPs) and Michael Jordan (six championships and three MVPs) are the goats of NBA basketball. Undefeated middleweight boxer Floyd Mayweather, with 50 and 0 record, is the "goat" of middleweight boxers.

Given these iconic sports greats and the logic presented here, shouldn't Marciano be rightfully included as the "goat" or at the very least, the top tier – top three, of heavyweight boxers of all-time with an undefeated record of 49 and 0, I believe? It's time to get-and-set the record straight now and give Marciano his proper due as one the very top tier - top three, or better yet the "goat" of heavyweight boxers all-time. Justice needs to be extolled on Marciano's greatness and achievements.

Marciano always won, never lost, never disappointed, and his courageous legend as a mighty and great champion for all-time will live on forever. Bravo, Rocco, Italy's favorite American son, beloved by all.

How the Son of an Italian Fisherman Became the Symbol of American Baseball

Joe DiMaggio, honorably remembered as the Yankee Clipper and as Joltin Joe, fulfilled a lifelong dream to become the symbol of American baseball. (The Official Site of Joe DiMaggio, joedimaggio.com)

By Al Bruno
La Gazzetta Italiana
February 2020

Editor's Note in Italian (italicized):
Quella dell'italo americano Joe DiMaggio potrebbe essere una comune storia di italiani di fine XIX secolo: figlio di pescatori originari delle Isole delle Femmine in provincia di Palermo emigrati in America alla ricerca di migliore fortuna, cresce in una famiglia numerosa. A causa delle difficili condizioni economiche, e costretto suo malgrado ad aiutare il padre ed i fratelli che gestiscono un'attività di pesca che non gli piace, mentre fin da bambino si interessa al baseball. E proprio questa passione che segnerà la singolarità del destino dell'uomo in seguito definito "Il più grande giocatore di baseball vivente." Approfittando dell'occasione offertagli da uno dei suoi fratelli – che lo raccomanda al dirigente della squadra di baseball dove lui stesso giocca – Joe diventa un idolo di qualsiasi appassionato dello sport maggiormente in voga negli Stati Uniti. Quando nel 1936 compare sul campo degli Yankees lo accolgono 25 mila bandiere tricolore issate dai suoi connazionali italoamericani.

How does an immigrant, Italian fisherman rear, endear, and ultimately prepare his gifted son to rewrite most of American baseball records and somehow rise up from the murky depths of the unforgiving sea to net and symbolize America's baseball best in grace and power?

That's the incredible story of Joe DiMaggio, a first-generation Italian kid, working the shores of Fisherman's Wharf, in northern San Francisco, from dawn-to-dusk, with his four brothers and by order of Papa DiMaggio. DiMaggio gloriously experienced and benefitted from the American dream, the postwar promise, for himself and for his financially-challenged family of 11.

"I would like to take the great DiMaggio fishing. They say his father was a fisherman. Maybe he was poor as we are and would understand," memorably writes Ernest Hemingway in "The Old Man and the Sea" (1952): The old man empathizes with DiMaggio's humble beginnings and presumes he grew up "poor" and would understand, the son of a fisherman.

Guiseppe and Rosalia, the native Italian parents, had nine children, five boys and four girls; Joe was son four in age chronology, rendered Guiseppe's namesake, and naturally more was expected. The oldest sons, Tom and Michael, diligently followed papa into the fishing business.

The third brother, Vince, and his younger or fifth brother, Dominic, decided against fishing full-time and chose to play baseball along with Joe, and both brothers would eventually play centerfield, as brother Joe did, in the major leagues.

Vince, the oldest of the three DiMaggio baseball brothers, led the way into professional baseball; he played 10 seasons and was a two-time, all-star with the Pittsburgh Pirates, retiring in 1946. Dom, the youngest DiMaggio and a seven-time all-star with the Boston Red Sox, played 10 seasons; he was considered to be one of the best center fielders of his generation, retiring in 1953; Joe retired earlier in 1951.

How did this unimaginable blessing happen to Joe, his two baseball brothers, and the DiMaggio family? In the Italian American home of the first generation that they grew up in, DiMaggio and his brothers and sisters spoke only Italian, cooked Italian, married Italian, and acted Italian. Acting Italian, simply put, meant placing the family first, above all else, the most important Italian mantra.

The oldest son unconditionally followed papa's lead, "senza parole" (in Italian), translating as 'no words, without discussion.' He inherently felt an incredible responsibility to support and make 'economic good' happen for the family's future: a burden and a blessing, simultaneously, for the oldest son to bravely encumber, accept, and importantly, turn-the-challenge into positive ends. This was not an easy calling for anyone. Tom and Michael did precisely that and more for Giuseppe; he was a proud papa.

Giuseppe was strict, relentlessly hardworking, and a successful fisherman in the San Francisco area, and he expected nothing less from his five sons, wanting all of them to become fiercely-focused fishermen, following father's, family footsteps, like he and his father before him had done, successfully, in

Joe DiMaggio and Guiseppe DiMaggio handle the crab catch as they did in their early days with 4 brothers in San Francisco Bay, earning their family's income for everyday living. (Photo by Dario el Siciliano)

Sicily. Like other native Italian fathers of the 1940s and 1950 eras, Guiseppe was revered, mirrored, and even feared by his children.

According to Italian cultural traditions, the children were never allowed to question the motives or decisions of the hard-working papa; and in doing so, those acts would be viewed as intolerable disrespect. Guiseppe was Sicilian, born-and-bred, and he made it abundantly clear to his nine children that they knew and respected 'what papa wants, papa gets.' That decision was final in his house, "senza parole, capieci?" This translates as 'no words, understand?'

The DiMaggio baseball brothers (left to right): Vince, Joe, and Dominic. (Photo is courtesy of Boston History Comes Alive).

His mother, Rosalia, was protective, intense, and encouraging with all her children. Her Catholic devotion and prayers was a stabilizing factor for the DiMaggio family; Rosalia had a strong, motherly belief in Joe as a youngster that Guiseppe did not share, especially about fishing, the family business.

DiMaggio showed very little enthusiasm about fishing with papa and his brothers; the smell would nauseate him, and he would do anything to get out of cleaning his father's boat, folding the nets, and bundling up the "crab catch" that night at Fisherman's Wharf: a dreaded and ridiculously, repetitive routine that Joe learned to passionately hate.

Joe would conveniently disappear to Guiseppe's displeasure and disdain, as oldest brothers Tom and Michael would predict, prompting Guiseppe to lash out, calling Joe a "good-for-nothing bum," "un disgraziato," a disgrace, and "un magabonu," a vilified vagabond.

"Italian sons were supposed to suffer shame and guilt for not following their fathers' ways," relevantly writes Andrew Rolle, in his book, "The Italian Americans: Troubled Roots." For Italian sons, following papa was often the only right thing to do, or they would likely face estrangement from the family forever.

Joe dropped out of high school in the 10th grade, and instead of working with papa and his brothers at the Wharf, he decided to sell bundles of newspapers and work at warehouses, offending Guiseppe's hope for him to become a fisherman.

Fortunately for him, brother Vince was soon signed by the San Francisco Seals, a minor league team; big brother encouraged Joe to come back to baseball because Vince was absolutely convinced that Joe was very 'talented and pure' in skills to earn a baseball payday; Vince knew all too well about Joe's talents.

The rest happened, almost magically for Joe, as his flawless style was now on display and being touted by national baseball writers as pure, graceful, and fluid. Joe's ease and perfection on-the-field left fans awestruck and clamoring for more.

Joe DiMaggio, the Yankee Clipper, is indelibly etched deep into America's, all-time, sports consciousness: DiMaggio achieved nine World Series championships, named American League MVP three times, selected a 13-time all-star, and garnered an astounding, 56-game, hitting streak with the Yankees: one of the greatest achievements in baseball history.

On the day of his passing in 1999, President Bill Clinton voiced these defining, memorable words to honor the venerable Joe DiMaggio: "This son of Italian immigrants gave every American something to believe in. He became the very symbol of American grace, power, and skill."

Dom DiMaggio: Beloved Boston Red Sox Hall of Famer

Dom DiMaggion was a 7-time, all-star center fielder for the Boston Red Sox in the 1940s and 1950s (Article and pic are courtesy of Baseball Wiki 2022).

By Al Bruno

Dominic "Dom" Paul DiMaggio (born February 12, 1917, in San Francisco, California) was a former, all-star centerfielder in major league baseball who played his entire career for the Boston Red Sox from 1940 to 1953. He was affectionately nicknamed "The Little Professor," partly as a result of his wearing glasses. An effective leadoff hitter, he batted .300 four times and led the American League (AL) in runs twice, 1950 and 1951, and in triples and stolen bases once each.

DiMaggio also led the AL in putouts and double plays twice each; he tied a league record by recording 400 putouts four times, and his 1948 totals of 503 putouts and 526 total chances stood as AL records for nearly 30 years. His 1338 games in centerfield ranked eighth in AL history when he retired.

His 34-game hitting streak in 1949 remains a Boston club record, also adding a 27-game hitting streak in 1951.

Of three baseball brothers who each became major league centerfielders: Joe DiMaggio was a star with the rival New York Yankees, while Vince DiMaggio played for five different National League (NL) teams. The youngest of nine children born Sicilian immigrants, Dom's small stature and eyeglasses earned him the nickname, "The Little Professor."

After breaking into the minor leagues in 1937 with the San Francisco Seals of the Pacific Coast League, Dom DiMaggio's contract was purchased by the Boston Red Sox following a 1939 season in which he batted .361 in his rookie season, becoming part of a .300-hitting outfield with Ted Williams and Doc Cramer. In both 1941 and 1942, he scored over 100 runs to finish third in the AL, and was among the league's top 10 players in doubles and steals; he was named an all-star both years. After missing three years by serving in the Coast Guard in World War II, he returned in 1946 with his best season yet, batting .316 to place fifth in the league, and coming in ninth in the MVP voting as Boston won its first pennant in 28 years.

Batting third, he hit only .259 in the 1946 World Series against the St. Louis Cardinals, but was almost a World Series hero for Boston. With two out in the eighth inning of game seven, he doubled and drove in two runs, tying the score, three to three, but he pulled his hamstring coming into second base and had to be removed for a pinch runner. The result was costly, as Harry Walker doubled to centerfield in the bottom of the inning, with Enos Slaughter coring from first base in his "Mad Dash" to win the game and World Series for St. Louis; had DiMaggio remained in the game, Walker's hit might have been catchable, or the outfielder's strong arm might have held Slaughter to third base. Leon Culberson had replaced DiMaggio in the outfield.

After an offensively disappointing year in 1947, DiMaggio rebounded in 1948 to score 127 runs (second in AL) with career highs in doubles (40), runs batted in (87) and walks (101). His 503 putouts broke Baby Doll Jacobson's AL record of 484, set with the 1924 St. Louis Browns; his 526 total chances surpassed the league mark of 498 shared by Sam Rice of the 1920 Washington Senators and Jacobson.

At the time, the marks ranked behind only Taylor Douthit's totals of 547 and 566 with the 1928 Cardinals in major league history; both records stood until 1977, when Chet Lemon of the Chicago White Sox recorded 512 putouts and 536 total chances. In 1949, DiMaggio batted .307 with 126 runs, and had his team-record 34-game hitting streak; ironically, the streak was ended on August 9 by an outstanding catch made by his brother, Joe. That year he made 400 putouts for the fourth time, tying the AL record by Sam West of the Senators and Browns; the mark was later tied by two other players before being broken by Chet Lemon in 1985.

In 1950, DiMaggio led the AL in runs (131), triples (11), and stolen bases (15) while hitting a career high .328. In June, he and Joe hit home runs while playing against one another, becoming the fourth pair of brothers to homer in the same game. Dom's stolen base total of 15 is the lowest stolen base total to lead either of the major leagues in a single season.

DiMaggio again led the league in runs (131) in 1951, when he had a 27-game hitting streak from May 12 to June 7. He retired in May 1953, after appearing in only three games that year as a pinch hitter, with a .298 batting average, 1680 hits, 308 doubles, 87 home runs, 1046 runs and 618 RBIs in 1399 games, He was selected an all-star seven times (1941-42, 1946, 1949-52). His career average of 2.98 chances per game remains the record for AL outfielders. The three DiMaggio brothers totaled 573 home runs (Joe 361, Vince 125, and Dom 87) – equaling the total of Baseball Hall of Famer Harmon Killebrew.

DiMaggio enjoyed a close friendship with teammates Ted Williams, Bobby Doerr, and Johnny Pesky, which was chronicled in David Halberstam's book, The Teammates. After retiring, he became a plastics manufacturer in New England. He was inducted into the Boston Red Sox Hall of Fame in 1995. He and his wife, Emily, to whom he has been married since 1948, have three children and several grandchildren.

It was once said of the DiMaggio brothers' talents: "Joe is the best hitter, Dom is the best fielder, and Vince is the best singer." "Who hits the ball and makes it go? Who runs the bases fast, not slow? Who's better than his brother, Joe? Dominic DiMaggio..."

In an article in 1976 in Esquire magazine, sportswriter Harry Stein published an "All-Time All-Star Argument Starter," consisting of five ethnic baseball teams. Dom DiMaggio was the left fielder on Stein's Italian team. He was unsuccessfully backed in the 1990s by Ted Williams (a committee member who died in 2002). Williams' motives were questioned, however, as the cronyism factor (noted in The Teammates) and Williams' so-far successful unfair attempt to block Gil Hodges from the Hall of Fame (confirmed by several committee members) came into question. Dom DiMaggio has since been eliminated from the Veterans' Committee list of finalist candidates, partly because of his short career and lack of batting power.

Dom DiMaggio died at his home in Marion, Massachusetts on May 9, 2009, from complications caused by pneumonia at the age of 92.

The Lorenzo Pietro "Yogi" Berra Baseball Story

Yogi Berra was the best, bad-ball hitter of all-time for the New York Yankees. Berra and the Yankees won 10 World Series championships together, and he was named American League MVP three times in his memorable baseball career. Berra was a courageous participant at D-Day (in Normandy) during World War II and was ceremoniously-decorated as a Navy gunner with the Purple Heart. (Yogi Berra Museum and Learning Center in Little Falls, NJ)

By Al Bruno

He was born on May 12, 1925, into an America that more than one President described as a "nation of immigrants." Lorenzo Pietro "Yogi" Berra was a first-generation, Italian-American who grew up in a St. Louis neighborhood called, "The Hill," where he was surrounded by recent immigrants, raised with a sense of community, and informed by Italian beliefs and traditions.

Yogi's father, Pietro, had come to the United States alone in 1909 from Malvaglio, a northern Italian town close to Milano. Temporarily leaving his wife, Paolina, and firstborn children, oldest sons Mike and Tony, in Italy, Pietro arrived through Ellis Island alongside thousands of other immigrants from across Europe.

The journey across the Atlantic was often a lonely and perilous experience; many were malnourished and became ill and hospitalized, upon arrival. After a brief stay in New York City, Pietro settled in St. Louis, his wife and children followed him soon thereafter. Once settled, Pietro and Paolina had three more children, John (third son), Yogi (fourth son), and Josie (daughter and baby of the kids).

Yogi often described The Hill as an ideal place to grow up. Like many other immigrant neighborhoods in the United States, The Hill was a tight-knit community where neighbors knew neighbors and extended families remained connected despite the upheavals of European and Italian immigration. If life there could be hard, Yogi nonetheless remembered his childhood as a happy time, punctuated by his love for baseball.

This is illustrated by writer, Harvey Araton, in his depiction of Berra and his immigrant parents, in Driving Mr. Yogi: "His respect and admiration for his father, Pietro, was retold and enduring, permanently leaving the poor tenant farms of northern Italy for the promise of America and a grueling but steady factory job, producing bricks and other clay products."

Yogi's baseball experiences started in his neighborhood, where local children played an informal, sandlot version of the game. After leaving school in eighth grade to help his family, Yogi joined working with his father in a brick and cement yard. Yogi graduated to American Legion baseball, for 13- to 19-year olds, showing himself to have the kind of baseball talent his three, older brothers had already demonstrated and more in overall potential.

Yogi's older brothers had left sports for the workplace at their father's insistence, yet Yogi attempted to do both, and he struggled to meet both demands placed on him. Italian fathers were traditional and demanding of their sons, especially about learning the trades:

"Pietro Berra was Old World all the way, demanding that his sons learn a trade, find a job, and leave children's games like baseball behind. Yogi's brothers all played recreationally, and one in particular – Tony, known as Lefty, was good enough to earn an invitation to try out with the Cleveland Indians, if only his father would have allowed it," writes Araton.

For sons of Italian fathers, it was simple: They followed their Italian fathers into the trades, and a college education was usually unaffordable and not an option. Therefore, the sons that obediently followed papa were the good and faithful sons and culturally applauded, and those not and dissenting were "disgraziata," the disgraceful.

Failing an Italian father's wishes usually had dire consequences for a dissenting son, like being shamed. Baseball regularly interfered with his brick and cement work to papa's dismay; Yogi kept working in the brickyard and playing baseball: the game he truly loved.

Yogi was indebted to his three older brothers for relentlessly lobbying and insisting that Yogi keep playing baseball because they intuitively knew, as believing brothers, that Yogi's baseball hitting skills were truly exceptional, and their kid brother was getting remarkably better at his craft with each passing week. After the war, the nation's pastime flourished for all from coast-to-coast, beautifully blossoming baseball's beginnings into a nation's passion, maybe a sports obsession in retrospect.

"If it wasn't for my brothers, I would probably have worked in a shoe factory or something," recalls Yogi, according to Araton, in Driving Mr. Yogi. "When Berra asked his father to imagine how much money the family might have made if all four Berra brothers had played ball, Pietro said, 'blame your mother.'"

Yogi's first glimpse of a possible professional career in the sport came in 1941, at age 16, when he joined Garagiola, a long-time neighborhood friend from The Hill, and tried out for their home team, the St. Louis Cardinals. Cardinal General Manager Branch Riley offered both young men contracts, but Garagiola was offered a signing bonus of $500. Yogi received a $250 offer and rejected it; Yogi languished.

"Branch Riley, the brilliant judge of talent, refused to sign the teenage Berra after a tryout at Sportsman's Park in St. Louis, saying that no kid who was all of five feet seven and not exactly built for speed would ever be more than a minor leaguer," writes Araton.

As fate would have it, it now seems, an American League coach contacted the New York Yankees on behalf of Yogi, and Yogi was signed by the Yankees, which included a $500 signing bonus. Yogi would start his professional baseball career with the Yankees, joining the Class B Piedmont League affiliate in Norfolk.

Almost immediately, World War II interfered with Yogi's new baseball career. At 18, he joined the Navy. He would see France, Italy, and North Africa through the lens of war. But it was direct on D-Day, at both Utah and Omaha beaches, dangerously placing Navy Seaman Berra at the epicenter of what was arguably WW II's, most iconic battle.

In fact, Berra served in the Navy as a gunner's mate on the attack transport, USS Bayfield, during the Normandy landings. A second-class seaman, Berra was one of a six-man crew on a Navy rocket boat, firing machine guns and launching rockets at the German defenses on Omaha beach, later receiving several commendations for his bravery during D-Day, including the Purple Heart, an American war hero.

When he returned from the war in 1946, Yogi joined the Yankees in 1947 with the great Joe DiMaggio, who would retire in 1951. Upon his arrival, Yogi was routinely ridiculed by the New York press for his small, physical appearance. One, insensitive reporter wrote that it was a good thing that he was a catcher because he would be wearing a mask.

There would even more mean-spirited jokes about Yogi's perceived intelligence, short stature, and appearance. Yogi felt those mean and discriminating comments toward Italians in those postwar years, and he endured it with class and purpose.

Yogi was not alone, as other celebrity Italian coaches like Vince Lombardi and Italian athletes, Joe DiMaggio and Rocky Marciano, experienced all kinds of discrimination because they were first-generation, Italian Americans: They were easy targets for ugly tormenting by an unrelenting New York press, but they, too, rose above it, as winners and champions always do. Like Yogi, Italian hall of famers Lombardi, DiMaggio, and Marciano all refused to follow their fathers' footsteps into the trades, like papa insisted, and they all succeeded in American sports.

The arrival of Casey Stengel in 1948 was the impetus and teaching that the young Yogi needed in refining his game. Between 1949 and 1953, the Yankees won five World Series in a row, a major league record that still stands. Stengel remained Yogi's role model as a player and an eventual coach, learning how to benefit the team and the individual players on it.

Yogi was an all-star for 15 seasons, won the American League MVP three times, was named a member of Baseball's All-Century Team, won 10 world championships as a Yankee great, and had his number, "8," retired by the NY Yankees.

In the batter's box, Yogi hit 358 home runs, had 1430 RBIs, and hit .285 in his 18-year career. Yogi is remembered for seldom striking out, one of the great bad-ball hitters of baseball, smashing bad-balls into earned, extra base hits.

As a baseball coach and manager, Yogi took home another championship ring as a coach for the 1969 NY Mets, later becoming a Mets manager. Yogi led the Mets to the National League Pennant in 1973; he left the Mets in 1975.

Yogi was back as the Yankees coach in

1976, winning the World Series in 1977 and 1978. In 1984, he was named Yankees manager and then was unexpectedly fired 16 games into the 1985 season.

While Yogi's accomplishments in baseball are the striking centerpieces of his legacy, his integrity and long-held principles are just as crucial; by design, the walls of the Yogi Berra Museum & Learning Center reflect the values that Yogi espoused and lived by: "Loyalty, passion, respect, cooperation, wisdom, service, generosity, selflessness, and citizenship, among them. Visitors to the Museum will get a sense for them as they take in Yogi's story – a story that has, with time, elevated him to the status of national treasure."

Yogi Berra transcended the world of sports to become an American icon. Few athletes have made such a transition. Yogi is a household name. He was a child of Italian immigrants, a World War II Navy gunner who served at D-Day, a record-holding athlete, a major league coach and manager, a husband and a father, son, an engaged community member, and a friend to many; he has done it all and more.

To be a war hero, a New York Yankees great, and a national treasure are truly remarkable, lifetime achievements, and the reasons why he will never be forgotten for all that he believed, fought for, and accomplished as an American hero; Yogi passed on September 22, 2015.

"Yogi" Berra and Famous Yogisms

Yogi Berra is pictured here in 1969 as an assistant coach for the New York Mets, winning the World Series that fall. (Wikimedia.com, Google Art Project)

By Al Bruno
La Gazzetta Italiana
July 2020

Over time Yogi Berra emerged as baseball's, unofficial ambassador and one of the game's, most admired representatives. Yogi's entangled speech automatically makes literary history because he is an American sports great that has never been fluid on word usage or close to clarity and understanding on what he has personally experienced in baseball or life.

While Yogi Berra's role in the history of American baseball is immeasurable, his ongoing legacy rests also on his enormous contributions to the American language. His so-called Yogisms, those unique and witty observations we have all heard before, are recognizable, and are attributable to Berra. By making those outrageous nonsensical statements, Berra unknowingly created a Yogi lexicon, a literary legacy for posterity, making him even more famous and remembered for in his passing.

Yogisms are memorable examples of double-talk, stating opposites or stating the obvious, deriving from a colorful icon and a multi-linguist extraordinaire of a different sort: a first-generation, Italian American war and sports hero, who only finished the eighth grade in order to help his family.

Importantly, Yogi was extraordinary in almost everything he did, including his unconventional use of language:

"In his own way and without intending to, Yogi became a literary figure, a man of language. The simplicity of his style appealed to an American audience already attuned to the pithy maxims of such public figures as Mark Twain, Oliver Wendell Holmes, and Dorothy Parker" (Yogi Berra Museum, 2020).

In time and with God's grace on the Berra family, Yogi found his passionate love for playing baseball to his best abilities, making his family, multitudes of friends, the Yankee organization, and a nation proud of his contributions. Here are some of the notable Yogisms famously uttered by Yogi over the years and documented for the record:

"It ain't over til it's over," is a famous Yogism that most do not know is actually attributable to Yogi. It is harmlessly repeated at sporting events that appear to be decided at the end of the game in the fourth quarter in a football or basketball game.

"It's déjà vu all over again," is another Yogism that is an example of double-speak and repetition. It is heard these days but not often. Again, most would recognize this as one of Yogi's best ones and is seldom quoted.

In fact, "Yogi said arguably his most popular Yogism after Mickey Mantle and Roger Maris hit back-to-back home runs during the 1961 season. Both players were vying to beat Babe Ruth's record of 60 home runs hit in a single season; Maris would go on to beat it when he hit his 61st home run in the final game of the season" (Yogi Berra Museum, 2020).

"When you see a fork in the road, take it," is a very recognizable Yogism. It is quoted often and most do make the association of the ambiguous meaning of this little statement as one of Yogi's best and laughable as well.

In fact, "While giving directions to his best friend Joe Garagiola to his house in Montclair, Yogi told Joe to take the fork. The fork was unique in that no matter which direction you chose, you would end up at Yogi and Carmen's house" (Yogi Berra Museum, 2020).

"I want to thank you for making this day necessary," is Yogism that relates the importance of distinguishing between day and night activities and the accurate words to make those important announcements.

In fact, "The first time this famous phrase was uttered was during 'Yogi Berra Night' in 1947 in St. Louis, when Yogi was being honored by his fans and friends from The Hill. There's debate on whether it was day or night, but Yogi could not recall the exact phrasing" (Yogi Berra Museum, 2020).

"You can observe a lot by watching," is a hilarious little Yogism that most recognize as well. Again, this is laughable and an example of unintentional double-speak, a Yogi-style redundancy.

"Nobody goes there anymore. It's too crowded," is another great Yogism that most would recognize. Two opposites in the same statement are nonsensical and laughable, too.

In fact, "Ruggeri's Restaurant was a hot spot in Yogi's old neighborhood in St. Louis. While talking with Stan Musial and Joe Garagiola, Yogi came out with this quip about the restaurant" (Yogi Berra Museum, 2020).

"Why buy good luggage? You only use it when you travel," is a funny Yogism that suggests Yogi is being practical and frugal about spending extra money on expensive luggage – something you only use when you travel. Yogi is a practical joker on this one, having one ask himself or herself, internally: "Why should I overspend for luggage?" Therefore, your luggage will wear out, not mine, Yogi's logic.

In fact, "Yogi's teammates often ribbed him about his luggage. Yogi's logic was his bags couldn't get worse, but theirs could" (Yogi Berra Museum, 2020).

"We were overwhelming underdogs," is another Yogism expressed enthusiastically by Yogi to describe those 1969 New York Mets and their amazing performance and comeback that fall. A rush of emotional enthusiasm is the precursor to a spontaneous Yogism, and this one is a great example of that spontaneity, as Yogi does his very, entangled best to retell memorable events.

In fact, "Yogi was talking to famed pitcher Nolan Ryan at the time, reminiscing about the 1969 Amazing Mets" (Yogi Berra Museum, 2020).

"You should always go to other people's funerals; otherwise, they won't come to yours," this one of his funniest Yogisms because what he is saying is so very true, but it begs the question: Who really knows or cares when you are dead anyway? This is a Yogism that is repeated often when it comes to attending funerals. It is a great party joke and Yogism to share.

For now, this is the last but not the least of all the possible Yogisms; they are chronicled and are often retold, and they endure.

While Yogi's accomplishments in baseball are remarkable and so are his legacy, integrity, and long-held values, among them: duty to country and citizenship. The walls of the Yogi Berra Museum & Learning Center in Little Falls, New Jersey, reflect the values that Yogi both espoused and lived by in his great life as one of America's, greatest sports heroes.

Italian Great Bruno Sammartino Becomes a Wrestling Hall of Fame Champion in America

Bruno Sammartino is pictured here with his wrestling heavyweight championship early in his career. Italian-born Sammartino physically suffered through World War II and then came to America, achieving the American Dream. Sammartino is remembered and still honored as "The Living Legend." (Wikimedia.com, Google Art Project).

By Al Bruno

Italian great and wrestling hall of famer Bruno Sammartino was a titan in the 1960s, 70s, and 80s, and even today, he is considered by many as one of the most honorable and great athletes in wrestling history.

For more than 11 years combined, during two title reigns, Sammartino was the World Wide Wrestling Federation Champion between 1963-71 and 1973-77 (4040 days). Sammartino headlined New York's famous Madison Square Garden 211 times, including 187 sell-outs, a record that still endures to this day.

"This is the story of a young man who grew up into a man who worked hard to become a hero to the Italian people. To be in the presence of Bruno Sammartino is to be in the presence of a unique and special individual who came up from nothing and rose to the top of his profession," writes Sal Corrente in Bruno Sammartino: The Autobiography of Wrestling's Living Legend.

Born in Pizzoferrato Abruzzi (Chieti), Italy on October 6, 1935, Bruno Leopoldo Francesco Sammartino was the youngest of seven brothers and sisters. Owing to the devastation of war-torn Italy, only three of his siblings lived into adulthood: Bruno, Paul and Mary. Originally, there were seven children born to Alfonso and Emilia, but four died (Anita, Sandrino, and two unnamed children) due to the lack of medical facilities. Alfonso left for Pittsburgh when Sammartino was an infant.

Sammartino's family often avoided the marauding German soldiers by hiding in the nearby mountains, Valla Rocca, in Abruzzi. It was an especially dangerous time as the Germans slowly withdrew north from the advancing Allies.

During their time in the mountains, many near-tragedies occurred, including three German soldiers almost killing off the village with a machine gun. Sammartino's mother, Emilia, would often slip into the town of Pizzoferrato to gather food for her family; she was detained during one trip and survived a German bullet to the shoulder on another occasion.

"I remember those times when Mom left us and went into town. We would hear the bombs exploding below. We would be petrified, worrying about whether she would return or not," writes Sammartino. "There were times when we didn't eat at all, sometimes for days."

Emilia was incredibly brave and fully aware of the danger that family was experiencing, saying to her kids: "Don't be afraid of my children, because soon we'll be in Heaven and there will be no cold, no more hunger, no more suffering. We'll all be together and we will be happy. It's going to be paradise," painfully writes Sammartino.

Life in the mountains was harsh on the young and skinny Sammartino; his health kept deteriorating. Emilia helped the young Sammartino battle a dangerous bout of pneumonia using hot blankets and leeches applied repeatedly over the course of a few weeks, making him feel better.

"Many people in our camp had died during this time from sickness and starvation. I remember the hell that it was for my own family. My brother Paul and my sister Mary were certainly not in the best of health after all we had gone through," writes Sammartino.

The German soldiers had left the town of Pizzoferrato, finally. "Everything lay in ruins and there were bodies everywhere. I remember seeing so many corpses of our own people, of the Germans, English, and some Polish. We had lived through so much hell that nothing else seemed to make an impact," writes Sammartino.

Just like so many Italian immigrants, Sammartino heard the stories of America and that the streets were paved with gold, and the family was elated at the opportunity. The long boat journey for the Sammartino family would begin on February 15, 1950, out of Naples.

"A big disappointment to us was that we missed seeing the Statue of Liberty, arriving late at night. The next day, mass confusion reigned...

"We were directed to stand under the letter that corresponded with the first letter of our last name, so we dragged our bags and waited for the big "S" for Sammartino," writes Sammartino.

They waited patiently for Sammartino's father, Alfonso, who left Pizzoferrato when Sammartino was an infant child: They almost did not recognize him. Alfonso was thrilled to see his family; it had been 11 years since Alfonso left Pizzoferrato to secure employment in America.

The shockingly-bony and sickly, 15-year old Sammartino arrived in the United States and settled with his father in Pittsburgh, Pennsylvania. Idolizing a Greco-Roman style wrestler named Batisti who had represented Italy in the Olympics (1930s), Sammartino began working out zealously at a local gym after school. He went from a frail 90 pounds to 225 pounds in just four years, earning a full scholarship to the University of Pittsburgh for wrestling and competing and eventually winning in statewide weightlifting contests.

By 1956, Bruno was working construction during the day and either lifting weights or working out with the University of Pittsburgh wrestling team. Sammartino displayed an uncommon discipline and consistency in his workouts: a weight-training marvel. He almost made the 1956 Men's Olympic Weightlifting Team.

In 1959, remarkably, Sammartino broke the world record in the highly-regulated, bench press contest with a record lift of 565 lbs., weighing only 270 lbs. at that time. Sammartino completed this lift while not wearing any elbow or wrist wraps. When he brought the bar down, he did not bounce it off his chest, but it sat there for two seconds before attempting the press.

His weightlifting reputation led him to compete in bodybuilding and won "Mr. Allegheny" in the late 1950s. In fact, Sammartino became known for strongman stunts in the Pittsburgh area, and sportscaster Bob Prince put him on his television show, and his popularity grew.

He appeared in some tag-team matches at Madison Square Garden in New York City. Low payoffs and unscrupulous promoters forced Sammartino to wrestle in Toronto.

In addition to his growing popularity in Toronto, Sammartino became popular in southern Ontario and wrestled in Welland and was really popular in Hamilton and Buffalo where he wrestled with Ilio DiPaolo on the same wrestling cards and even worked together as tag-team partners from Abruzzi, Italy, rallying immigrant Italian people from northwestern Pennsylvania, Western New York, and southern Ontario.

Toronto's growing and vibrant Italian population helped to make Sammartino a very lucrative gate attraction. Eventually, Sammartino returned to the United States, and in 1963, he won the World Wrestling Federation's heavyweight title, against Buddy Rogers at Madison Square Garden in New York City, pinning Rogers in 48 seconds with his back-breaker, succumbing to one of Sammartino's, signature closing moves.

In retrospect, Sammartino was worried, at first, wondering whether he would be received well by the non-Italian fans, but he wasn't, to his great delight and appreciation. Instead, Sammartino was embraced by virtually all and soon became popularly revered, known as the people's champion, "The Living Legend," in the New York City area: An American dream came true for the young Sammartino from Abruzzi, Italy.

Throughout the 1960s and 70s, as wrestling's popularity grew, Sammartino headlined cards around the country and even other parts of the world. One event featuring Sammartino in Caracas, Venezuela, attracted an estimated crowd of 40,000. In Australia, Sammartino managed to sell out for 21 consecutive nights, an attendance record back then.

Sammartino's primary venue remained Madison Square Garden, the Mecca of pro wrestling in the United States. It was the Garden, in 1971, where Sammartino lost his long-held title to Ivan Koloff, known as the "Russian Bear." After the pin, Koloff slowly walked across the ring while the referee raised his hand three times, and the announcer came into the ring with championship belt.

Fearful of a potential riot, he did not present the belt to Koloff. Koloff the ring while Sammartino stayed inside to keep the crowd's attention off Koloff. As Sammartino left the ring, Sammartino's faithful fans began weeping at the loss, observers noted. Sammartino held the wrestling title for almost eight years.

Eventually, on December 10, 1973, Sammartino regained the WWF Heavyweight Championship by defeating Stan Stasiak, who had won the title from Pedro Morales nine days earlier in Philadelphia.

In his second reign as champion, in 1976, Sammartino suffered a legitimate neck fracture in a match against Stan Hansen at Madison Square Garden, when Hansen improperly executed a body slam and dropped Sammartino on his head. He managed to wrestle an additional 15 minutes and performed the planned finish of a stoppage due to blood.

The rematch was highly touted and called the "1976 Match of the Year" by a number of wrestling magazines. After having an opportunity to recover and train, Sammartino scored a decisive, steel cage match win over Hansen around the WWF circuit.

In early 1977, after suffering the broken neck and many other ailments, Sammartino informed promoter Vince McMahon Sr. that he was done with his second reign, which ended on April 30, 1977, when he was defeated by Superstar Billy Graham in a controversial ending.

"My father took me to see professional wrestling at the DC Coliseum in 1966. My father introduced me to Bruno after his match. He shook my little hand, said something in Italian and signed an autograph for us," recalled Leonardo Solimine in Italian-srus.com.

"Bruno was a giant to me then, and for that simple kindness one night so long ago, he remains a giant," writes Solimine.

"I believe that America gave me the opportunity to live my dream, which was to be a champion. I still sometimes wake up and I'm afraid somebody's going to pinch me and tell me it was a dream, that I am not in America, but back in the Abruzzi hills and mountains, starving and hiding from the German troops…For me, it is a privilege to be an American," writes Sammartino in his autobiography.

Mario Andretti:
The Italian Driver of the Century

Mario Andretti is pictured here at the German Grand Prix in August 1969. Italian-born Andretti suffered through World War II and then came to America and achieved unimaginable success in race car driving for him and his family. (Wikimedia.com, Google Art Project)

By Al Bruno
La Gazzetta Italiana
August 2020

His passion for motor racing as a youngster in Italy would be fulfilled in America in 1955, arriving with his hopeful family in New York Harbor and looking for a new life with opportunities.

Mario Gabriele Andretti was born in Montona, Italy (now Croatia), about 35 miles from the northeastern city of Trieste. World War II broke around the time he was born, at the beginning of 1940 on February 28, along with twin brother, Aldo, to his parents (i suoi genitori), Alvise and Rina Andretti.

When the war ended, the peninsula of Istria, which is where Montona was located, became part of Yugoslavia. So the Andrettis were forced to stay inside a communist country. The family stuck it out for three years, hoping that the only world they had ever known would right itself.

In 1948, they decided to leave and eventually ended up in Lucca near Tuscany, for seven years, 1948 to 1955, the Andrettis lived in a refugee camp. They lived in one room with several other families – with blankets separating each one's quarters. It was not just 'pick up and go.'

Formal requests for visas had to be submitted to the American Consulate. Only so many people were given visas at one time.

When they reached a quota, there would be no more granted.

Mario Andretti, a youngster at that time, recalls: "Many people were trying to leave. Some were going to Argentina, some to Australia, and some to Canada. Everyone followed their imagination. And some people stayed. Whatever you thought was best bet" (Mario Andretti biography, 2020).

On the morning of June 16, 1955, the Andrettis cruised into New York Harbor aboard the Conte Biancamano, the Italian ocean liner, an Andretti family of five with $125 and no one could speak English. Mario and his twin brother, Aldo, were 15, culturally confused, in a new, English-speaking world.

Before journeying to New York Harbor, the young Andretti twins had gone to Monza, Italy in 1954 to watch the Italian Grand Prix, vividly remembers Andretti: "In those days, motor racing was more popular than any other sport in Italy, including soccer. In the 1950s, Ferrari, Maserati, and Alfa Romeo were the top players in Formula One. And the world champion at that time was Alberto Ascari (Mario's idol)," writes Andretti.

A few days after arriving in America, the Andretti boys discovered a race track – right near their home in Pennsylvania. It was a half mile oval track, which was different from what they had seen in Europe; the cars were modified stock cars, not sophisticated grand prix cars like they experienced back in Italy.

"There was a lot of speed. And it looked very, very do-able to us. We (Mario and Aldo) were on a mission…The first time I fired up a car, felt the engine shudder and the wheel in my hands, I was hooked," vividly writes Andretti about his instant love for racing in his book, What's It Like Out There (1970).

The 1960s were incredibly momentous for the Andretti team, tallying 21 modified stock car wins in 46 races in 1960 and 1961. The Andretti racing team kept winning remarkably, and Mario drove with a passion and joy that few, if any, have equaled.

Mario's most celebrated win in the Indianapolis 500 came in 1969. He led a total of 116 laps and established 15 of 20 new records set during that memorable event. Mario scored a total of nine wins and five pole positions that season and went on to win his third national Indy Car title; he ended the decade with a total of 30 victories and 29 out of 111 Indy Car starts.

Mario's racing success was nowhere near a foreseeable hope in his early Italian days; Mario recalls those difficult days after the war, in a Yugoslavian refugee camp, with his papa, waiting anxiously for their visas, affirming to him: "I am looking at your future, where I think would be the best solution for you kids to have opportunities, and he was correct: He was right because if we had remained in Italy I don't know whether I could have pursued what is my first passion and the only passion I really had career wise" (Mario Andretti biography).

Andretti's winning ensued, efficiently and magically at times, and he took the checkered flag 111 times during his career, a career that stretched five decades. He won the Indianapolis 500, Daytona 500, the Formula One World Championship and Pikes Peak Hillclimb. He won the Indy Car National Championship four times and was a three-time winner at Sebring.

He was named Driver of the Year in three different decades (the 60s, 70s, 80s), Driver of the Quarter Century (in the 90s) and the Associated Press named him Driver of the Century in January, 2000. Andretti is an American racing icon, considered by many to be the greatest race car driver in the history of the sport.

These days Mario is a spokesman, associate, and friend to top executives around the world. He works with Bridgestone Firestone, MagnaFlow, Mattel, Phillips Van Heusen, Honda, and GoDaddy.

Healthy and fit, Mario looks like he could slip right back into the cockpit of a race car and often does, in the two-seater which allows for a passenger to sit behind the driver and truly experience the speed and pressure that comes with open-wheel racing. Mario remains vibrant, pursuing other passions, still working at a number of personal business ventures, including a winery and petroleum business.

Mario remains one of the most popular interviews in racing and the most voice in motorsports.

Immigrant Italian Leo Nomellini Achieved the Halls of Fame in Football and Wrestling

Italian Leo Nomellini achieved the halls of fame in football and wrestling. Nomellini was a great competitor, a revered strong man, and gentleman giant in his era. (Wikimedia.com, Google Art Project)

By Al Bruno
La Gazzetta Italiana
April 2020

Leo "The Lion" Nomellini, a star tackle for the San Francisco 49ers from 1950 – 63 and member of both the Pro Football and NWA Wrestling Halls of Fame, is forever remembered as that tough-and-gritty, football Italian kid and all-around athlete: He was born on June 19, 1924, in his native town of Lucca, Italy.

Nomellini immigrated to Chicago, Illinois, as an infant with his family. Because he had to help support his family, he dropped out of high school early on, working in a foundry as a young adolescent; as a result, young Leo had to pass up playing high school football, his true love as a youngster. Importantly, the economic needs of his Italian family was first, above all, the most important mantra of Italian children to Papa and Mama Nomellini.

Relevantly, this was also true of first-generation, Italian great, Lawrence "Yogi" Berra, leaving school in the 8th grade to help his family, working in a brick yard with Papa Berra; Italian great Rocky Marciano left high school in the 10th grade to work in a shoe factory with Papa Marciano. These were standard practices for Italian sons, serving the family needs first.

Nomellini played in his first football game while stationed at a Marine base in North Carolina as a member of the Cherry Point, NC, Marines team (during World War II). After serving in the Pacific, Nomellini returned from the war effort to develop into an All-American football player at Minnesota and was named to the College Football Hall of Fame in 1977.

Nomellini played in 174 straight regular-season games and counting all appearances, including 10 Pro Bowls, he played in 266 pro contests, and he was the number one draft choice of the 49ers in 1950. The "Lion" had everything needed to eventually be an all-time, pro great size, 6'3" and 260 lbs., speed, agility, aggressiveness, dedication to the game, superb conditioning and the willingness to go the full 60 minutes of any game.

Sometimes he played both ways, garnering him incredible among his NFL football peers. Nomellini was one of the few players ever to win All-NFL recognition on both offense and defense. He was named all-league at offensive tackle in 1951 and 1952 and then received All-NFL honors defensive line play in 1953, 1954, 1957, and 1959. In 1969, he was inducted to the NFL Hall of Fame. In 1979, Nomellini was also inducted into the National Italian American Sports Hall of Fame.

When he finally retired at 39 after 14 years of battering the enemy, Nomellini was tagged "indestructible." It was a tag he truly earned and appreciated. "I really like to play football. It's tough, and it's hard and no pro football owners can pay a player enough for the punishment they take. You just have to like it – and I do," emphasized Nomellini.

Promoters lured Nomellini into the wrestling ring in the off-season and after retiring from the 49ers, ready to seize his power and strength; Nomellini was an instant success and became a wrestling superstar in Northern California.

Later in his wrestling career, officials signed him to a much-anticipated match with the World's Wrestling Champion, Lou Thesz. Nomellini won by disqualification and walked away with the NWA Championship; however, the decision was reversed and Thesz remained the champ.

That decision would always be remembered by the fans, clamoring that Nomellini was robbed of the championship belt. Nomellini was inducted into NWA Hall of Fame as well in 2008.

After Nomellini's passing on October 17, 2000, former 49ers quarterback, Y.A. Tittle, a Nomellini teammate from 1951 to 1960, said "Let just put it this way: Leon was one of kindest, gentlest, biggest tough men you'd ever want to meet. He was big and strong, a weightlifter."

Tittle continued, "More than that though, he was a great human being. He never had any bad things to say about anyone. He wasn't a gossiper…He was a guy you could have fun at, and he'd poke fun at you. He's a friend I hate to see go."

Joe Perry, who was a fullback and 49ers teammate of Nomellini, observed this: "Nomellini was as strong as three bulls. He'd slap you on the back and knock you 20 feet." His physical strength was amazing.

Nomellini was asked by a trainer to test a new strength machine and to their surprise, "Leo exploded the strength machine and blew it apart. The trainer made a big mistake in telling Leo to pull as hard as he could," recalls Perry. After that incredible demonstration of strength, Nomellini quickly established himself as the strongest, most physical player on the 49ers roster and for good reasons.

Former Viking Bob St. Claire had a particular friendship with Nomellini. "We were close, very close," St. Claire recalls. "You know he was born in Lucca, Italy, and raised by his Italian grandmother in Chicago. Every time we'd go to play the Bears, we'd go over to his grandmother's house and they'd stuff us with good Italian food. We'd end on the living room floor, we were so stuffed."

Former 49ers teammate, Gordy Soltau, played with Nomellini also at the University of Minnesota, and said this about Nomellini, "He was a great teammate and one of the best lineman we ever had. He loved to play and he loved people."

Coach Geno Auriemma:
From Montella to UConn

UConn Coach Geno Auriemma is pictured here at the World Championship Games in 2014. Auriemma is the winningest, D-1 coach in college women's basketball history. (Wikimedia.com, Google Art Project)

By Al Bruno
La Gazzetta Italiana
June 2020

Editor's Note in Italian (italicized):
Questo Articolo tratta dell'allenatore Geno Auriemma nato a Montella, un paese piccolo nella regione Campania. Lui e emigrate dall'italia negli stati uniti quando era ragazzino. Lui e sua famiglia non sapevano né la lingua inglese ne la cultura Americana. Auriemma dovera imprarare la lingua rapidamente per aiutare i suoi genitori a comunicare. Auriemma aveva una passione per gli sport e giocava a calcio e baseball quando era adolescente. Quando fu al liceo, fu introdotto al basket. Lui qui sviluppa una passione per questo sport. Auriemma prese differenti posizioni come allenatore in diverse università. Quando era allenatore dell'Università di Connecticut per la squadra delle donne, ebbe eccellenti risultati per l'universita. Sotto il suo controllo, la sua squadra vinse 43 stagioni, andò diciassette volte nelle Final Four, ebbe sei stagioni perfette, e vinse 11 campionati. Auriemma fu nominato allenatore dell'anno per le università americane otto volte, sette volte allenatore dell'anno in un'altra lega, e tre volte allenatore d'America. Auriemma fu fantastico ed ebbe ancor più successo quando divenne l'allenatore per la squadra nazionale anche per le Olimpiadi. Auriemma e ancora oggi una leggenda nel mondo di basket.

The dream of coaching women's college basketball was never even a remote thought in 1961 for Geno Auriemma, age seven, confused, and journeying to a multiethnic, changing America from the town of Montella, located in southern Italy, in the Campania region.

Geno's humble life, as he knew it then, originated from the poor beginnings of a backward, little Italian town (where he was born and raised) where piped-in, gas heat and running water were considered to be luxurious living items; the progressive impetus of a new, American daily life would radically and forever change this naive Italian kid, his parents, and his younger brother and sister.

"I arrived in Norristown, Pennsylvania, not being able to speak English. I don't know the customs. I don't dress the right way. I feel out of place, so I'm constantly self-conscious and unsure of myself," vividly remembers and writes Auriema in his book, "Geno: In Pursuit of Perfection."

From birth on, Auriemma was a natural leader, in pursuit of perfection, and this mantra was firmly ingrained in his physical being and in his DNA. When his family immigrated to the United States from Italy in 1961, it was not uncommon for this seven year-old, Geno, to help his parents, Donato and Marciella, interpret, negotiate, and often remedy English language issues.

Astoundingly forward-thinking for a child, he voluntarily rose up to the challenge of being the unconventional and relentlessly assisting, assuring, assuming kid. Auriemma did so by interpreting tax statements, making mortgage payments, and communicating parents' concerns to lawyers.

He was the oldest son and much was expected; he instinctively guided and taught his younger brother, Ferrucci, and younger sister, Anna, the new language and the American ways.

This was an incredible display of leadership and initiative for this treasured gem, the oldest son of the Auriemma family, placing the family's needs first: the most important Italian mantra culturally instilled in Geno by his Italian parents. He was the oldest son and, therefore, he delivered in remarkable fashion, honoring his Italian parents.

"At this point, I'm talking to my parents strictly in English. It is hard for them, but necessary for me. I know they need to understand English. They also need to speak Italian to me, to make sure I never forget Italian," writes Auriemma about those early years in Norristown.

Those were important, cross-cultural communication lessons that happened out-of-life's necessity, simultaneously, in both native Italian and English: new learning and linguistic adaptation in its purest, pluralistic format.

"I lived a different life than most fourteen- and fifteen-year-old kids my age. I am on my own with a lot of responsibility. Don't get me wrong, I never felt unsafe or unloved, just not that connected," writes Auriemma. His family was a safe haven and cultural security for Auriemma.

For Auremmia, soccer was his first love, coming from Italy, but he soon became very interested in baseball, as his first sport, and he did well. In his sophomore year, however, he learned to appreciate the game of basketball imparted to him, by then Coach Buddy Gardler, at Bishop Kenrick High School.

In 1978 and 1979, Auriemma worked as an assistant coach at Saint Joseph's University; he then returned to be the assistant coach at Bishop Kerrick, his alma mater, until 1981, the year he earned his BA. Auriemma then accepted an assistant coach job with the University of Virginia and worked there until 1985.

Auriemma remained 'old school' in pedagogy, tough and gritty, in his approach to coaching; he adopted and molded his style to that of Coach Gardler: demanding, fair, and unassuming. "I was fortunate enough to do what I love to do – and that is to teach and coach," writes Auriemma.

"I am a hard-ass," admits Auriemma. He pushes his players hard, emphasizing, "I demand sometimes more than they can give. But I don't know what that is until I find out what they can't give."

Importantly, it's incumbent on a coach to obtain a baseline on performance, an assessment, using the collected data and observations to understand what players can and cannot do. That is informed, insightful coaching for any sport.

"I push them, prod them, challenge them, and take them to the brink. I don't want them ever to land face first in a hot bed of coals. Believe me. It hurts," writes Auriemma.

"He's the guy everyone loves until he gives it to you straight, and then you hate him for it. But underneath the anger, you know what he's saying is true," writes his former All-American and now professional, 10-time, all-star player Diana Taurasi. "He forced me to be somebody special, and I will always be grateful."

Candid and honest, it describes Auriemma, but they are just labels. Auriemma transcends all of that – he continues to contribute and transform women's basketball into what it is today.

Before Auriemma arrived at the University of Connecticut (UConn), the women's basketball program had only one winning season in its history. Amazingly, since his arrival in 1985, the Huskies have had only one losing – his very first year with the team.

Since his arrival in 1985, the UConn women's basketball team has won 43 regular season tournament titles, advanced to 17 Final Fours, posted six perfect seasons, and won 11 national championships.

Auriemma is an eight-time, AP College Basketball Coach of the Year, seven-time Naismith Coach of the Year, and three-time American Athletic Coach of the Year; his cumulative record at UConn remains the best winning percentage in the history of the sport.

Auriemma was the head coach of the United States women national basketball teams from 2009 through 2016, during which time his team won the 2010 and 2014 World Championships; he garnered gold medals at the 2012 and 2016 Summer Olympics, going undefeated in all four tournaments.

"We have won 11 national championships, and we've never taken any of them for granted. Every one of those championships is special," emphasizes Auriemma.

Remembering a Friend: Phil Scaffidi

NU basketball great Phil Scaffidi at Niagara Falls in 1976

By Al Bruno.
La Gazzetta Italiana
December 2018

Editor's Note in Italian (italicized):
Membro della Greater Buffalo Sports Hall of Fame dal 2005, Phil Scaffidi e stato un atleta straordinario che si e distinto nel calcio, nella pallacanestro, nel baseball e nell'atletica sulla pista del St. Joseph's Collegiate do Buffalo, vincendo numerosi premi durante il terzo e quarto anno di università. Adorato dai tifosi della sua citta, e stato probabilmente uno dei tre migliori atleti and emergere dallo Stato di New York. Il coraggio, la determinazione e la perseveranza dimostrati sul campo gli hanno permesso di affrontare e combattere un tumore diagnosticato gli nel 1979, che lo ha poi ucciso l'anno successivo a soli 23 anni.

NFL Hall of Fame quarterback Jim Kelly's courageous fight against cancer sad-

Phil Scaffidi was drafted by the Pittsburgh Pirates to play shortstop

dens me and thousands of other Western New Yorkers. As we continue to pray for Jim's recovery, I cannot help but to similarly remember a great local kid, a 4-sport phenom, a champion, a dear friend, and a member of the Greater Buffalo Sports Hall of Fame named Phil Scaffidi. Posthumously inducted in 2005, Scaffidi, like Kelly, showed us great courage and perseverance in battling cancer.

Scaffidi excelled in football, basketball, baseball, and track at St. Joseph's Collegiate Institute in Buffalo. He earned All-Catholic honors in all 4 sports in his junior and senior years: Phil was certainly an extraordinary athlete, thus making him special and celebrated by local sports fans.

In football, Phil was an All-Catholic quarterback, impressively running Coach Tom Reddington's veer offense and often optioning and bursting off-tackle into the secondary for long runs and touchdowns.

In basketball, although not a great scorer, he was a ball hawk on defense, running down and taking possession of every 50-50 ball because of his incredible, closing speed; aptly put, he was the consummate point guard, dribbling and penetrating past defenders, getting to the paint, and distributing the ball to open teammates for easy buckets. Scaffidi led the Marauders to Manhattan Cup Championships in 1973 and 1974, under St. Joe's Coach Dick Bihr, and was named Tournament MVP in 1974.

Phil's prowess in baseball was nothing short of spectacular as a standout shortstop, who could put on a baseball skills clinic, almost to perfection: hitting, fielding, firing Philly fastballs, stealing bases, and scoring runs. In track, Phil's sprinter speed not only gained him recognition in the 100-yard dash, locally, but he also was a member of the national, record-setting, 4 x 4, 880-yard, relay team at the Penn Relays in 1972, honoring St. Joe's Coach Bob Ivory with an unforgettable, sprinter performance for the ages.

"Scaffidi was probably one of the three best all-around athletes ever to come out of

Phil Scaffidi was an All-Catholic quarterback at St. Joe's Collegiate Institute in Buffalo

Western New York," said Joe Wolf, St. Joe's athletic director. After graduating from St. Joe's in 1974, Phil was drafted by the Pittsburgh Pirates as a shortstop in the ninth round of the 1974 major league draft and played two years of Class A pro ball before returning to play basketball at Niagara University (NU) where he was offered a scholarship by then Coach Frank Layden, prior to the 1975-76 season. Coach Layden immediately inserted Phil to his starting point guard position at NU, and led the Purple Eagles to a berth in the National Invitation Tournament (NIT) in Spring 1976.

Sadly, Phil was diagnosed with adrenal cancer in 1979; Phil had surgery and amazingly returned to NU's line-up in 1980, breaking the NU assist record before a packed house crowd on-hand to witness Phil's courage and history being recorded. "He got a standing ovation, took the ball up to the stands and gave it to his dad, which was touching," recalls Joe Wolf, then St. Joe's Athletic Director.

The cancer returned, unfortunately, and on March 23, 1980, Phil passed away; he was only 23.

Tragically taken too soon, Phil's legacy is far-reaching and still painfully affects me today when admirable qualities like courage and perseverance are mentioned, I think of Phil and become emotional. Phil was humble, inspiring, kind, and very approachable: Phil was the prince of North Buffalo and Kenmore; he is and will continue to be sorely missed.

Importantly, Phil's life is a resonating reminder of what great men do with their lives in extraordinary ways. God blessed Phil on earth, and God continues to bless Phil in Heaven.

Quarterback Rick Cassata Realizes Inductions into Three Sports Halls of Fame

Ottawa quarterback Rick Cassata rolls out to the right, stretching the defense

By Al Bruno
La Gazzetta Italiana,
November 2020

OUTSTANDING HIGH SCHOOL athletes frequently possess the tools of stardom in more than one sport and indeed the Great Buffalo Sports Hall of Fame features more than a few multi-sport notables. Even among the crowd, certain athletes stand out, including a player widely considered to be the best three-sport athletes ever produced locally on the high school level in Western New York (WNY) – Rick Cassata.

A product of Buffalo's Lower West Side, Cassata was schooled by the old-time, Italian kids, most of whom were older; but those Italian kids soon recognized that the younger "Rico" was unusually strong, a diamond-in-the-ruff, with overly-muscular thighs, a great arm, and a competitor. Those Italian boys would hit him harder and punish him more because they knew he could take it, and they knew they were making him better by the week.

Cassata played a lot of grueling games at the south end of Busti Avenue on the Lower West Side: the football training and baptisms began there on those grassy fields, sometimes under the lights. In many of

Syracuse quarterback Rick Cassata is pictured with future, NFL Hall of Famers Floyd Little and Larry Csonka. Former NFL coach Tom Coughlin was Cassata's wingback and is pictured in front of Csonka

those grueling and battering football scrimmages, Cassata would intentionally get roughed-up, thrown-on-his-head, swatted, and gang tackled with a nastiness to hurt, a typical display by those competitive, Italian kids of the Lower West Side with attitude. Certainly what would follow was the issuance of pummeling pain to get Cassata off-the-field and laugh, so that Cassata would painfully remember them.

Yet, unexplainably and uncommonly determined, like the great Italian ones, Rocky Marciano and Ilio DiPaolo, young Cassata would get up again-and-again in determination: He was inspired to throw, run, and catch like few before his time on the Lower West Side in the early 1960s. The legend of quarterback Rick Cassata, the grit and determination of an Italian kid and champion, was formed and developed there on that playing field on South Busti Avenue on the Lower West Side.

Then, the Cassata family moved to Tonawanda, and the young Cassata displayed that he possessed exceptional, football skills, touting a strong arm. In view of this, it was 1961 and not everyone liked Italians: Some called him "that 'dago kid' from the West Side."

In response, Cassata served notice of future, athletic greatness at Tonawanda High School early on in eighth and ninth grades. A strong-armed quarterback, Cassata achieved All-Niagara Frontier League (NFL) honors as a junior in 1962, and added All-WNY and All-American citations in 1963. Cassata paced the Red Warriors to a share of the NFL title in 1962 and later to an undefeated championship season in 1963.

Basketball and baseball provided additional showcases for Cassata, athletic talents; he led his basketball team to an AAA Sectional championship in 1962, and a year later achieved All-NFL status as a forward.

Cassata's contributions were recognized with selection to the NFL All-Decade team for the 1960s; he was no less a terror on the diamond; the hard-hitting, hard-throwing, shortstop and pitcher won an NFL batting title in 1963 and All-NFL and All-WNY

Ottawa quarterback Rick Cassata rallies his Rough Riders on the winning drive to the Grey Cup Championship against Edmonton in 1973, winning 22 to 18, and Cassata was named the game's MVP.

honors in 1964. Cassata was drafted in baseball by the New York Yankees and Washington Senators.

During his senior year at Tonawanda HS, football scouts from Miami University and Notre Dame came calling because he was the number one prospect for the Irish, even more highly than eventual Heisman Trophy winner Terry Hanratty. Cassata decided to stay close to home by choosing Syracuse University.

With Cassata and NFL hall of famers Larry Csonka and Floyd Little in the backfield, the mid-1960s was a golden gridiron era for the Orangemen, and bowl appearances capped off each of Cassata's last two seasons in college. Although the 1966 Gator Bowl featured a fine performance from Cassata, he saved his best for last. In a memorable 1967 clash in the Hula Bowl, before a nationwide audience, Cassata soundly outplayed his counterpart, UCLA quarterback and Heisman Trophy winner Gary Beban, capturing the game's MVP award.

Cassata also captained the Syracuse Orangemen his senior year and faced another fork in the road after graduation, as scouts from New York Yankees and Washington Senators crowded pro football scouts on his doorstep. Instead, Cassata opted for the Canadian Football League. Cassata flourished as a quarterback in the wide-open CFL and his stellar nine-year career north of the border.

One thing about Cassata's stats to remember is that he had arguably the best backfield combination at running back/fullback with Floyd and Csonka when compared to others, but still went to win a Grey Cup.

Cassata joined Saskatchewan in 1968, serving as the backup to Ron Lancaster. In 1969, he moved to join Winnipeg. In 1970,

Cassata joined the Jersey Jays of the Continental League, the farm club of Cleveland Browns, and Cassata returned to the CFL with the Ottawa Rough Riders in 1971. Cassata played four seasons in Ottawa, in the era between the retirement of hall of famer quarterback Russ Jackson and the arrival of two other hall of fame quarterbacks, Tom Clements and Conredge Halloway, in 1975.

In 1971, Cassata split the quarterbacking with the former duties with NFL quarterback Gary Wood, and then took over as the undisputed #1 quarterback in 1972, when he had his best season. He threw 357 passes and completed 50.1 of them for 2,548 yards.

In 1972, strangely, Eddie MacCabe. a columnist for the Ottawa Journal, published a letter to the editor by Terry McKinney of Oxford Station near Kemptville. McKinney was critical of Cassata, saying that "he had a candy arm."

Cassata was so offended that he got in his car, drove to Oxford Station, and pounded on McKinney's door. When McKinney's wife answered the door, she thought – or was actually hoping, according to McCabe - that the quarterback was not going to deck her husband, appealing to Cassata, "I told him not to write that letter to the editor."

Cassata did not do that but instead, he marched out McKinney onto the street, told him to stand still, marked off 70 yards, and as McCabe put it, threw a ball so hard that it nailed itself into McKinney's chest to his amazement. The candy arm was actually a cannon arm and McKinney had a welt to prove it.

In 1973 and 1974, including a Grey Cup win with the Ottawa Rough Riders against Edmonton Eskimos, 22 to 18, in 1973. Cassata shared quarterbacking duties with veteran Jerry Keelin.

After being moved and playing with Hawaiians of the Word Football League (WFL) in 1975, Cassata brought six years of proven experience from the CFL and was the Ottawa Rough Riders most valuable player in the 1973 championship game.

In that memorable win, Cassata brought Ottawa back from a 0-7 deficit with a 38-yard , touchdown strike to split end Rhome Nixon in the first quarter when it appeared that Edmonton might run away with the game, after Roy Bell's 33-yard, TD romp.

But it was Cassata's passing that set the stage for Jim Evenson's 18-yard, touchdown run in the third quarter which gave the Rough Riders a 19-10 lead and put the game beyond reach.

"The whole key to my game is that there are 31 guys who believed in me in their special way," said Cassata. "It didn't matter what the knockers said. My guys believed in me, including head coach Jack Gotta.

"Before the game, Gotta told me that I was calling the shots. He said if I wanted to throw the ball 80 yards, to go ahead. Or run as many times as I liked, even though we knew Keeling couldn't have played," said Cassata.

Gotta commented that Cassata was his kind of guy, one who plays a tough, physical game. The Rough Rider head coach also left two situations that turned the game around for Ottawa.

"We hadn't shown a great deal of offense and Edmonton looked tough in the first two quarters," said Gotta. "Then Cassata starts hitting his passes."

The quarterback and Grey Cup MVP commented further, "You don't know how good it was to come back, after the half-time break and seeing us leading on the scoreboard – it was a lift."

An athlete with tremendous ability, Cassata played out his option and signed with the Hawaiians. Cassata was a scrambler, who liked to take off with the ball, and he had an excellent arm and was a great leader on the field. In fact, future NFL running backs Calvin Hill and Duane Thomas played with Cassata during his time with the Hawaiians.

In his football career, Cassata tallied 8,365 passing yards and threw for 39 touchdowns. As a positive result, Cassata was inducted into the Buffalo, Tonawanda, Ottawa, and CFL Halls of Fame.

In 1984, Cassata purchased what is now known as the Sawyer Creek Hotel, 3264 Niagara Falls Boulevard in North Tonawanda near Niagara Wheatfield. Rick Cassata has retired and his son, Brett, runs the restaurant and bar, creating a North Tonawanda dining mainstay and area landmark.

At the 2002 Buffalo Sports Hall of Fame ceremony and as he starts off his induction speech, Cassata recalls, looking to the sky and with arms wide open, yelling, "Hey, mom, look at me now." All the sustained efforts, and Cassata had finally made it: from the Lower West Side to Tonawanda to Syracuse University to the CFL, meritoriously earning his way into the Buffalo Sports Hall of Fame. His mission is complete.

Cassata is proud of his WNY roots, which he still maintains, and the Greater Buffalo Sports Hall of Fame is equally proud to call him a member.

Rick Cassata Passed on Yankees' Baseball Offer

Rick Cassata was drafted by the New York Yankees to play shortstop, passing on the offer to play shortstop to play quarterback in the CFL, and earning him induction into the CFL, Ottawa, and Greater Buffalo Sports Halls of Fame.

By Al Bruno
La Gazzetta Italiana,
January 2021

Editor' Note in Italian (italicized):
Rick Cassata, un giocatore italiano di football, vinse il premio MVP nel "Grey Cup Championship" nel 1973. Nel 2002, fu introdotto nel "Greater Buffalo Sports Hall of Fame." Quando era uno studente di scuola superiore, gioco a calcio, baseball, e football. Malgrado il fatto che ebbe l'opportunità di giocare il football per una squadra professionale in Canada. Siccome era atleta bravissimo, gli fu riconosciuto un premio per la sua abilità eccezionale in tutta la sua vita.

Rick "Rico" Cassata was inducted into the Greater Buffalo Sports Hall of Fame in 2002 for his quarterback play with the Ottawa Rough Riders of the Canadian Football League (CFL), winning the MVP award in the Grey Cup Championship in 1973 and highlighting a nine-year, CFL career.

However, in 1964, after graduating from Tonawanda High School, Cassata had the opportunity and choice to play shortstop for the New York Yankees, potentially, for two decades in the 1960s and 1970s, much like Derek Jeter demonstrated in his remarkable, two-decade journey into the Baseball Hall of Fame in Cooperstown, NY.

Cassata was the object of many baseball's affections before being courted to play baseball for the Yankees and even the Washington Senators, who both prioritized and drafted Cassata as their future, franchise shortstop.

In fact, Cassata's baseball and football contributions were recognized with the selection to the Niagara Frontier League (NFL) All-Decade Team for the 1960s. The hard-hitting and hard-throwing shortstop won the NFL batting title in 1963 as a 17-year old junior, inviting baseball scouts to all of his baseball games during his junior and senior years.

Cassata's junior year was an awesome baseball season for the Tonawanda Warriors, hitting an amazing .422, winning the NFL batting title, and leading the league in extra-base hits. Uncommonly, Cassata possessed eye-catching, power-hitting skills for a shortstop like few others. Cassata's stellar play in baseball unanimously garnered him the All-NFL and All Western New York honors in 1964.

Cassata's fielding skills were flawless: His agile footwork, speed, and his uncanny ability, often off-balance, to successfully turn double plays were superb; he certainly possessed a great arm for those powerful, across-the-diamond throws (assists) to nail hopeful base runners from tallying an easy hit with their legs.

Cassata had a complete baseball game, a talented youngster: His batting skills were rare, special, and appreciated more; his hitting skills are still marveled at by those that saw it happen for themselves in those memorable 1963 and 1964 baseball seasons.

"The stands would be packed, standing room only, when Rick played at home (Veteran's Park) with fans and scouts from all over. Rick's bat speed and hitting display was a thing of beauty," remembers Allen Chester, a minor league baseball player from yesteryear in the 1950s and a longtime, baseball coach in the city of Tonawanda.

After the lure of professional baseball was considered, Cassata decided on his passion and ultimately accepted a football scholarship to be the future quarterback for the Syracuse Orangemen, unknowingly joining future football hall of fame teammates Floyd Little, Larry Cszonka, and Tom Coughlin in the fall of 1964.

Cassata was not allowed to take the diamond until his senior year at Syracuse, when his football scholarship service was completed. In the 1960s, scholarship athletes were forbidden from participating in other varsity sports. To no one's surprise, Cassata was an impacting newcomer to the infield line-up and was one of the best baseball players as a hitter and fielder that year, after foregoing three years of possible eligibility.

"Rick Cassata is the best athlete to ever come out of Tonawanda," recalls Larry Margaris, who played for the Tonawanda Warriors from 1962 to 1964, playing side-by-side with the multi-talented Cassata. "Football, basketball, baseball, boxing, pocket billiards, he could do it all."

Margaris expounded on what he observed, experienced, and assessed about Cassata's athletic talents: "There haven't been a lot of quarterbacks who could throw a football like Rick. I would play catch with him and I would swear he was going to throw the ball through me. In gym class one time, I saw Rick throw a softball 302 feet."

Given the major league prospect of signing with the Yankees back in 1964, Cassata admits even today that he would still choose football over baseball, if he had it to do all over. He passionately affirms: "I love quarterbacking more than baseball still. At that time, I had to ask myself, do I want to be a quarterback or a baseball player? I wanted to be a quarterback. There was no other choice."

Admittedly, Cassata added: "It would have been nice to have had both pro football and pro baseball careers, but my knees could never be able to endure it."

Buffalo's Tony Masiello: College Basketball Player and Mayoral Hall of Famer (Part 1)

Tony Masiello, #22, was an all-star and captain of the Canisius College basketball team in the late 1960s. (Permission from Tony Masiello).

By Al Bruno,
La Gazzetta Italiana,
August 2021

Editor Note in Italian (italicized):
Tony Masiello, l'ex-sindaco di Buffalo, NY, è stato recentemente onorato nella "Mayoral Hall of Fame" per il suo servizio alla città per trentacinque anni. Inoltre, è conosciuto per la sua carriera nel basket quando era all'università Canisius College. Per il lavoro da sindaco e il suo atletismo, lui è stato eletto dagli altri "Hall of Fame," un onore che poche persone possono vantare. Questo gruppi di professionali sono: Cardinal Dougherty High School, Canisius College Hall of Fame, Pre-70s All-Century Team, Greater Buffalo Sports Hall of Fame, e il Metro Atlantic Athletic Conference Hall of Fame. Questi onori sono notevoli perché secondo lui non ha ancora finito di raggiungere i suoi obiettivi.

Few hall of famers are recognized as hall of fame honorees in two professions, and former Buffalo Mayor Tony Masiello accomplished that and much more in his celebrated life in Canisius College basketball history and, more recently, in public service for 35 years, including three, four-year terms as mayor.

As the oldest of seven children (i.e. five sons and two daughters), much was expected of first-son Masiello, per traditional Italian credo and determined by family necessity. Hence, a young Masiello was summoned into action soon after his birth in 1947. He was raised and bred for leadership as a promising youngster on Buffalo's Italian West Side in the 1950s and 60s, residing at 1336 West Avenue and nestled in a blue collar, hard-working neighborhood. Basketball was young Masiello's first love: Masiello and his basketball brothers (Vito, Michael, and Johnny) practiced and honed their early basketball skills in the backyard with Tony literally holding court and where lessons were learned, using that hoop that Masiello's father nailed to a tree as their goal.

Young Masiello learned about caring and education from his mother, Bridget Masiello; he learned about the importance of rigor and commitment by observing his father, Dan Masiello, thereby embracing his "hard work" values as a 30-year, city sanitation worker: As the oldest and first-son of proud Italian parents, he had no choice but to succeed - failure was not an option.

Masiello was the first of the family to attend Coronation of the Blessed Virgin Mary School, a small two-story building that had no gym but was located close enough to home so Mrs. Masiello could watch her children walk to school. The Masiello brothers, Tony and his younger brother, Vito, led the school's basketball team to its first diocesan championship.

To no one's real surprise and based on athletic merit, Masiello earned basketball scholarships at Cardinal Dougherty HS and then at Canisius College that paid his

Tony Masiello drives past a defender for an easy layup. (Permission from Tony Masiello).

tuition and fees. "Tony always showed that fighting spirit. I knew then Tony had great leadership, not just because he was tall and good-looking, even ruddy, but he was always a gentleman, respectful, and very appreciative," remembers former Coronation Monsignor Richard S. Amico.

As a youngster at 6'4" with solid basketball skills, Masiello recalled having dreams of playing professional basketball. "I spent all day and night in gyms and on playgrounds throughout the city of Buffalo (i.e. Butler Mitchell Athletic Club, Knights of Columbus, Delaware Park Basketball Courts, Schools 19 and 52, and the Reese Basketball Courts). Sports helps you at an early age to relate to people from different neighborhoods, different colors, and different walks of life."

Masiello was a three-year starter at Cardinal Dougherty HS, averaging 18 points as a junior and was league-leading scoring champ in 1965 with 21 points per game. He led his team to the Manhattan Cup Championship in 1963, was runner-up in 1965, and named to the All-Tourney team at the Hoyle Tournament in Pennsylvania.

At Canisius College, Masiello helped lead Griffs' teams to victories over powerhouses such as Georgetown, Providence (ranked #3 in D-1 in 1967), Seton Hall, St. John's, Xavier, and Syracuse; he was selected as the 15th all-time best at the Canisius College 150 Sesquicentennial Anniversary in 2019.

In his final game against Niagara and Calvin Murphy, Masiello amazingly netted 35 points. Masiello saved his very best to the end. Masiello was 13 for 24 from the field, most of his buckets coming on swishers from 15 to 20 feet out; he was nine for 10 from the charity stripe, including two free throw makes in the final seconds of the game to seal an 81 to 79 most memorable win before a packed house at the Memorial Auditorium, leaving Masiello physically exhausted afterward and restraining his emotions.

"I owed this game to my school – Canisius. I also owe it to my coaches, Mr. MacKinnon and Mr. Markey. I am deeply moved by it all. I am happy, and I am sad – happy because we won and sad because, for me, it's all over. My basketball career at Canisius is over. I will never forget my four years at Canisius," passionately said Masiello immediately after the game. Masiello talked about his future, "I want a chance to play basketball in the NBA or in the ABA or Europe – anywhere. I just want a chance."

In a column and tribute written by Phil Ranallo of the Buffalo's Courier Express the next morning (March 10, 1969), justly affirmed Masiello as a future hall of famer for Canisius College Men's Basketball, saying for the annals and for posterity:

"Tony Massiello, the Canisius College captain with the mighty heart – with his magnificent performance Saturday night against Niagara – took his place among the great Golden Griffin basketball warriors of all-time. The gallant young man truly belongs," wrote Ranallo.

"Tony Masiello, at 6 feet 4 inches, spent three years in the basketball jungle – the snake pit under the backboards – and did battle with the redwoods of the sport, those athletes who stand 6 feet and 9 inches and taller," acknowledged Ranallo.

Coach MacKinnon emoted a heartfelt compliment to Masiello after his last game, "Tony is one of the greatest, most dedicated players I've ever coached. With Tony, from the first game he played for me right through tonight, it's always been the same. It's been the team first and Tony second."

Masiello earned his Bachelor's degree from Canisius College in 1969, and Masiello was drafted in the third round by the Indiana Pacers of the ABA in the 1969-70 season but did not make the final roster. Masiello tried out for the new first-year Buffalo Braves and did not make the team, unfortunately. Locally, most believed that Masiello should have made the Braves team.

Deservingly, Masiello was inducted into the Cardinal Dougherty HS Hall of Fame (1980), Canisius College Hall of Fame (1982) and the Canisius College Pre-70s All-Century Team (2019), Greater Buffalo Sports Hall of Fame (2007), and the Metro Atlantic Athletic Conference Hall of Fame (2012). Masiello is married to Kathleen Masiello (nee McCue) and has two daughters with her: Ariel and Madeline. He has a third daughter, Kim, with his first wife, Donna Abraham. Presently, Masiello is the president of Masiello, Martucci, and Associates, a governmental lobbying firm in Buffalo.

Tony Masiello's Political Career in Buffalo Kicked Off in 1971: 35 Years of Service (Part 2)

Former 3-term Buffalo Mayor Tony Masiello is pictured. Masiello has 35 years of government service as an elected councilman, state senator, and mayor. He is now the president of Masiello, Martucci and Associates in Buffalo, serving clients in lobbying and governmental relations consultations. (Permission from Tony Masiello).

By Al Bruno,
La Gazzetta Italiana,
September 2021

Editor's Note in Italian (italicized):
Tony Masiello si e laureate al Canisius College. Dopo la laurea, ebbe l'opportunità di giocare a basket da professionista ma non riusci. Dunque, insegno in un istituto professionale e piano piano divenne attiva nel partito democratico. Nel 1971, vinse un'elezione che diede inizio alla sua carriera politica. Masiello fu eletto al senate statale per New York. Lui si è guadagnato il nome di "the people's senator." Lui fu anche il leader in molte commissioni. Nel 1993, vinse l'elezione per sindaco di Buffalo. Lui fu fondamentale nei finanziamenti governativi per la città, specialmente per la polizia, i vigili del fuoco, e scuole pubbliche. Fu una persona importante e rispettata nella città.

IN 1969, TONY MASIELLO earned his Bachelor's from Canisius College, and he was the third-round draft pick for the Indiana Pacers of the ABA in the 1969-70 season but did not make the final roster. Masiello tried out for the new Buffalo Braves, a first-year NBA franchise, in 1970, but he did not make the team, unfortunately; locally, most believed he should have made the Braves. "That really was the hardest hit I had up until I was 22 years old. All of a sudden, I had to find a new vehicle to translate all those energies... all that drive, all that competitive spirit."

Masiello taught business at St. Joseph's Collegiate Institute and sold insurance for a year in the interim (1970-71). He was always active in the Democratic Party, up until this time; Masiello had no particular plans for politics, but party boss Joe Crangle came calling on campaigning.

In 1971, Democratic Party boss Joe Crangle asked Masiello to run for the North District Councilman seat. The incumbent dropped out and Masiello won in a close race against another candidate, becoming one of the city's youngest elected officials ever; he was elected to an at-large seat on the council, served as democratic majority leader in 1974, and he then served as chairman of the council finance committee.

The unrest of the Vietnam War dominated television and newspaper coverage and reporting. In fact, Masiello went for his required physical exam for the Vietnam draft but was declared ineligible because of a childhood injury that left him legally blind in his left eye. "When the war started, I think I was gung-ho on beating communism. I bought into that type of hype. But as the war gradually evolved, I started to learn more about why we were there, what was happening there. I read about the anti-war demonstrations. I saw them from a distance, but I wasn't really the demonstrating type."

Masiello shifted his political direction and broadened his base in NYS, and he first ran for the state senate in 1980, and the Democratic Party did not endorse him. However, Masiello went on to win the primary and subsequently won this special election; he went on to win the democratic endorsement for the state senate in 1982, 1984, 1986, and 1988, and he served as NYS state senator from 1981-1993, sitting in the 184th, 185th, 186th, 187th, 188th, 189th, and 190th NYS Legislatures. Masiello's senate district originally comprised many Buffalo and other parts of Erie County. During his final year of his Senate service, his district encompassed part of Buffalo, as well as Grand Island, Tonawanda, and Niagara Falls.

As state senator, Masiello served as a "people's senator." Some of the highlights of the senate career include keeping Columbus Hospital open; fighting to save the Connecticut Street Armory and the Richardson Building in the Psychiatric Center; saving jobs and keeping his hometown of Buffalo constantly receiving grants and financial aid, to help keep many local businesses operational. The largest investment of public money in Western New York was $241 million, and Masiello was instrumental in lobbying Governor Cuomo's office to secure this funding.

In the NYS Senate, Masiello ascended to minority whip and served as chair of the democratic conference; as a senator, Masiello served as the ranking minority member of various committees, including the child care committee and the energy committee. Masiello was re-elected to the office of state senator in 1990 and 1992.

On November 2, 1993, Masiello easily won the mayoral general election in what seemed certain from the onset of the campaign, to become Buffalo's first new mayor in 16 years, thus succeeding Mayor James D. Griffin. Masiello's 36,092 votes was 68% of the total vote. Republican Richard A. Grimm received 9,277 votes while Conservative candidate Eugene Fahey received 7,566 votes.

Masiello ambitiously outlined his vision for the mayor's office:

"This is an awesome responsibility. It's a big task. We are inheriting some problems, but they are not insurmountable. I get excited to think about putting Buffalo on the map and turning around the image of a smokestack, snow, and the chicken wing capital of the country to a progressive, exciting city with vibrant neighborhoods, an exciting waterfront, and a place where people want to live."

Masiello promised to change the way city government worked, if elected, saying:

"One thing it will do is bring new and younger people to help run the government. There's a staleness about city government. This city hasn't moved into a new era. I don't think (the administration) is aware of the value of new management techniques, principles, and computers. In many ways, we're a Flintstones-era type of government."

Masiello emphatically made the plea for unity and common purpose, moving forward in Buffalo:

"It is a day of dedication to the simple idea that we are one people united by common purpose. We could not have chosen a more fitting symbol of that idea than the steps of this majestic building. Stretched across the entrance are symbolic columns that represent bundles of needs bound together with cable wire. The message of the architect of City Hill was the same message of the Masiello campaign – the strength of Buffalo lies in our unity, and our danger is rooted in discord.

"The better we are at recognizing common goals, the better able we will be to solve and provide solutions to common problems. Working together, respecting each other, understanding our differences, and uniting to bring our hearts and minds to the work of building a better Buffalo, that's what last year was all about…that's what today is all about…and what I promise all of you is that my administration will continue to do that…To each of you as concerned citizens of the city (Buffalo) that we love."

As mayor, in fact, Masiello doubled the amount of state aid to Buffalo and convinced the federal and state governments to fund the re-engineering of both the Buffalo Police and Fire departments. Working with Governors Cuomo and Pataki, Masiello secured state and local funding for projects like the HSBC Arena, the Buffalo Niagara Medical Campus, and the Theater District expansion.

Targeting investments such as these, along with efforts to spur development on Buffalo's Inner Harbor Waterfront, expanding downtown housing and securing funding for the return of automobile traffic to Main Street are focal points of Buffalo's award-winning Queen City Hub Plan: The blueprint for over $1 billion of investment that's already spawned a wealth of new housing and business development in downtown Buffalo.

One of the architects of the Joint Schools Construction legislation, Masiello played a key role directing over $1 billion of state investment into the renovation and transformation of Buffalo's Public Schools. He built on that initial investment with the Mayor's Livable Communities Grant Program, encouraging block clubs and community groups to undertake projects that produce measurable and physical and visual improvements in the neighborhoods where these schools are located, thus maximizing impact. Masiello successfully forged bonds with decision-makers at every level of government.

A nationally recognized expert on brownfield reclamation, Masiello focused on cleaning polluted land up to standard and on making former brownfields shovel-ready for redevelopment. Convincing HealthNow, Blue Cross/Blue Shield's parent company, to locate its company's headquarters at the old Buffalo Gas Works site, Masiello brought home a project with a total economic impact of almost $2 billion – the largest private sector development in downtown Buffalo since 1967.

For almost four decades, Masiello honorably served Buffalo and Western New York (WNY) as its elected councilman, state senator, and mayor. His commitment and duty to community service made an indelible contribution to the Buffalo and WNY governmental landscape. A heartfelt sense of caring and unity for a greater Buffalo characterized his tenure like no other – Tony Masiello is a remarkable Buffalo legend.

Coach Dick Vitale: "I Am Living the American Dream"

Coach Dick Vitale is pictured here at a press conference. (Wikimedia.com, Google Art Project).

By Al Bruno
La Gazzetta Italiana,
January 2022

Editor's Note in Italian(italicized):
Dick Vitale è un telecronista sportive sul canale ESPN. E anche conosciuto per quando era allenatore di basket. I suoi genitori emigrarono dall'Italia. Vitale racconta sempre che i suoi genitori vennero senza niente, neanche un'istruzione formale. Secondo Vitale, però, loro furono maestri della dedizione nel lavoro duro. Vitale racconta come non potera dire "non posso" in casa. Veramente, erano due parole impronunciabili perché loro vissero una vita dignitosa malgrado il fatto che iniziarono con nemmeno un centesimo in tasca. Vitale ha avuto tanto successo nella sua carriera. Con ESPN, aveva programmi sugli sport ai quali dava le sue opinioni. Attualmente, è ancora una voce rispettata del basket. La prossima volta che sentirai la sua voce, pensa come quelle due parole "non posso" abbiano influenzato la sua vita.

In 1973, few knew of Dick Vitale outside of those residing in the tri-state region; he is a first generation Italian American, who was born in 1939 in Passaic, New Jersey, to John and Mae Vitale, Italian immigrants, both working tirelessly in the clothing industry to give him a better life in America, indeed.

"I am living the American dream," Vitale passionately emphasizes. "My mom worked in a factory and sewed coats, until she suffered a stroke. Then she continued to sew coats in our cellar, dragging her leg as she worked. I learned about love, family, and loyalty. I watched as my dad pressed coats in a factory. He told me that I needed to get an education so that I could do other things in life," writes Vitale in his autobiography.

"I cannot thank my mom and dad enough for instilling in me to never use the word, can't. My mom and dad did not have a formal education but they had doctorates of love. They told me that if you give 110 percent all the time, beautiful things will happen. I may not always be right, but no one can ever accuse me of not having a genuine love and passion for whatever I do. ESPN and many sporting organizations have been grateful enough to recognize this," writes Vitale.

Now in 2021, he is known almost everywhere in "Sports America" where he enjoys his legendary status as a hall of fame basketball coach and active ESPN broadcaster: all in one, storied, ambitious lifetime.

Vitale's roots are teaching the game he has loved since childhood: basketball. Following graduation from college, he got a job teaching at Mark Twain Elementary School (Garfield, NJ) and coaching junior high football and basketball. He began coaching at the high school level at Garfield High School, where he coached for one season (1963-64).

Vitale then earned four state sectional championships, two consecutive state championships, and 35 consecutive victories during his seven years at his alma mater, East Rutherford NJ High School; he joined Rutgers University for two years (1970-72) as an assistant coach, helping Phil Sellers and Mike Dabney, two cornerstones on an eventual NCAA Final Four Team in 1976.

Young Vitale got his break in 1973 and was named the head basketball coach of the University of Detroit, compiling a winning percentage of .722 (78-30), which included a 21-game winning streak during the 1976-77 season when the team participated in the NCAA Tournament. Vitale gained basketball coaching notoriety and became celebrated nationally. In April 1977, Vitale was named Athletic Director at the University of Detroit and later that year was named the United Fund's Detroit Man of the Year. In May 1978, he was named head coach of the NBA's Detroit Pistons, which he coached during the 1978-79 season prior to joining the ESPN broadcast team.

In 1979, Vitale began working with ESPN as a college basketball broadcaster and has been contributing as an analyst ever since. His thorough knowledge of the game is presented in an enthusiastic, passionate, sometimes controversial, but never boring, style. Vitale has distinguished himself with ESPN by spontaneously spewing his riveting and conjured, basketball insights and memorable quips. Vitale makes an indelible impression on audiences. He is that vivacious personality that there is no substitute for.

ESPN has televised two nationally acclaimed Vitale specials: "The Game of Life," which first aired December 1991 and "Game Plan For Life," which first aired December 1994. Both were motivational speeches delivered to high school players at basketball camps. ESPN's Jock James CD – of which Vitale is a focal part – is now multi-platinum after selling more than six million copies, containing Vitale quips often played at basketball arenas. His popular merchandise line distributed through Tandem Enterprises includes autographed basketballs, shirts, and hats.

Remarkably, the always-energetic Vitale is a favorite endorser among a wide variety of major corporations. He is also one of the nation's most requested public speakers, providing motivational speeches to numerous leading corporations and organizations which have since raised millions of dollars across the U.S. In 1987, he signed an exclusive contract with the Washington Speakers' Bureau.

Vitale is quite the philanthropist. He is on the Board of Directors of the V Foundation, non-profit organization dedicated to finding a cure for cancer and founded in 1993 by ESPN and the late Jim Valvano (and an organization which has since raised millions of dollars). He has co-chaired with Mike Krzyzewski and the Jon Saunders V Foundation Golf Classic and hosts an annual V Foundation Gala in Florida which gathers numerous celebrities to raise money and honor individuals such as Krzyzewski, Bob Knight, and Pat Summit.

Vitale has also authored nine books, including one children's title, Dickie V's ABCs and 1-2-3s (2010). Dick Vitale's Fabulous 50 Players and Moments in College Basketball (2008) and Dick Vitale's 2003's Living a Dream (Reflections on 25 Years, Sitting in the Best Seat in the House) were both co-authored by Dick Weiss.

In addition, Vitale has been selected for nine halls of fame: National Italian Sports Hall of Fame, the Elmwood Park, NJ Hall of Fame (2001), the Five-Star Basketball Camp Hall of Fame (2003), the University of Detroit Hall of Fame, the Florida Sports Hall of Fame in 1996 and the East Rutherford Hall of Fame (1985), the National Collegiate Basketball Hall of Fame (2008), and the Naismith Memorial Hall of Fame (2008).

Academically, Vitale graduated from Seton Hall University with a bachelor's degree in business administration. He also earned a master's degree in education from William Paterson College and has 32 graduate credit hours beyond the master's degree in administration.

Born in East Rutherford, NJ, in 1939, Vitale and his wife, Lorraine, have two daughters, Terri and Sherri, who both attended the University of Notre Dame on tennis scholarships, both graduating with MBAs. Vitale's proud involvement with Notre Dame includes the endowment of the Dick Vitale Family Scholarship, presented annually to an Irish undergraduate who is participating in Notre Dame sporting activities and not receiving financial aid. Recipients have included the school's Leprechaun mascot, cheerleaders, and band members as well as players.

Legendary Coach Jim Valvano: Never Quit Campaign and the V Foundation

Coach Jim Valvano is pictured here after a big Wolfpack win in 1983. (Wikimedia.com, Google Art Project)

By Al Bruno
La Gazetta Italiana
December 2021

Editor's Note in Italian (italicized):
Jim Valvano era un allenatore ben conosciuto quando stave nel North Carolina State University. Benché sia morto quasi 30 anni fa, è ancora ricordato per il suo talento di allenatore. Valvano era anche un giornalista televisivo che lavoravano per il canali ESPN ad ABC. Lui aveva tre regole per la vita quotidiana che sempre diceva: una persona deve ridere, pensare, e piangere. Queste tre azioni, secondo lui, fanno della vita piena. Purtroppo, è morto del cancro dopo una lunga battaglia.

First-generation, Italian American Jimmy Valvano closely followed on the Italian pioneering trail that Dick Vitale did in the 1970s for men's college basketball.

Valvano is remembered most, competitively, for coaching the North Carolina State University's Wolfpack to the unlikely and miraculous garnering of the NCAA Division 1 Men's Basketball Championship in 1983 from the highly-favored University of Houston Cougars, dramatically beating Houston at the buzzer with a dunk by Lorenzo Charles, 54 to 52, and ecstatically running around the center of the basketball court, looking for someone to hug and celebrate with. This was a candid and spontaneous moment of total human elation in climbing the mountain of success, finally reaching the pinnacle of college basketball in D-1 championship competition: lost in the wonderment of the moment.

Rob Goldberg insightfully wrote in 1993 for The Bleacher Report: "At the beginning of the 1983 season, the entire roster practiced cutting down the nets like teams do after winning championships. This was apparently an event that the coach had every one his squads do over the years. This alone is something that gives his team confidence and the belief that it is capable of winning it all...Every decision that Valvano made ended up working out during that 1983 season. Although the coach never was able to win another title (national championship), his legacy was never diminished."

Valvano demonstrated his remarkable winning ways as head coach at NC State from 1980 to 1990. He led the Wolfpack in one of greatest Cinerella stories in college basketball history, culminating as winners of the 1983 NCAA championship. During his ten seasons at NC State, Valvano's teams were the ACC's tournament champions in 1983 and 1987, and they were regular season champions in 1985 and 1989. In addition to gloriously winning the 1983 NCAA championship, the Wolfpack then advanced to the NCAA Elite 8 in 1985 and 1986.

It all began following his graduation in 1967, earning a Bachelor's degree in English from Rutgers University, Valvano began his coaching career at his alma mater, Rutgers University, where he was appointed freshman coach and the assistant for the varsity. In fact, Valvano recalled that he had discussed how he planned to use one of Coach Vince Lombardi's memorable speeches on his Rutgers freshman basketball prior to his first game as their coach; he mentioned that he accidentally told the team to "fight for the Green Bay Packers," humiliating him forever.

His 19-year career as a head coach basketball coach began at John Hopkins University in Baltimore for one year before being tapped to be an assistant at the University of Connecticut for two years. Following that, he was the head coach at Bucknell, Iona, and finally at NC State (1980 – 1990), his final tenure.

From 1964 – 1967, Valvano played point guard for Rutgers University. During his senior year, Valvanno helped lead the team to a third-place finish in the exclusive 1967 National Invitational Tournament; Valvano was named Senior Athlete of the Year.

After his coaching career, Valvano became a broadcaster for ESPN and ABC Sports. In 1992, Valvano won a Cable ACE Award for commentator/analyst for NCAA basketball broadcasts. From time to time, he was paired with basketball analyst Dick Vitale, dubbed the "Killer Vees," with similar voices and exuberant styles. The two even made a cameo appearance, playing the role of professional movers, V & V Movers, on an episode of The Cosby Show.

Valvano is remembered, too, for his sustained and courageous fight against cancer and his memorable address to the nation at the 1993 ESPY audience on March 3, 1993. Remarkably and from the heart, Valvano told the viewing audience for posterity: "To me, there are three things we should do every day. We should do this every day of our lives. Number one is to laugh. You should laugh every day. Number two is think. You should spend time thinking. And number three is, you should have emotions moved to tears, could be happiness or joy. But think about it. If you laugh, you think, and you cry, that's a full day. That's a heck of a day. You do that seven days a week, you're going to have something special…Cancer can take away all my physical abilities. It cannot touch my mind. It cannot touch my heart, and it cannot touch my soul. And those three things are going to carry on forever…Keep your

Coach Jim Valvano signals to his players to run the number four play against Duke in 1983. (Wikimedia.com, Google Art Project)

dreams alive in spite of problems, whatever you have. Work hard for your dreams to come true…"

And then again, spontaneously and passionately, he declared: "Don't ever give up. That's what I am going to do with every minute left. I will thank God for the day and moment I have." Great applause ensued, and the tears flowed from the faces of those sports celebrities and media personnel in attendance, demonstrating an outpouring of love and appreciation for Jimmy Valvano's courage and his passion for coaching.

Less than two months after that most memorable moment at the ESPY Awards, Valvano died at age 47. Jimmy V will never be forgotten; his inspirational words and most importantly, his creation – the V Foundation still lives on and thrives upward into perpetuity, continuing to raise millions of dollars for cancer research, in his name and long-lasting legacy in American sports.

Valvano is a first generation Italian American and the son of Rocco and Angelina Valvano, both Italian immigrants; Valvano's father, Rocco, was born and raised in Guardio Lombardi, Avellini, in Campania, Italy.

Valvano was born and grew up in Queens, New York, in 1946. In his honor after his early and tragic passing in 1993, the V Foundation was established and flourished with millions of dollars raised in charitable donations as a cancer research center, assisting cancer patients nationwide.

Coach Mike Krzyewski, the legendary head coach of Duke University Men's Basketball, reflected in a deep heartfelt commentary on Coach Valvano: "Jimmy formed the V Foundation during the last couple months of his life. We would laugh, joke and cry at the hospital together. One night he said, I want to try to fund researchers to attack cancer. I want you to be on my team. He recruited me during that time. His wisdom and his ability to think beyond his life was incredible."

DIANA TAURASI'S BASKETBALL STARDOM SHOWCASED AT 2020 TOKYO OLYMPICS

WNBA all-star Diana Taurasi is pictured here in a game as a member of the Phoenix Mercury team. (Wikimedia.com, Google Art Project).

By Al Bruno
La Gazzetta Italiana
October 2021

Editor's Note in Italian (italicized):
Diana Taurasi, la figlia di un immigrante italiano, ha partecipato alle Olimpiadi quest'estate. Ha aiutato la squadra Americana a vincere la quinta medaglia d'oro nella pallacanestro. Taurasi ha detto che da sempre lavora duro in tutto quello che fa perché ha visto i genitori fare tanti sacrifici per la loro famiglia. La mamma è emigrata dall'Argentina ed il padre dall'Italia. Taurasi è andata in Connecticut per l'università per giocare a basket. A parte le Olimpiadi, Taurasi e la sua squadra hanno vinto tre campionati internazionali.

FIRST-GENERATION, ITALIAN American Diana Taurasi's basketball stardom shined brightest and was showcased for all to witness worldwide at this past summer's, 2020 Tokyo Olympics where she amazingly garnered her fifth, consecutive gold medal (in 2004, 2008, 2012, 2016, and 2020) with the USA women's basketball team. Bravo, noi la ringraziamo.

Powerful, all-encompassing words like winner, legendary, and immortality meritoriously describe Taurasi's unprecedented contributions in women's basketball: In the past 22 years, Taurasi has repeatedly proven to be the best in professional, college, and Olympic competition in the history of women's basketball.

Taurasi is deeply appreciative and quick to credit her Italian father, Mario, and her Argentinian mother, Liliana, for their love and instilling in her that fiery competitiveness she displays on the hardwood. Relevant to note, Mario was a professional soccer player in Italy for several years, excelling as a goalkeeper; Mario met and married Liliana in Argentina, and they emigrated to Southern California in 1978 before they had Diana in 1982 and her older sister, Jessika, two years earlier, settling in the small yet diverse agricultural town of Chino, California.

Taurasi vividly recalls: "I watched dad go to work every day from 6 am to 6 pm as a sheet metal worker in a factory, no matter what, not because it was fun. I remember, one time, dad had accidentally cut off the tip of one of his fingers, and he just went

Diana Taurasi applauds one of her Phoenix Mercury teammates on the sidelines. (Wikimedia.com, Google Art Project).

to work the next day." Watching her dad do the same routine, working 60 hours a week rubbed off positively on young Taurasi, slowly building the foundation of her grit, toughness, and work ethic that has been on display for the past 22 years. Taurasi's eventual rise to success was not an accident or an automatic thing that just happened: She acquired it, a learned behavior, as a desired result.

Growing up in the Taurasi household meant they interchangeably spoke three languages (English, Italian, and Spanish), and they ate Liliana's ethnic Argentinian and Italian cuisine, no American-food exceptions were allowed for Taurasi and older sister, Jessika. Food was Liliana's love language: It spoke for Liliana and Mario from their hearts, and the Taurasi household was full of affection – this was clearly obvious to anyone who was invited to dinner there.

Older sister, Jessika, remembers the lessons she and Diana learned from her parents, Mario and Liliana: "My parents clearly showed us and told us 'Look, we moved here (to America) to have a better life for our kids. We didn't want you to have holes in your shoes and one pair of clothes. We moved here, we sacrificed to give you a better life.'"

Diana agrees and is forever appreciative, saying: "I wake up every morning and I feel like I owe them more. They picked up and came to another country, didn't know the language, maybe knew two or three people, because they knew there was just something better for our family here than in Argentina at the time. And they didn't do that lightly. So, for me, my feeling is, whatever I've been able to give them, I owe 100 times more." It's a feeling of deep appreciation that persists inside Taurasi to this day, even if she has conquered every mountain top in women's basketball.

While growing up in Chino, Taurasi's athletic gifts soon emerged as a standout soccer and basketball player by the time she was in the eighth grade and felt perplexed on whether to focus exclusively on soccer or basketball, not wanting to disappoint Mario's inherent love for soccer. At 6 feet and 163 pounds with speed and agility, she was the ideal point guard, displaying uncommon dribbling, passing, and three-point shooting skills and wizardry like few before her. However, soccer was the number one sport in the Taurasi household.

Selflessly and objectively as pensive Italian fathers usually can be, Mario assured his young and talented daughter, Diana: "You should choose basketball because you will have more opportunities. You are special in basketball." Dad was instinctively right, and Diana never looked back, passionately began perfecting her basketball skills and carving out her future legacy in women's basketball lore.

Dozens and dozens of college scholarship offers came pouring into the Taurasi household, after graduating and gaining statewide and national recognition at Don Antonio Lugo High School in Chino where she was also named the 2000 Naismith and Parade Magazine National High School Player of the Year.

Learning of Taurasi's high school basketball prowess and success immediately prompted the venerable, UConn Huskies Women's Basketball Coach Geno Auriemma, an Italian immigrant himself, to travel to Chino and enjoy a warm, memorable visit with Diana and her parents; Auriemma had a firsthand familiarity with the cultural circumstances, challenging and urging the highly-recruited Taurasi, saying to her: "If you want to be something different and if you want to become someone special, come to Connecticut (UConn) with me," instantly bringing Taurasi's parents to a tearful flow of joy.

Soon thereafter, Mario and Liliana discussed the highly-coveted scholarship offer with Diana, and Mario and Liliana gave Diana their blessings, advising her to go to Connecticut with Coach Auriemma. No one could have scripted it better at that important time in Diana's life: It was poetry-in-motion and a match made-in-heaven. Diana chose UConn where she would sojourn to Storrs, Connecticut, on her first major step to a storied and unimaginable, basketball legacy for the ages.

Taurasi began her collegiate career at UConn in the 2000-2001 season. Playing primarily point guard for Coach Auriemma, Taurasi led the Huskies to three consecutive NCAA Division I championships (in 2002, 2003, and 2004). She received many personal accolades at UConn, including the 2003 and 2004 Naismith College Player of the Year award, the 2004 Wade Trophy, the 2003 and 2004 Honda Sports Award, and the Associated Press Player of the Year award. Coach Auriemma called Taurasi, "The best basketball player I have ever coached on the collegiate and Olympic levels of competition."

In the Women's National Basketball Association (WBNA), Taurasi was drafted first overall by the Phoenix Mercury in the 2004 WNBA draft. Taurasi has won the WNBA Rookie of the Year Award (2004), three NBA WNBA championships (in 2007, 2009, and 2014), one WNBA Most Valuable Player Award (2009), and two WNBA Finals MVP Awards (2009 and 2014). She has been selected to nine WNBA All-Star teams and 10 All-WNBA teams. In 2017, Taurasi became the WNBA all-time leading scorer and in 2021, she became the first player to surpass 9,000 points.

In 2017, Taurasi married former Phoenix teammate Penny Taylor, who is currently the Phoenix Mercury Director of Player Development. In 2018, Taylor gave birth to the couple's son, Leo Michael Taurasi-Taylor, who is now three years old.

REMEMBERING JAKE LAMOTTA: BOXING MIDDLEWEIGHT CHAMPION AND HALL OF FAMER

Jake LaMotta is pictured here in his boxing prime in December 1950, celebrating after a victory over Tiberio Dimitri (Courtesy of theguardian.com, photo by Corbis).

By Al Bruno
La Gazzetta Italiana
March 2022

Editor's Note in Italian (italicized):
Jake LaMotta e nato in la città di New York in 1922 dove lui si impara male cose per la morale della nazione in le strade di "The Bronx." Il figlio di due immigrati italiani, LaMotta era cattivo e litigavo molto con gli altri ragazzi. Però, positivamente, LaMotta anche si impara usare le sue mani di pietra per il pugilatore per le strade e questo regalo fu la forza nella sua vita. A 19 anni, divenne un pugile professionista e ebbe tanti incontri molto conosciuti in questo sport. La Motta ha realizzato il suo sogno americano, "The American Dream," come un campione di pugilato in peso medio. In tutto, LaMotta vince 83 e perde 19 incontri di boxe. LaMotta purtroppo rovina la sua carriera quando decide di barare nello sport per ottenere il sostegno della mafia. Fu l'inizio della fine della sua carriera. Nel 1954, LaMotta va in pensione. La sua vita fu piena di problemi severi. LaMotta espose sette moglie e ebbe due figli e quattro figlie. LaMotta morì nel 2017 e aveva 95 anni.

First-generation, Italian American Jake LaMotta is remembered for his hall of fame boxing career, winning the middleweight championship in spectacular fashion at Madison Square in New York City on June 16. 1949, while realizing his longtime boxing goal and achieving the "American Dream."

LaMotta survived a turbulent upbringing in the Bronx, experiencing a rough, seedy, and even criminal early life as a teenager and beyond into his 20s, as LaMotta would later confess in his book, but it was what he possessed in his hands and what how he battled in the ring that made him different and special: His boxing tenacity, toughness, and slugging power made him a dangerous fighter in the ring, respected by all, and feared by opponents.

Ring Magazine, a respected publication on boxing, ranks LaMotta as one of the 10 greatest middleweight champions of all-time. In 106 total fights, LaMotta 83 wins (30 by knock-out), 19 losses, and four draws. He was inducted into the International Boxing Hall of Fame in the inaugural class of 1990.

It needs to be referenced and illustrated that LaMotta was born-and-bred in the Bronx to Italian immigrant parents; his father was from Messina, Sicily, and his dad introduced him to a hardened, seedier lifestyle in the Bronx, forcing young Jake to fight other boys to entertain neighborhood adults, who threw pocket change into the ring for enticement. LaMotta's father gladly collected the money and used it to pay the rent: a practical matter.

Young LaMotta had valuable pre-training in boxing, and he capitalized on those pugilistic skills in the old garages and back alleys of the Bronx; he learned to box while in a reformatory in upstate New York, where he had been sent for attempted robbery, reports confirmed. After fighting all comers and remaining undefeated in local matches, LaMotta was convinced to turn professional at age 19 in 1941, and the LaMotta legacy was born, battling and bleeding in the Bronx.

LaMotta's boxing tenacity and ferocity to take countless punches and deliver power punches and flurries distinguishes him in boxing history and for the annals.

"There is much more to LaMotta than a granite chin. LaMotta was a clever boxer who executed the nuances of the game with fine precision. While he was able to absorb punches with little problem in the ring, he was also adept at rolling with punches to minimize the damage. He likes to play possum in the ring, lulling opponents into a false sense of confidence before unleashing his own attack. And, perhaps above all, he had a tremendous will to win. His aggressive unrelenting style, earned him the nickname, 'The Raging Bull,'" as he is accurately described in the International Boxing Hall of Fame (Canastota, NY) annals in 1990.

A six-fight series with Sugar Ray Robinson largely defines LaMotta's career. They met for the first time in 1942 in New York, and Robinson earned a 10-round decision, victimizing Robinson with his first loss in 41 fights. Robinson, who fought once in between the three weeks, garnered a decision in the next fighting encounter.

The rivalry would resume in 1945, and Robinson took a 10-round decision in New York. In the interim, LaMotta was also busy fighting a slew of other top-ranked opponents. LaMotta beat world-class fighters, ranging from welterweight to heavyweight. Among his victims Fritzie Zivic, George Kochan, Tommy Bell, Bert Lytell, Jose Basora, Bob Satterfield, Holman Williams, and Tony Janiro.

On November 14, 1947, LaMotta was knocked out in the fourth round by Billy Fox. Suspecting the fight was fixed and it was, the New York State Athletic Commission withheld purses for the fight and suspended LaMotta. The fight with Fox would come back to haunt him later in his life during a case with the Federal Bureau of Investigation (FBI).

In his testimony and later in his book, LaMotta admitted to throwing the fight to gain favor with the Mafia so he could get his title shot; to justify his action, LaMotta stated that he had no other options at the time. All agreed the fix was a certainty and their staging was inept. LaMotta would write:

"The first round, a couple of belts to his

head, and I see a glassy look coming over his eyes, Jesus Christ, a couple of jabs, and he's going to fall down? I began to panic a little. I was supposed to be throwing a fight to this guy, and it looked like I was going to end up holding him on his feet…By the fourth round, if there was anybody in the Garden who didn't know what was happening, he must have been dead drunk."

LaMotta openly confessed in court to cheating the sport of boxing, stating for posterity:

"Make these boys see. It wasn't fear. It wasn't cowardice. It was even money. It was the only way. The only way to get my shot: it was mine. I'd earned it. Nobody would give me a chance, five years as an uncrowned champion. I deserved that shot. I did what needed to be done."

The thrown fight and a payment of $20,000 to the Mafia got LaMotta his title fight against World Middleweight Champion Marcel Cerdan.

On June 16, 1949, met Cerdan and won middleweight championship in the 10th round by technical knock-out (TKO), despite being significantly behind on points. Cerdan and LaMotta were scheduled to meet in a rematch, but the plane carrying Cerdan back to the United States crashed, and Cerdan was tragically killed.

In 1950, LaMotta successfully defended the middleweight crown against Tiberio Mitri and Laurent Dauthuille. Trailing on the scorecards, LaMotta staged a miraculous 15th-round knockout of Dauthuille to retain his middleweight belt. That set the sixth and final meeting between LaMotta and Robinson.

LaMotta and Robinson met on February 14, 1951, at Chicago Stadium, and this time LaMotta's middleweight crown was at stake. As the fight ensued, Robinson began to build a comfortable lead. Although LaMotta absorbed a tremendous amount of punishment, LaMotta refused to fall. Finally, in the 13th round, the referee stopped the fight, and LaMotta lost his middleweight crown to Robinson.

LaMotta fought through 1952, was inactive in 1953, and retired after three fights in 1954.

LaMotta had a troubled personal life and was married seven times; he admitted beating his wives and his possessiveness with his wives caused issues and arguments. In one incident in his early life, he almost beat a man during a robbery.

Based on his 1970 book, Raging Bull: My Story, the film, Raging Bull, released in 1980, was initially only a minor box office success, but it eventually received overwhelming critical acclaim for both director Martin Scorsese and actor Robert DeNero.

In February 1998, LaMotta's elder son, Jake LaMotta, Jr., died of liver cancer. In September 1998, his younger son, Joseph LaMotta died in the crash of Swissair Flight 111. La Motta has four daughters including Christi by his second wife, Vikki LaMotta, Elisa, Mia, and Stephanie. He married his seventh wife, his longtime fiancée Denise Baker, on January 4, 2013.

LaMotta remained active on the speaking and autograph circuit and worked as a witty, stand-up comedian, publishing several books about his career, life, and his memorable fights with Robinson.

LaMotta passed away on September 17, 2017, in a nursing home in Florida; he was 95 years old.

CFL Hall of Famer Angelo Mosca Won 5 Grey Cup Championships (Part 1)

Angelo Mosca is pictured here as a member of the Hamilton Tiger Cats of the CFL. (Courtesy of the CFL Hall of Fame).

By Al Bruno
La Gazzetta Italiana
October 2022

Editor's Note in Italian (italicized):
Quest'articolo parla della vita di Angelo Mosca, un atleta molto famoso per la sua carriera nel football e nel wrestling. Suffrì una vita, in quanto piena di abusi e povertà non ebbe un'infanzia felice e per questo, dovette lavorare sodo per migliorare la sua vita. Lui cominciò ad allenarsi e giocare ai football. Dedicò tanto tempo agli sporti. Dopo il liceo, andai all'Università di Notre Dame per giocare a football. Nel 1959, ebbe l'opportunità di giocare per i Philadelphia Eagles, ma decise poi di giocare il football professionistico in Canada. Mosca aveva tanti tifosi ma anche tanti nemici perché aveva un azione di giocca molto aggressiva durante le partite. La sua carriera, tuttavia, fu ricca di successi e vittorie.

THE 1960S, 70S, AND 80S were great football and wrestling times for first-generation, Italian American Angelo Valentine Mosca, growing up in Waltham, Massachusetts, never imagining that he would someday develop into a sports celebrity and legacy in Canada and North America.

Mosca grew up in the hard-scrabble streets in the north end of Boston, embedded in the gambling and prostitution district of the city. As fate would have it in his favor, Mosca's physical gifts would eventually empower him to become an international sports celebrity for his exploits on the gridiron and in the wrestling ring: A rags-to-riches story of an incredibly-determined and physically-gifted Italian American kid who overcame the near impossible to achieve both the American and Canadian Dreams in one lifetime.

Thankfully for Mosca, his size, speed, and incredible athletic ability in football rescued Mosca from a potential life of waywardness and criminality by means of gambling and hustling in the streets to make-a-living, a seedier and scammer existence that he was introduced to as a youngster by his father, the well-known Italian "bookie" in the neighborhood. Young Mosca was born to an Italian immigrant father from Syracusa, Italy, also named Angelo, and a second-generation Italian American mother, named Agnes, who was ethnically mixed, half-Italian and half-black.

Unfortunately, Mosca grew up impoverished, as the oldest and physically largest of six siblings, and unfairly subjected to physical and verbal abuse from his misguided alcoholic parents.

"My dad beat us and was always screaming at us about being black. I didn't fully get what was supposed to be wrong with us kids, and I certainly didn't know how the black part fit in. All the kids in the neighborhood liked us. I even used to organize neighborhood baseball games: The Italian kids would play the Irish, and we never lost a game," writes Mosca in his 2011 book with Steve Milton, Tell Me to My Face, published by Lulu Canada.

"I wasn't proud of being poor and I was willing to work hard so I wouldn't stay poor. I realized now that as a child I didn't want to be dependent on anyone. I began working all the time, and I hustled too, both long before I was a teenager," writes Mosca. Several years later, young Mosca had tolerated enough in a dysfunctional household and left home, at age 16, to live with relatives.

"I had started playing football at high school, and I was working out in the Waltham Boys Club like a maniac. No one else worked out back then, but I had an idea in my mind of being totally independent, and becoming stronger and tougher was part of it. Being good at sports was my rebellion. Sports were becoming my guiding light, with them I'd have probably ended up in jail," writes Mosca.

At 6'4" and 275 lbs., combining power and agility, Mosca became a highly-recruited, defensive lineman and was recruited by over 60 colleges and universities. After choosing and playing for the University of Notre Dame, the premier college football team in the country, for two years, Mosca had to transfer, sojourning across-the-country to University of Wyoming to finish his college playing days.

Mosca was drafted by the Philadelphia Eagles of the NFL in 1959 in the 30th round (350 overall); he had already decided to play in the Canadian Football League (CFL) in 1958 and 1959 for the Hamilton Tiger-Cats. Mosca was traded to the Ottawa Rough Riders in 1960 and 1961, before joining the Montreal Alouettes in 1962. He played his remaining years, from 1963 to 1972, in Hamilton.

Mosca's play was remarkable, it was noticed, and it was publicized by local and national media, repeatedly, in his distinguished 16-year, CFL career: a five-time, all-star, appearing in nine Grey Cups and winning five of them, four with Hamilton (1963, 1965, 1967, and 1970) and one with Ottawa (1960). He was inducted into the CFL Hall of Fame in 1987, the Hamilton Sports Hall of Fame in 2012, and the Ontario Sports Hall of Fame in 2013.

In a 16-year CFL career, running from 1958 to 1972, Mosca proved to be about as dominant a defensive lineman as the game could hope to see, playing left defensive tackle for Hamilton and lining up, side-by-side, with all-star John Barrow from 1958 to 1959 and then again from 1963 to 1970, fortifying a veritable wall up the middle, disrupting running plays, and preventing most teams from having success against Hamilton on the ground.

Mosca was on the roster for three different CFL teams, but he is indelibly linked to his time in Hamilton. Not least because he represented them between 1962 and 1972 (his return to the team) when Hamilton went 98-51-5. Hamilton earned 12 consecutive playoff berths during his years with them, appearing in six Grey Cups and winning on four occasions.

Mosca especially remembers how glorious that 1967 Hamilton team really was, the Grey Cup winners.

"The 1967 Hamilton Tiger-Cats were the greatest football team I've ever seen assembled in Canada. I always say it was the core of the team that all came of age at the same time. Zuger, Barrow, Ceppetelli, Henley, and myself were all 28, 29, 30 years old and full of experience. Ceppetelli was the center, Jon Hohman and Bill Danychuk were the guards, Charlie Turner and Ellison Kelly were the tackles. That was the greatest offensive line I've ever seen. We had Tommy Joe Coffey and Tommy Grant catching the ball, and Dave Fleming and Willie Bethea, running the ball," writes Mosca.

"The Grey Cup win was the sixth straight game that we didn't allow a touchdown, and in the three playoff games, including the Cup, we allowed all of four points. Nobody's ever going to convince me that our club wasn't the greatest team this country has ever seen. Four points in three games at the most important time of the year? Forget about it," writes Mosca.

During the years he was in Ottawa, the Rough Riders went 17-11 and won the 1960 Grey Cup. In 1963 and 1970, Mosca was named Outstanding Lineman in the East and runner-up, Outstanding Lineman in the CFL. In recognition of his outstanding play in Hamilton, Mosca was placed on the Tiger-Cats Wall of Honor, and he was only the second Hamilton player to have his shirt number (68) retired.

Despite Mosca having an illustrious CFL career, there is still a play that stands out: A tackle in the 1963 Grey Cup game that saw Mosca controversially knock BC Lions star running back Willie Fleming out of the game. The question was, did Mosca kick him in the head while he was down? A short, online video shows the hit, but it is inconclusive after review. Some viewed it as accidental and others still argue the other way, calling it a "cheap shot." The referees did not flag it or consider it a dirty play at the moment it happened, but the British Columbia (BC) fans and media did. BC fans never grudgingly forgot it or forgave Mosca.

In 1964, the CBC news magazine program featured a 10-minute documentary about Mosca, dubbed "the meanest man in the game." Mosca explains, "I created an image and everyone thinks I am dirty. There's no such thing as dirty play, unless you're kicking people in the face."

Mosca further explains: "Hey, it just happened, it wasn't a late hit, I came from about 45 yards away to make the play and slid over the top of him." Clearly, it can be viewed as a late hit but not a cheap shot as critics dissected and overstated the controversial hit by the ensuing Mosca, charging toward the ball carrier.

That controversial hit by Mosca on Fleming has astonishingly persisted for almost five decades in some of the minds of CFL players that played in that memorable, 1963 Grey Cup championship game: There are varying opinions on what happened and the consequences it had on the championship outcome, lingering in the airspace like an ominous black cloud, clamoring for a downpour of rain. Ironically it would seem, that day came 48 years later in Vancouver.

In 2011, the grudges that persisted came to a vicious head when Mosca and former BC Lions quarterback Joe Kapp, well into their seventies at the time, got into a fight at a CFL Alumni Association charity luncheon and fundraiser in Vancouver to assist CFL retired players needing some help with medical and rehabilitation costs. Important to note, strangely, one of the objectives of the luncheon was to revisit that 1963 controversial hit on Willie Fleming and determine whether it was, in fact, a late hit.

A video of the 2011 event shows that Kapp shoved a daisy flower in Mosca's face twice on stage, prompting Mosca to swing his cane in his left hand, striking Kapp in the right side of his face, cutting him and knocking his glasses off his face. Kapp immediately charged the seated Mosca and punched Mosca in the face, knocking him off his chair and stage, landing on the ground, and ending the unforeseen skirmish in bewilderment by all in attendance.

Mosca and Kapp were both overtaken by it all, startled, and humiliated by their unprofessional behaviors. "It's a shame it happened," Mosca told the CBC in November 2011. Kapp responded this way: "The altercation should have been avoided there because it was a celebration of teamwork and togetherness in the country (Canada)."

Kapp recalled the incident: "Somebody hit me on the side of the head with a cane – a club – so I had to respond. I don't think there is a person anywhere that wouldn't respond the way I did."

Contrarily, Mosca said things got heated after he had a "dead-ass flower" shoved in his face, recalling: "I don't care if you're the king or the queen, you're not going to shove something in my face and get away with it."

Unforeseeably, the video of the Mosca and Kapp skirmish went viral, recovering over 647,000 views on YouTube and mentioned on ESPN's Monday Night Football and on Fox TV's The O'Reilly Factor. The unusual, worldwide publicity resulted in Mosca and Angelo Mosca, Jr. appearing on the Phil Donahue Show as well. Kapp was invited to the Donahue interview, but he declined the invite to the show.

To his creative credit, Mosca has always thought big and about big picture scenarios with entertainment value like few celebrities before him; inventively again in his illustrious career, Mosca auctioned off the cane he used against Kapp at the following year's luncheon for $7700, with the charitable proceeds going towards the CFL Alumni Association's "dire straits" fund for struggling former players: Good public relations work by Mosca again is realized for a great humanitarian cause.

Angelo "King Kong" Mosca Becomes Legendary in Canadian Wrestling (Part 2)

Angelo Mosca is pictured here as the legendary wrestler King Kong Mosca in the 1970s and 1980s. (Wikimedia. com, Google Art Project).

By Al Bruno
November 2022
La Gazzetta Italiana

Editor's Note in Italian (italicized):
Angelo Mosca fu un canadese che ebbe un'eccellente esperienza nel wrestling oltre 40 anni fa. Fece parte del club di wrestling in Canada ed è famoso per la sua forza e le sue manovre. Nel 1980, con Andre the Giant combatte contro Big John Stud e Crusher Blackwell. Vinsero senza troppo litigi. Nel 1982, lotto di nuovo contro Big John Stud e in una gabbia chiusa. Dopo un incontro lungo e sanguinoso, Mosca vinse. Dopo la carriera, importante, Mosca diventò giornalista sportivo. Purtroppo è morto nel 2021.

After retiring from the CFL, Angelo Mosca reinvented himself into a star with a villain, a mean-man personality, in Canadian professional wrestling like he had done in the CFL, benefitting from his already-established, heel reputation: It was an easy transition for the motivated Mosca. Mosca was almost an instant success in wrestling, and he eventually became a recognized wrestling star throughout Canada and North America.

Mosca was introduced to wrestling by Montreal promoter Eddie Quinn; he wrestled all across North America, earning the nickname, Angelo "King Kong" Mosca and later known as "Big Nasty." Mosca was always placed at or near the top of the wrestling card from 1972 until the early 1980s, and almost always as a heel or villain, even in Toronto, a style he imported from his playing days in the CFL.

King Kong Mosca would make his long-awaited debut at Toronto's Maple Leaf Garden on June 21, 1971, against the Sheik, the villain of villains. Allan Ryan, a reporter, wrote of Mosca's debut in the next day Toronto Globe and Mail:

"Mosca gave the Sheik trouble. Angelo Mosca, evidently so unnerved at hearing Torontonians actually cheering for him, erred on a flying tackle, wrapped himself around a ring-post and ultimately, lost his wrestling assignment against the Sheik last night. In the autumn, Mosca is a 270 pound lineman with the Hamilton Tiger-Cats and seems to rate the most verbal abuse when the Toronto Argonauts are hosting other Canadian Football League teams at CNE Stadium. He forgot that a Maple Leaf's wrestling crowd would throw roses to Adolph Hitler had he faced the Sheik."

After losing to Andre the Giant on December 23, 1976, at Maple Leaf Garden (MLG), Milt Dunnell, of the Toronto Star, wrote that "Mosca still confesses to villainous impulses since he left the refining influences of the Tiger-Cats," Dunnell quoted Mosca, saying: "I am a pretty tough character. I am. The heavyweight champion is in demand."

"Wrestling is very much an individual business, and more than that it's a dog-eat-dog business. I often refer to it as a whore's business. You learn not to trust people and you sell yourself for money.

"When I broke in, a lot of wrestlers had never been athletes. They didn't have to be. Some wrestlers, all they did was tell stories about other guys, so eventually I learned to travel alone so that stories never got back to the promoter's office. That's why I was known as kind of a loner in the business," writes Mosca in his book in 2011, Tell Me To My Face, with Steve Milton.

"You have to have an imagination in wrestling. It is your job to create an image. That's why there were a lot of stereotypes, a lot of them racial. Once you have an image, you need to nurture it. A good way to do that was to keep using the same line, the same verbiage, over and over again until people knew what you might say at any given moment," writes Mosca.

Mosca fought the likes of wrestling greats like Ivan Koloff, Big John Studd, and the Iron Sheik and beat all of them; in fact, Mosca teamed up with the great Andre the Giant and memorably defeated Big John Stud and Crusher Blackwell on November 6, 1980.

In the early 1980s, in the World Wrestling Federation (WWF), Mosca gained momentum and became a lead face, using a "sleeper" as his finishing move. Mosca began wrestling all over the world and became an international wrestling star, showcasing his wrestling skills in Australia, Hawaii, the South Pacific, and Japan.

In 1981, Mosca became a top challenger to WWF Champion Bob Backlund's world championship belt but was unsuccessful in winning the belt. On June 19, 1981, Mosca would face off against arch-rival Ivan Koloff in a tough, bloody battle that he won, appearing in newsprint the next day, "Angie still hears the cheers," Kevin Boland of the Toronto Sun, wrote, then quoting Mosca: "I built this image of a guy who loved to be hated, and now it's different. All of a sudden, it changes. People like me, really like me. That's the way it goes in this game. One night you're the good guy, the next night you're the villain."

Mosca won an anticipated Canadian Wrestling Championship match with champion Big John Studd in a steel cage, and it arrived on January 17, 1982. The two faced off down on the ramp as Mosca waited for Studd to climb the stairs. Mosca attacked Studd, and the bout was on. Mosca, bloody and beaten, emerged from the cage as the new champion would begin his fourth reign with the title.

In the mid-1980s, Mosca became a part-time color commentator and promoter, wrestling for WWE TV tapings in Ontario from August 1984 until January 1985. After being fired by the WWF, Mosca promoted the NWA in Ontario from 1985 to 1987. He and Milt Avruskin hosted a TV show featuring compilations of NWA matches.

Mosca organized a NWA card in Hamilton in February 1986 called "Moscamania" that drew an excellent house of 12,000 spectators, but the follow-up a year later drew only 3,200 spectators; he retired from wrestling in 1986.

Mosca's son, Angelo Mosca, Jr., had a brief but successful wrestling career, winning the NWA Eastern States Heavyweight Championship three times, defeating champion Ivan Koloff three times in 1984; Angelo Mosca, Jr. was enthusiastically managed by his father, Angelo Mosca, Sr., who reminded everyone of his support and love for Angelo, Jr., because "blood is thicker than water."

Angelo Mosca, Jr. revealed that his father is funny and loves a practical joke, and it can be heard in his distinct, powerful voice: "It's animated but in many ways, it's intimidating, too. It's his voice and his demeanor." His sister, Jolene, calls their father's voice "commanding" but that he can also "be tender with it when he wants to."

In his distinguished career in professional wrestling, Mosca achieved great success across-the-continent, earning the following titles/championships: the American Wrestling Association British Empire Heavyweight Champion (AWA, 1 time), National Wrestling Association (NWA) Southern Heavyweight Champion (Florida, one time), NWA Florida Tag-Team Champion (one time with Bobby Duncum), NWA Georgia Heavyweight Champion (one time), NWA United States Champion (San Francisco, one time), NWA Canadian Heavyweight Champion, Toronto, five times from 1980 to 1984), NWQ Tri-State Brass Knuckles Champion (one time), and the Stampede North American Heavyweight Champion (one time). Years after retiring from wrestling Mosca was inducted in the Canadian Wrestling Hall of Fame (1989) and the Stampede Wrestling Hall of Fame (1990).

Bill Apter, a wrestling commentator, said this about Mosca, the wrestler: "Angelo Mosca was one of the meanest, toughest, human beings in the world, but he had the heart of a teddy bear. He is one of the nicest guys I have ever met."

Mosca had his share of adversaries inside and outside the wrestling ring, but the guys who wrestled against him acknowledge his wrestling greatness. Here is a sample of some of those wrestlers and their comments:

Jim Ross, a fellow wrestler, remembers Mosca: "You are one of the greatest football players and wrestlers of all time, and you went to Notre Dame. And you beat my Oklahoma Sooners in Oklahoma. I was there."

Ricky Steamboat, a fellow wrestler said this about Mosca: "I remember all the times in the late 70s you hammered me. If I could live as long as you have, I might have a second chance at a wrestling career." Bill Eadie, a fellow wrestler known as Ax, said: "We go back a long time, my friend. I followed your football and wrestling careers. I wish I was there."

Importantly, Mosca's was able to capture his images and experiences about his wrestling career through writer Steve Milton's insightful remarks:

"The most conspicuous thing about Angelo Mosca has always been his size. He was a big kid, a big football player, a big wrestler, and he is still a big man. Bigger than life sometimes. Angelo doesn't do small things. Not in his body, his face, his voice, his strengths, his weaknesses, his passions, his anecdotes, his history, his secrets," writes Milton.

"It's fitting that Angelo came of age just as television was moving heavily into his two sports: football and wrestling. During and after his athletic careers, TV kept him famous and he, in turn, made good for TV. His face filled the screen unforgettably and his it-could-only-be-Mosca voice added to the over impression," writes Milton. Mosca believed he had television appeal, asserting: "I think I was born to be an entertainer." Most would probably agree.

People love personality, and Mosca had personality in spades: A big, tough, and nasty reputation that he developed in football proliferated in wrestling and beyond. Mosca created his own personal brand, and companies flocked to him; he promoted it all: donuts, Chevy trucks, spaghetti, and even snowmobiles. In 1970, Mosca was everywhere. His infamous Schick razors commercial was the perfect union between the spokesperson and the brand. Mosca was the perfect pitchman, public speaker, storyteller, and actor, appearing in 60 TV commercials, in TV shows, and even in the movies.

"Angelo Mosca has many faults, and he would be the first to tell you that. But he is a man with a heart in the right place who is starting to regret some of the pain he caused. He is a guy you want in your corner, and as your friend. And I would tell him that. To his face," writes Milton.

In February 2015, sadly, Mosca was diagnosed with Alzheimer's disease. Mosca has lived in and around Hamilton for many years and currently lives in St. Catherines, Ontario, with his wife, Helen, a real estate agent. He first met Helen in 1996 at a Tiger-Cats game, and they married in 1998. He had divorced once and widowed prior.

Mosca faced countless storied rivals on the football field and in the wrestling ring. However, his biggest rival, Alzheimer's disease, is a form of dementia: It kills brain cells, resulting in problems associated with memory, thinking, and behavior. It's an invisible disease, and the process begins long before the person begins to exhibit symptoms.

"On a day to day basis, you wouldn't even notice anything was wrong. But if you're with him the whole day, you start noticing he repeats things and forgets things," states his wife, Helen Mosca.

Without a cure, the only way to treat it is through patience and understanding. "I just take one day at a time. So far, we haven't had many problems. It might be a little slower, but I get it done," points out Mosca.

Sadly in 2021, Mosca passed away at age 84. He is survived by his wife Helen, his son Angelo Mosca, Jr., and his daughter Jolene Mosca.

Giovanni "Nino" Benvenuti: America's, Most Beloved Italian Boxer During 1960s

Giovanni "Nino" Benvenuti is pictured here brandishing his earned gold medal in welterweight boxing at the 1960 Rome Summer Olympics. (Wikimedia.com, Google Art Project).

By Federico Pasquali
We The Italians
February 16, 2020

Giovanni "Nino" Benvenuti had a phenomenal, hall of fame boxing career in Italy and the United States during the 1960s, becoming a champion in the welterweight, light-middleweight, and middleweight divisions in his illustrious career. Benvenuti achieved a record of 82 wins, seven losses and one draw (tie) in 90 professional bouts, with 35 wins by knockout. In 1992, Benvenuti was inducted into the International Boxing Hall of Fame.

He is currently ranks No. 32 in BoxRec's ranking of the greatest pound-for-pound boxers of all-time. In 1968, Benvenuti was voted Fighter of the Year by The Ring Magazine. After retiring from boxing, Benvenuti became a successful businessman, TV pundit, and city counselor in Trieste, Italy. He opened a high-class restaurant and maintained a strong friendship with his former rivals, Monzon and Griffith.

Benvenuti was born in Isola d'Istria, at that time in Italy (now in Slovenia). After World War II, his family fled to Italy due to the consequences of the war treaty and the hostilities created by the Yugoslav Government. In 1961, Benvenuti married Giuliana Fonzari; they had four sons and adopted a Tunisian girl. They later divorced, and Benvenuti married Naid Bertorello, with whom he had one daughter.

Sixty-three years ago Italy, in particular its capital, Rome, showed itself to the world in all its modernity. Fifteen years after the end of the Second World War, the Bel Paese had closed most of the wounds of the atrocious war and launched itself toward the famous economic boom of the 1960s.

It was a sport event to give impetus to this period of rebirth: the Olympic Games in Rome, Italy, in short time, the Capital city transformed itself from a peripheral city to a European metropolis, thanks to the building of many modern infrastructures, But the 1960s Games where also the first to be broadcast on television to various countries and the first to put disabled athletes on a par with able-bodied athletes with the birth of the Paralympics.

Among the thousand stories of that magical summer, two left an indelible mark in the following years. Both were written by boxers: one African-American, the other Istrian-Italian. The first was Cassius Clay, who won the gold medal in Rome at a very young age, a success that launched him into the professional world where a few years later, converted him to Islam, changing his name to Muhammad Ali.

The other was Nino Benvenuti, who in the years following his Olympic gold medal became a legend of international boxing for all and in particular those immigrating to the States.

Benvenuti, always with a fate crossed with the United States, won several awards: "Fighter of the Year" in 1968, entering the International Boxing Hall of Fame in the following years: in 2022, named "Man of the Year" by the Associazione Culturale Italiana di New York;" in 2016, the solemn entry into the National Italian-American Sport Hall of Fame. Five awards, all "made in the USA," obtained by a few boxers in history.

But his fame in the States before these awards, and it's tied to a particularly unbeatable figure in those years: Emilie Griffith. Born in Saint Thomas, Virgin Island, Griffith moved to New York as a young boy and immediately started boxing with excellent results. He had a reputation as a great fighter and in 1962, he won the world welterweight title against Cuban Benny Paret: Griffith beat him hard in the ring so much that Paret died nine days later. Benvenuti and Griffith fought for title three in what is considered one of the biggest battles in world boxing.

The first match was held at Madison Square Garden in New York City on April 17th, 1967, and in Italy, about 18 million people followed it on the radio: the highest ever listeners for a radio report after the 1970 World Cup semifinal between Italy and Germany. Griffith was defending the world belt of middleweights, fighting at home and also having history on his side; until then, only one European boxer had won a world title in the United States. But the thousands of Italian who immigrated to the States present at Madison Square Garden supporting Benvenuti: who, surprisingly, won by points in Rome.

On September 29th of the same year, at Shea Stadium in Queens, there was a rematch and Griffith took back the world title. On March 4th, 1968, at Madison Square Garden, the last match between the two saw Benvenuti as the winner, becoming the idol of the Italian Americans.

Benvenuti's career continued successfully and for another two years, he successfully defended the world title. On November 7th, 1970, Monzon in Rome, Benvenuti lost to Argentina Carlos and was unable to regain the title.

Benvenuti's career ended in 1971, becoming a radio and television commentator on boxing, a position that brought him back to the United States for many years to comment on the most prestigious matches. Today Benvenuti is 85 years old and is still very active in the world of sports as a commentator and testimonial for sporting events. And he is still recognized today as one of the Italian sports legends both in Italy and in the United States.

Baseball Hall of Famer Tommy Lasorda Embodied "Dodger Blue" For Eight Decades

A young Tommy Lasorda is seen here early in his baseball hall of fame career as a pitcher for Kansas City. (Wikimedia.com, Google Art Project).

By Al Bruno

"Tommy Lasorda will always remain the embodiment of Dodger blue," memorable words that are inscribed in the Baseball of Fame in Cooperstown, NY. "For more than eight decades, he was the face of the Los Angeles Dodgers."

Lasorda was born September 22, 1927, in Norristown, Pennsylvania, the son of Italian immigrants. His father, Sabatino, was from Tollo, the Abruzzo region of Italy, and his mother was Carmella (Cavuto) Lasorda, His father worked as a meat-packing plant and a truck driver. He was the second of five brothers, who all went into the restaurant business.

Lasorda refused to follow his father's and

brothers' footsteps into their work occupations. He loved playing baseball and excelled as a left-handed pitcher. The Philadelphia Phillies signed him after he graduated from high school in 1945. After pitching briefly in the minors, he joined the Army until 1947.

After his return, Lasorda joined the Schenectady Jays of the Canadian-American League in 1948. He set a league record by striking out 25 batters in a 15-inning game on May 31, 1948, a game in which he drove in the winning run. The Dodgers acquired him in 1949.

Lasorda signed with the Montreal Royals of the International League in 1950. He was a star pitcher for a total of nine seasons and is the winningest pitcher in the history of the team. He led Montreal to four straight Governor Cups from 1951 to 1954, and a fifth championship in 1958 when he was selected for the International League's Most Valuable Pitcher Award.

Lasorda broke into the majors in 1954 as a left-handed pitcher with the Brooklyn Dodgers. After two seasons in Brooklyn, he was traded to the Kansas City Athletics (1956). Playing in abbreviated stints, however, Lasorda never established himself as a major-league player.

He did not see major league playing time after the 1956 season and finished his career in 1960 with the Royals. In 2006, Lasorda was elected to the Canadian Baseball Hall of Fame.

Lasorda's first off-field assignment with the Dodgers was as a scout from 1961 to 1965. In 1966, he began managing at the lowest rung in minor league baseball, with the rookie-level Ogden, Utah, Dodgers of the Pioneer League. After spending three years managing in rookie ball, Lasorda was promoted all the way to skipper of the Dodgers' AAA Pacific Coast League farm clubs, first with the Spokane Indians (1969-71) and then the Albuquerque Dukes (1972).

Lasorda was extremely successful at the minor league level, winning five pennants in seven seasons, guiding the careers of many future Dodgers who would form the nucleus of Lasorda's contending MLB teams.

In 1973, Lasorda became the third-base coach on the staff of Hall of Fame manager Walter Alston, serving for almost four seasons. He was widely regarded as Alston's heir apparent, and he turned down several major league managing jobs elsewhere to remain in the Dodger fold. Finally, Lasorda became the Los Angeles manager on September 29, 1976, upon Alston's retirement.

Lasorda led the team to consecutive National League championships in 1977 and 1978. Over 20 years at the helm of the Dodgers, Lasorda was not a great strategist, but there was no doubt he was able to inspire teams with his rah-rah style. He was not always the best of talent, either. In 1993, Lasorda questioned whether then-Dodger Pedro Martinez, because of his slight build, had the size and stamina to be a starting pitcher in the major leagues.

Lasorda's views led the Dodgers to trade Martinez to the Montreal Expos where Martinez began to build his Baseball Hall of Fame numbers. Many also blame Lasorda for overworking pitchers, especially Martinez, and to a lesser extent, Orel Hershiser, eventually shortening their careers.

Lasorda's final game was a 4-3 victory over the Houston Astros at Dodger Stadium; attendance was 35,467 on June 23, 1996. The following day, June 24, 1996, Lasorda drove himself to the hospital complaining of abdominal pains, and in fact, he was having a heart attack. He officially retired on July 29, having compiled a 1599-1439 record as a manager. His 1599 career wins ranks 15th all-time in MLB history with a .526 winning percentage.

To note, Lasorda had a .508 winning percentage in 61 postseason games. Dodger clubs provided some of the best moments in baseball in the 1980s.

Remarkably, Lasorda managed nine players who won the National League Rookie of the Year award. The Rookie of the Year winners came in two strings of four consecutive players. From 1979 to 1982, he managed Rick Sutcliffe, Fernando Valenzuela, Steve Howe, and Steve Sax. From 1992 to 1995, Lasorda managed Eric Karros, Mike Piazza, Raul Mondesi, and Hideo Nomo. Before retiring in 1996, he had also managed that year's Rookie of the Year, Todd Hollandsworth.

After retiring, Lasorda became an executive with the Dodgers. He was inducted into the Baseball Hall of Fame in 1997 as a manager. Lasorda came out of retirement to manage the United States team at the 2000 Summer Olympics in Sydney. He led the Americans to the gold medal, beating heavily favored Cuba, which had the gold medal at the two previous Olympics.

He was hospitalized in early 2021 and passed away on January 21, 2021, at age 93. On September 21, 2021, the Dodgers announced the death of Lasorda's widow, Jo, at age 91.

The Pride of Pittston

NFL Hall of Famer Charley Trippi is pictured here as a running back for the University of Georgia in 1946. (Wikimedia.com, Google Art Project).

By Joe Di Leo
Per Niente
Summer 2023

When the Industrial Revolution took place in the 19th century, 90 per cent of the world's sulfur came from Sicily. Sulfur emits suffocating hydrogen sulfide gas, making it difficult to breathe for the men and boys who worked 12 hour days in a stifling atmosphere– temperatures reaching above 100 degrees Fahrenheit with 100 per cent humidity.

They often worked naked because the human body can't survive these conditions clothed. The Sicilians earned low wages and often considered themselves slaves. In spite of fueling the Industrial Revolution of Northern Europe, they failed to be part of any of the profits.

At the turn of the century the underground extraction of crude oil produced sulfur as a by-product. This was a far cheaper and safer way of obtaining sulfur, and Sicily lost its global monopoly. Thousands and thousands of sulfur miners and their families lost their livelihood. Like the Irish at the time of the potato blight, Sicilians moved to America in a mass exodus.

Giuseppe Trippi and Giovanna Attardo were born in Montedoro, Sicily. Both their fathers were sulfur miners. In 1912, Giuseppe, 18, left Sicily for America, and the following year the Attardo family followed. Immigration and marriage records indicate that Giuseppe's destination was Buffalo, N.Y. In 1915 Giuseppe and Giovanna were married in Buffalo, then moved to join Giovanna's family in Pittston, Pa., a coal-mining town that attracted immigrants from Montedoro mainly because of its familiarity with the small sulfur town in Sicily.

Ironically, Giuseppe escaped the sulfur mines of Sicily only to work at the coal mines of Pennsylvania. The Trippis raised five children: Angelina, Salvatore, Maria, Calogero, and Jenny. It was Calogero, (Charley) who would become one of the great athletes of that era and the pride of Pittston.

Charley grew up playing football, basketball and baseball. He was an outstanding All-State football star at Pittston High School and played amateur and semi-pro baseball. After graduating from high school at 19, Trippi was offered a football scholarship to the University of Georgia. Immediately, Charley had an impact on Georgia's team, playing halfback on the undefeated freshman team. Midway through his sophomore season (1942-43), coach Wally Butts switched All-American halfback Frank Sinkwich to fullback and inserted Trippi at the halfback position.

Trippi finished the season with 1239 total yards. The Bulldogs won the Southeastern Conference (SEC) championship and earned a bid to the Rose Bowl, where Trippi rushed for 130 yards en route to a 9-0 victory over the University of California at Los Angeles. Trippi was selected the Rose Bowl's most valuable player.

Trippi missed the next two-and-a-half seasons while serving in the Air Force in World War II (1941-45). He returned to school for the last six games of 1945 and, in the season finale against Georgia Tech, set SEC records for passing yards and total yards in a single game. Trippi captained the Bulldogs in his senior year, leading the 1946 team to an undefeated SEC championship season and a Sugar Bowl victory and winning the Maxwell Award as college player of the year. He also played baseball at Georgia and was named to the All-American team. In his senior season he batted .450, with 28 steals.

In the 1945 NFL draft the Chicago Cardinals chose Trippi as a "future pick." Subsequently, in 1947, Trippi signed a $100,000 contract with the Cardinals. That year he also signed a baseball contract with the Atlanta Crackers, an AA team in the Southern Association, for a $10,000 bonus and a monthly $500 salary. He played just one season and batted .338, seventh best in the league among batters with more than 100 at bats. After that season he gave up baseball to concentrate on football.

Trippi headed to Chicago and became a member of "The Dream Backfield." In his first season, he was named All-Pro and led Chicago to the world title. In his nine seasons with the Cardinals, he played halfback, quarterback and safety, and punted and returned kicks. When he retired, he led the NFL in total offense. He is the only NFL Hall of Famer and one of only three men in NFL history with more than 1000 yards rushing, passing, and receiving. Trippi was inducted into the College Football Hall of Fame, the Georgia Bulldog Circle of Honor, the Arizona Cardinals Ring of Honor, the Pro Football Hall of Fame and the Pennsylvania Sports Hall of Fame. Trippi was also named to the NFL's 1940s All Decade Team. The football stadium at Pittston Area High School is named Charley Trippi Stadium in his honor, and his Georgia Bulldog number 62 has long been retired.

Charley Trippi, the Pride of Pittston, died at his home in Athens, Ga., on October 19, 2022. He was 100 years old.

Note: The original Sicilian birth and immigration records of Trippi's father and mother were found by Ange Coniglio, director of the Genealogy Station at the Buffalo Italian Cultural Center.

See www.bit.ly/GenealogyStationCCI to set up an appointment to research your ancestors.

Remembering Carmen Basilio: From Onion Picker to Champion to Boxing Hall of Fame

Carmen Basilio is pictured here in his second bout against Sugar Ray Robinson in 1958, a championship match that Basilio narrowly lost (Courtesy of The Ring magazine).

By Al Bruno

First generation Italian American Carmen Basilio (born April 2, 1927) lived the American Dream as an American professional boxer who was the world champion in both the welterweight and middleweight divisions, beating Sugar Ray Robinson for the middleweight title. An iron-chinned pressure fighter, Basilio was a combination puncher who had great stamina and eventually wore many of his opponents down with vicious attacks to the head and body.

In 1957, The Ring magazine named Basilio Fighter of the Year, and he won the Hickok Belt, a trophy that was awarded to the top professional athlete of the year. The Boxing Writers Association of America (BWAA) named him Fighter of the Year in 1955 and 1957. Basilio also holds the distinction of The Ring magazine's Fight of the Year in five consecutive years (1955-59), a feat unmatched by any other boxer.

In 2002, Basilio was voted by The Ring magazine as the 40th greatest fighter of the last 80 years. He was inducted into the International Boxing Hall of Fame in the inaugural class of 1990. In his glorious boxing career, Basilio had an overall record of 56 wins (27 by knockout), 16 losses, and seven draws.

Basilio's arduous journey from poverty to prosperity in boxing defines Basilio's determined life and legacy.

"Carmen Basilio, who rose from abject poverty, toiled as a boy in the onion fields of Canastota, New York, and dreamed one day of becoming a boxing champion... His remarkable career is a story of survival and perseverance during a fascinating time in boxing history. His refusal to deal with the mobsters who controlled boxing in the 1950s is a testament to his core value of living an honorable life on his own terms," insightfully writes author Gary B. Youmans in his book, The Onion Picker: Carmen Basilio And Boxing In The 1950s.

Basilio was the second oldest son of Italian immigrant Joseph and Mary Basilio, of Canastota, and he was one of four sons and he had six sisters for a total of 10 children. Joseph Basilio left Italy in 1904 aboard the Germania, journeying to America via Ellis Island. In fourth grade, young Basilio told his classmates he was going to be a boxing champion, and naturally, the class laughed. His teacher thought it was a disgusting thought, but the ambitious young Basilio believed in his dream, and it came true for him years later. He fought with great determination because he had to feed his six sisters, he would always say.

Basilio began his professional career by facing Jimmy Evans on November 24, 1948, in Binghamton, New York. He knocked Evans out in the third round and five days later, he beat Bruce Walters in only one round. By the end of 1948, he had competed in four bouts.

He started 1949 with two draws, against Johnny Cunningham on January 5 and against Jay Perlin 20 days later. Basilio campaigned exclusively inside the state of New York during his first 24 bouts, going 19-3-2 during that span. His first loss was at the hands of Connie Thies, who beat him in a six-round decision on May 2, 1949. He fought Cunningham three more times during that period. Basilio won by knockout in two rounds in their second meeting. Cunningham won by a decision in eight rounds in their third fight, and Basilio won by a decision in eight rounds in their fourth fight.

In the middle of the 24-bout span, 1950 rolled over, and Basilio met former world champion, Lew Jenkins, winning a 10-round decision.

For fight number 25, Basilio decided that it was time to campaign outside of New York State. So he went to New Orleans, where he boxed his next six fights. In his first bout there, he met Gaby Farland, who held him to a draw. He and Farland later had a rematch, Basilio won by a knockout in the first round. He also boxed Guillermo Giminez there twice, first beating him by knockout in eight rounds and then knocking him out in nine rounds. In his last fight before returning home, he lost by a decision in round 10 to Eddie Giosa.

For his next seven bouts, Basilio only went 3-3-1, but he avenged his loss to Giosa by winning a 10-round decision over him in Syracuse.

In 1952, Basilio went 6-2-1. He beat Jimmy Cousins among others that year, but he lost to Chuck Davey and Billy Graham. The draw he tallied that year was against Davey in the first of their two meetings that year.

In 1953, Basilio started winning big prize fights and rose in the welterweight division rankings. He secured his first world title fight, against Cuba's Kid Gavilan for the world welterweight championship.

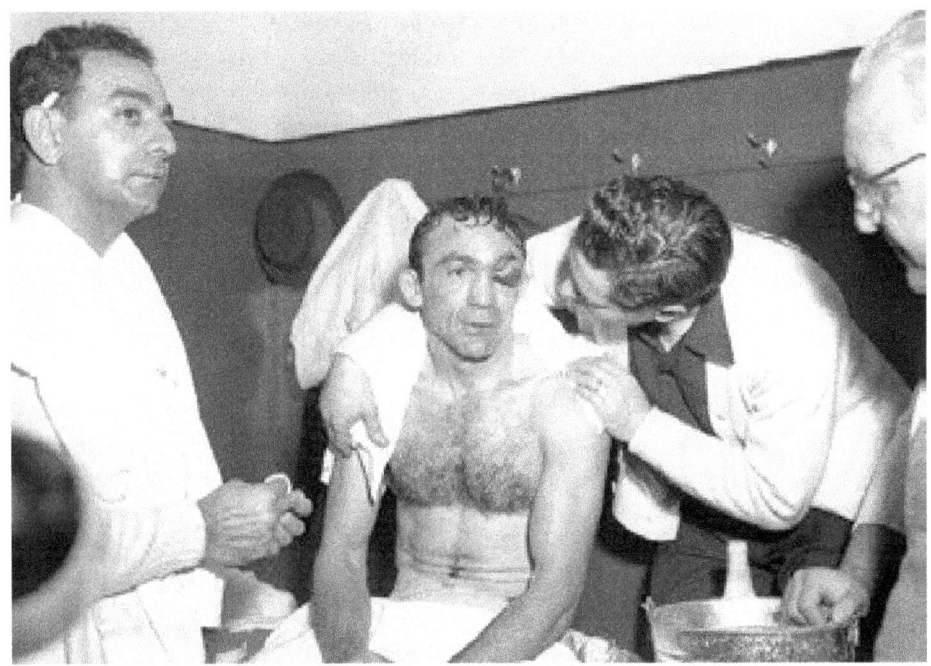

Carmen Basilio sits dejectedly with a severely-injured left eye after losing his second championship match to Sugar Ray Robinson (Courtesy of The Ring magazine).

Before fighting against Gavilan, he beat former world lightweight champion Ike Williams and had two more fights with Graham, avenging his earlier loss to Graham in the second bout between them with a 12-round decision win and a draw in their third bout. Basilio lost a 15-round decision to Gavilan and went to a fourth meeting with Cunningham, this time winning by a knockout in round four. Then, he and French fighter Pierre Langois began another rivalry with a 10-round draw in the first bout between the two.

In 1954, Basilio went undefeated in eight bouts, going 7-0-1 with two knockouts and defeating Langois in their rematch by decision.

In 1955, Basilio began by beating Peter Muller by decision. After that, Basilio was once again the number one challenger and on June 10 of that year, he earned his second world title opportunity against world welterweight champion Tony DeMarco. Basilio became world champion by knocking out DeMarco in the 12th round.

After winning the title, Basilio had two non-title bouts, including a 10-round decision win over Gil Turner, before he and DeMarco met again, this time with Basilio as the defending world champion. Their second fight yielded the same result as their first bout: Basilio won by a knockout in round 12.

For his next fight, in 1956, Basilio lost his title in Chicago to Johnny Saxton by a decision in round 15. Saxton's manager, mafioso Frank "Blinkey" Palermo, was later jailed along with partner Frankie Carbo for fixing fights. Basilio said of losing his title to the referees' decision: "It was like being robbed in a dark alley." In an immediate rematch that was fought in Syracuse, Basilio regained the crown with a round nine knockout, and then, in a rubber match, Basilio retained the belt with a knockout in the second round.

After that, Basilio bulked up in weight and challenged aging 36-year-old world middleweight champion Sugar Ray Robinson, in what may have been his most famous fight. He won the middleweight championship of the world by beating Robinson in a 15-round split decision on September 23, 1957. The 13th round of that fight is considered one of the greatest rounds in boxing history. When asked about that 13th round, Basilio said, "I couldn't remember a thing."

"Leading up to the fight, Robinson had angered his opponent with his arrogance and one-sided demands. Basilio entered the ring with one goal in mind: the destruction of Sugar Ray Robinson. The matchup was much more than a battle for a world championship. This fight was 'personal,'" writes Youmans. "He gave me the brush off, and I lost my respect for him right there and then. He was an arrogant guy," recalled Basilio years later.

The day after defeating Robinson for the middleweight championship, Basilio had to vacate his welterweight belt, in accordance with boxing's then rules. In 1957, Basilio won the Hickok Belt as the top professional athlete of the year.

In 1958, Basilio and Robinson met in a memorable rematch on March 25 and Basilio was perceived as the underdog. Reporter Howard Cosell informed Basilio that he had just polled 10 sport writers and nine had chosen Robinson by knockout. When Cosell asked Basilio for a comment, Basilio said, "Nine of them are wrong." Cosell chuckled.

Robinson barely regained the title with a controversial 15-round split decision. Although Basilio's left eye was totally swollen shut from the sixth round on, many of the ringside press thought Basilio won the fight, and most in attendance believed they were right.

From that moment on and until his retirement in 1961, Basilio fought only sporadically, but three of his last fights were attempts to regain the world middleweight title, losing twice to Gene Fullmer by a TKO in round 14 at San Francisco and by a TKO in round 12 in Fullmer's home state of Utah (in Salt Lake City), and also later, when he lost a 10-round decision to defending world champion Paul Pender.

In between those fights, Basilio was able to beat Art Aragon by knockout in eight and former world welterweight champion Don Jordan by decision in round 10. His fight with Pender for the title was also his last fight as a professional boxer.

"To be a good boxer, you have to have a type of mentality that is rare. Carmen Basilio is the rarest of boxers. There has never been anyone quite like him. A stand-up guy who would outwork anybody to achieve his goals. He's number one in my book," writes Angelo Dundee, his corner man, and the corner man as well for legends Muhammad Ali, George Foreman, Sugar Ray Leonard, and Jimmy Ellis.

Hall of Fame Wrestler Ilio DiPaolo was a dear friend of Basilio, and he visited DiPaolo in Buffalo often. His older son, Dennis DiPaolo, remembers Basilio well, "Carmen Basilio was a great storyteller and humorist at many celebrity events. Carmen was a pallbearer, along with quarterback Jim Kelly, at my father's funeral. He was a second father to me in so many ways. We were able to recognize him in 1996 at the Legends of the Auditorium in Buffalo, New York."

After Basilio retired from his glorious boxing career, Basilio was very passionate about his love for boxing: "Nobody could ever change my mind about being a boxer. My mother had a fit and wanted me to quit boxing, a dirty rotten game. I would tell her I am going to be a world champion. I eliminated my parents' debt. When I made enough money boxing, I walked into the house, and I laid down the mortgage and the deeds. My dad had tears in his eyes."

In 1960, Basilio testified before the United States Subcommittee on Antitrust and the Monopoly during its investigation of the International Boxing Club of New York and the influence of organized crime on boxing.

Carmen Basilio is pictured here in a Senate hearing, testifying mafia involvement in fixing prize fights (Wikimedia.com, Google Art Project).

Basilio told the Subcommittee about Frankie Carbo and Frank "Blinkey" Palermo and Carbo's aide, Gabriel Genovese, a cousin of Mafia Don Vito Genovese who was convicted in 1959 of being an unlicensed boxing manager. He called for a house cleaning of professional boxing. His testimony revealed that his former managers had to pay off organized crime for his title shots and he essentially had a behind-the-scenes career in Genovese.

Evidence submitted to the Subcommittee showed that Basilio's on-the-record managers, John DeJohn and Joseph Netro, paid Carbo frontman Gabriel Genovese $39,334.41 and approximately $25,000, respectively, during the time Basilio fought for and defended his welterweight and middleweight titles.

After his retirement, Basilio worked for a time at the Genesee Brewery in Rochester, NY. Later on in his life, Basilio, a high-school dropout, taught physical education at LeMoyne College in Syracuse. Basilio, who also was a member of the United States Marine Corps at one point in his life, was able to enjoy his retirement. Basilio was associated with a sausage company run by his brother, Paul, where he worked as a salesman.

During the 1970s, his nephew, Billy Backus, became world welterweight champion after having a shaky start to his boxing career, and Basilio declared on the day that Backus became champion that, to him, Billy's winning the title was a better feeling than his winning of boxing titles in prior years.

In 1990, Ed Brophy decided to build the International Boxing Hall of Fame in Canastota, New York, to honor the two world champions born there: Basilio and his nephew, Billy Backus. Although Backus is not a member of the International Boxing Hall of Fame, Basilio is, along with many of the fighters he battled inside the ring.

In the late 1990s, Basilio became seriously ill, requiring triple-bypass heart surgery. Doctors were able to repair his heart.

Basilio was interviewed for an HBO documentary on Sugar Ray Robinson called, "The Bright Lights and Dark Shadows of a Champion." He mentioned that although he respected Robinson's talents in the ring, he did not like him as a person.

In 2010, "Title Town USA, Boxing in Upstate New York" by historian Mark Allen Baker was published by The History Press in 2020 and identifies Canastota as the epicenter of Upstate New York's rich boxing heritage. The book includes chapters on both Carmen Basilio and Billy Backus.

Basilio died in 2012 at age 85. He is survived by his wife, Josephine Basilio.

The Catch

Al Gionfriddo is pictured here as an outfielder for the Brooklyn Dodgers in 1947. (Wikimedia.com, Google Art Project).

By Joe DiLeo
Per Niente (2017)

THE GREAT THING novelist Philip Roth described took place on October 5, 1947. It was Game Six of the World Series. Outfielder Al Gionfriddo, a little-used reserve, made a racing, twisting catch in deep left-center at Yankee Stadium. He robbed Joe DiMaggio of extra bases or a three-run homer and saved the game for the Brooklyn Dodgers. Alas, that would be the last time the 25-year-old ever played in the majors. Yet more than 60 years later, his spectacular grab remains a potent memory.

Albert Francis Gionfriddo was born March 8, 1922, not far from Pittsburgh in Dysart, Pennsylvania. He was the seventh of

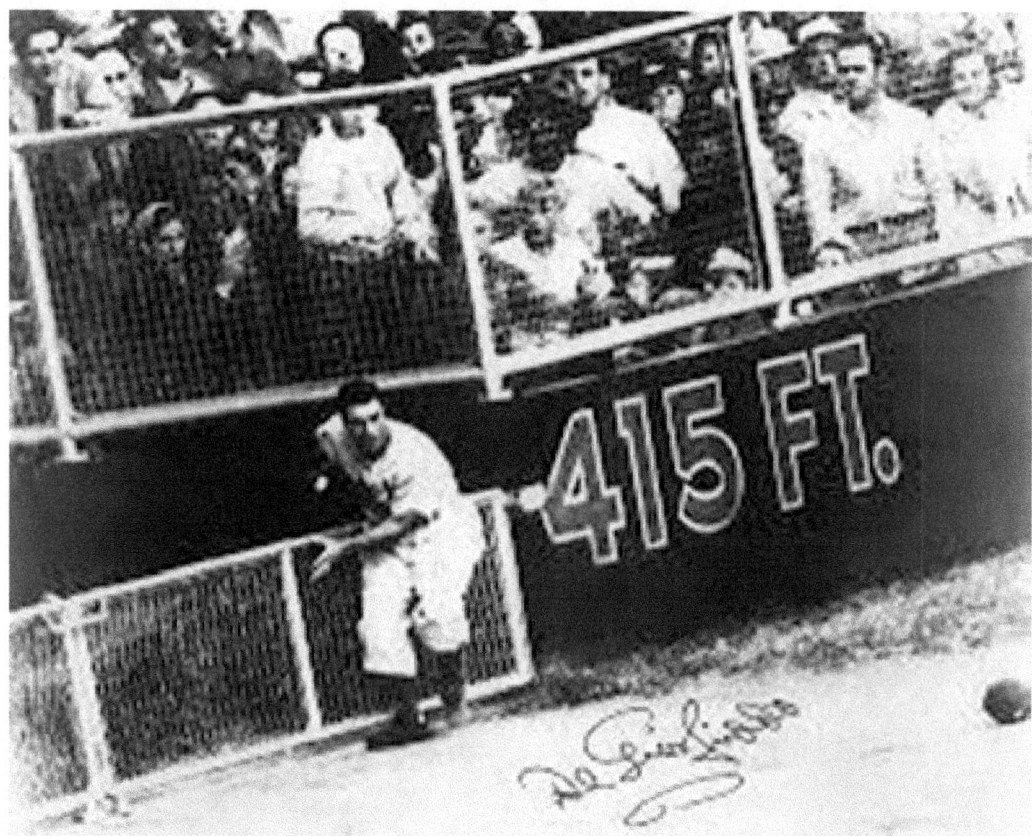

Al Gionfriddo makes a phenomenal grab, The Catch, off a 415-foot blast off the bat of Joe DiMaggio. (Wikimedia.com, Google Art Project).

the 13 children born to Sicilian immigrants Paolo Gionfriddo and Rosa Rametto. Paolo worked in the coal mines and Rosa raised the family. Although they conversed solely in Italian they wanted their children to grow up American and thanks to sports they did.

In high school Al excelled in baseball and football. As a running back, he was good enough to win a scholarship to St. Francis University in nearby Loretto, Pennsylvania. But baseball was his first love. At age 19 in 1941, before graduating from high school, he turned pro. A scout for the Pittsburgh Pirates noticed Al while observing his play in the area's American Legion state tournaments. This was a blessing for Al as he had been working in the coal mines along with his father. Baseball would save him from the mines, although his father felt that he should stay.

Al was assigned to the Oil City Oilers, a Class D farm team of the Pirates. Although he was only 5'6" and 160 pounds he batted .334 with 7 homers and 58 RBIs. He had another good season the following year batting .348 hitting 7 home runs and knocking in 82 runs while making the league's all-star team.

Al served briefly in the Army during World War II. After his military stint he was promoted to Albany in the Class A Eastern League where he batted .329 and scored 130 runs. In 1947 Pittsburgh sent him to the Brooklyn Dodgers where he developed a friendship with Jackie Robinson. Al reminisced how Robinson would wait for the other players to finish showering before he would take his. One day he approached Robinson and said " Jackie, what are you waiting on? I'm not accepted any more than you are, but we're part of the team. Let's go." He also made sure that Robinson's locker was right next to his.

The Dodgers won the National League Pennant and faced the New York Yankees in the 1947 World Series. Al's role in the series would be the same as during season. He was a bit player who would pinch hit, run or come into the game in later innings for defensive purposes. The Yankees won the first two games of the series. The Dodgers came back beating the Yanks in games 3 & 4. The Yankees beat the Dodgers 2-1 in the 5th game.

Game Six drew a crowd of 74,065 — a World Series record at the time. The Dodgers led the Yankees 8-5 going into the bottom of the sixth inning when Gionfriddo was brought in to replace Eddie Miksis in left field. The Yanks first batter lined out. Then Snuffy Stirnweiss walked. Yogi Berra singled after Tommy Henrich fouled out.

The stage was now set for Joe DiMaggio. Two outs and two men on the base. Then Red Barber, calling the game on the Mutual radio network, set the scene for the moment that would last for the rest of Al Gionfriddo's life and beyond:

"Joe DiMaggio up, holding that club down at the end. Big fellow sets, Hatten pitches — a curveball, high outside for ball one. Sooo, the Dodgers are ahead, 8-5. And the crowd well knows that with one swing of his bat this fellow's capable of making it a brand-new game again. Outfield deep, around toward left, the infield over shifted. Here's the pitch, swung on — belted! It's a long one deep into left center — back goes Gionfriddo! Back- back-back-back-back-back...he makes a one-handed catch against the bullpen! Ohhh-hooo, Doctor!" The normally unflappable DiMaggio had already reached second base, and he kicked the dirt in anger.

Ironically that was the last Major League game that Gionfriddo would play. In 1948 the Dodgers sent him down to Montreal in the International League. He remained with Montreal for a few years then transferred to St. Paul for the 1951 and 52 seasons. He continued playing ball in the minor leagues finishing his career in 1956 with the Visalia Cubs in the Class C California League by hitting (.354-9-73) retiring at the age of 35. Gionfriddo played just 4 years in the Majors with a .266 batting average. His 12 year Minor League lifetime average was .311.

After his playing days ended, Al remained in California. Working numerous jobs to support his wife and children. He eventually becoming an insurance salesman and became involved in the restaurant business. He loved playing golf and when younger had a single digit handicap.

Six days after his 81st birthday, on March 14, 2003, Al was enjoying his favorite pastime — a round of golf when on the fifth green he was stricken by a fatal heart attack.

Former Dodgers manager Tom Lasorda, who had been Al's roommate in Montreal, commented, "He was an outstanding ballplayer and friend. He wore the Dodger uniform proudly, and we're losing a great Dodger."

Al Gionfriddo will always be associated with his "thrill of a lifetime" feat from October 1947. "I've signed thousands of that picture," Al remarked. "You think, 'Geez, how in the world do these people remember?' They were there when they were teen-agers, I guess, and they tell their sons, their grandkids. His wife said "He used to say, 'If all the people that said they were there that day actually were there, Yankee Stadium must have held a million."

Part Two

Italian Immigration Issues

How it used to be:
Early Italians Arrive at Ellis Island

Early Italian immigrants arrive at Ellis Island in 1905, nervously looking for their luggage. (Photo by Lewis W. Hine, Wikimedia.com, Google Art Project)

By Al Bruno
Artvoice
February 16, 2020

More than 12 million immigrants passed through Ellis Island between 1892 and 1954 – with a peak of 1,004,756 entering the United States in 1907 alone, and most were Italians. In fact, most Italian immigrants arriving at Ellis Island in 1907 were processed in a few hours.

"It varied from person to person, but for 80 percent, the process took a few hours, and then they were out and through," he says. "But it could also take a couple days, a couple weeks, a couple months or, in some rare cases, a couple of years," writes Vincent Cannato In American Passage: The History of Ellis Island.

"At the end of the day, less than 2 percent are rejected. The process was not really to keep lots of people out; the goal was really to sift out the wheat-from-the-chaff and sift out those who are 'undesirable.' Those who passed inspection were simply sent on their way with no official paperwork," writes Cannato.

"It's hard a thing to wrap your mind around because we live in such a bureaucratic world today."

In 1907, a passenger manifest document was created from the point of departure, which included each passenger's name. According Barry Moreno, historian and librarian at the Ellis Island Immigration Museum, the process went something like this:

"Before the ship was allowed to enter into New York Harbor, it had to stop at a quarantine checkpoint off the coast of Staten Island where doctors would look for dangerous, contagious diseases such as smallpox, yellow fever, plague, cholera and leprosy," writes Moreno in History.Com.

"First- and second-class passengers (billionaires, stage stars, merchants, businessmen and the like) were interviewed and allowed to disembark once the ship docked. In 1907, no passports or visas were needed to enter the United; no papers were required at all. This was a paperless period. All you had to do was verbally give information to the official when you boarded the ship in Europe and that information was the only information used when they arrived," further writes Moreno.

"The passengers were put aboard small steamboats and brought to Ellis Island. First up was a medical examination by military surgeons. The doctors had to know a few words of instruction in many languages, and only 10% were detained for further examinations or questioning," writes Moreno.

Those that were detained were fortunate to get the help from the Italian Welfare League, tracing back to its beginnings in the resettlement work of the American Red Cross's Italian Committee at the end of the First Word War. At the time, thousands of Italians had just returned to their American after having fought in the Italian Army during the war.

"By the late 1920's, a branch of the Italian Welfare League was opened on Ellis and held a unique position on the island – it had become the only aid society exclusively assisting Italians. At Ellis Island, the League helped Italians in trouble, particularly detained aliens and immigrants who were being held under warrant or deportation. America's immigration laws and policies were laden with bureaucratic red tape which led to thousands of people temporarily detained, or worse, being held for special inquiry investigations and hearings," writes Moreno in The Story of the Italian Welfare League.

"From the 1920's through the 1940's, the League also stretched out a helping hand to alien nationals who have lived in the United States for a while but had fallen on dark days and were not facing deportation for having violated one or more of the immigration laws," writes Moreno.

"Some were being expelled because they have been convicted of having committed a crime, some for having fallen into a life of pauperism and beggary, others for not having a valid Italian passport and having entered the United States illegally, and still others for having committed one of the crimes of moral turpitude, such as white slavery prostitution, or giving birth to illegitimate children. The League provided advice, winter coats, clean clothing, and sympathy," writes Moreno.

The Italian Welfare League permeated into the community through immigrants who had succeeded in making a successful transition into American life as advocates and translators for those Italian immigrants just arriving from Italy, a commendable model of Italians-helping-Italians; out of necessity, it worked, remarkably.

High school educated, first-generation, young Italian males with service and union jobs became a resource and advisor to Italian families: a cultural and collegial sharing, creating valuable and lasting relationships in the community. The post-World War II spirit to become helpful and honorable sons was embraced and adopted by progressive-minded, Italian families.

Likewise for example, first-generation, Italian sporting greats like Joe DiMaggio, Lawrence "Yogi" Berra, Rocky Marciano, and Vince Lombardi all refused to follow their fathers' footsteps into their respective trades. DiMaggio did not want to become a fisherman; Berra did not want to become a bricklayer; Marciano did not want to become a shoemaker; and Lombardi did not want to become a butcher and meat distributor.

Marciano's father, Peirino, would repeatedly urge his oldest son, Rocco, fueling him emotionally to do something "special" and ridding himself of oppressive factory work and imminent poverty.

What Marciano feared most was poverty for his parents, especially, and he felt, as the oldest and good son, compelled to lift his family out of poverty forever; he wanted to make his immigrant parents, Peirino and Pasqualina, proud most, family first: the most important Italian mantra.

In the 1940's and 1950's, Lombardi worked with his father, Enrico, in the butchering and meat distribution business in Brooklyn, NY. Enrico worked tirelessly and Vince followed, knowing full well that hauling around 200 lb. slabs-of-beef, in-and-out of walk-in coolers routinely, was not the kind of work he wanted to do for the rest of his life.

At first, these first-generation Italian greats obeyed and followed their fathers into the trades, working side-by-side with them and realizing this was not the end game and success they wanted for themselves and parents. Their fathers led the way with exemplary work habits, modeling vocational readiness and applications while striving for perfection; no shortcuts were allowed.

"You don't do things right once-in-a-while. You do them right all-the-time," Papa Ernie Lombardi would shout at a young, aspiring Vincent. This was a commonplace mantra articulated in most Italian households during that time.

Obediently, these Italian sons did those grueling jobs while their fathers imparted the intangible qualities that would eventually translate into their great athletic efforts on the playing fields and arena, as they would later fortunately experience in life: DiMaggio hated cleaning his father's fishing boat; Marciano hated the oppressive conditions of factory work; Berra did not want to work in a brick and cement yard; and Lombardi had a huge disdain for hauling around 200 lb. slabs of beef, but they accepted the grind and did the work, commendably.

"Italian sons were supposed to suffer shame and guilt for not following their father's ways," relevantly writes Andrew Rolle in his book, The Italian Americans: Troubled Roots. For Italian sons, following papa was often the only right thing to do, or they would face 'estrangement' from the family forever.

These first-generation Italian sons were very special in their efforts and determination, overcame the odds against them, and were encouraged to be trailblazers in competitive, physically-demanding sports like football, baseball, boxing, wrestling, and even weightlifting: They intuitively knew they possessed the physical skills for sports but lacked the academic abilities needed to go farther in the white-collar professions.

These Italian sons very much wanted to forge their own distinct identity, helping their families see, experience, and benefit from the "American dream." They succeeded in unimaginable ways for all to appreciate, emulate, and retell for years to come.

The Great Arrival and the Dawn of Italian America

Italian immigrants arrive in Boston Harbor in 1915, while an Italian boy in front joyfully salutes "La Bella America" (Courtesy of Boston Public Library).

By Tony Traficante,
Italian Sons and Daughters
of America (ISDA)

Poverty, natural disasters and war drove millions from Italy. The Great Arrival transformed the nation's cultural landscape and led to the creation of Italian America.

They scrimped and saved to buy a ticket to America and today they gathered in the village piazza about to leave everything familiar – family, friends, and loved ones. There was a group of families, single men, husbands, fathers, and sons. Amid weeping and hugs, promises were made to send money home, and return soon, or send for them. Many, however, would never return, and some would never see families or friends again.

But, in spite of the anguish of the departure, they were upbeat, hoping to find fortune and a better way of life.

The Italians were leaving out of necessity and desperation. Four million Italians, many from the "Mezzogiorno," the southern areas of Italy, immigrated to the United States between 1890 and 1920. The southern regions of Italy suffered more significant hardships than the north, where there were better advantages of industry, education, and quality of life.

Other factors contributed to the migration of the southern Italians, among them poverty, unemployment, a scarcity of farming land, high taxes, and natural disasters.

During years of disastrous volcanic eruptions at Mount Vesuvius and Mount Etna, surrounding towns sustained enormous casualties. A violent earthquake, in 1908, rocked the southern part of Italy, creating a tsunami with such crushing force it decimated more than 100,000 Italians, and laid bare vast areas of Messina and Reggio di Calabria.

The Italians traveled from small southern communities and hamlets, going by whatever means available – train, bus, horse and cart, and even via "l'asino." Arriving at a departure port, most likely Naples, the immigrants underwent humiliating fumigation of body, clothes, and goods, a document verification, and then a cursory medical exam.

This memorable image shows Italian immigrants in crowded and unsanitary conditions in the boat's steerage class during their treacherous voyage to America (Wikimedia.com, Google Art Project).

Herded aboard ships, they were directed to third class, crowded "steerage" compartments located at the very bottom of the boat. The steerage halls were lined with rows of metal bunks stacked two high. They were primitive, unsanitary, and claustrophobic. Privacy was non-existent, and amenities were basic.

Bedding consisted of straw mattresses covered with a piece of canvas sheeting. A life preserver was their pillow. They were given a lightweight blanket, and a set of metal eating utensils consisting of a form, spoon, and tin lunch pail.

Third class meals were meager and far from gourmet. There were no dining tables or chairs; the Italians made do by sitting on bunks, floors, or when permitted al fresco on deck. Traveling steerage class was a most unpleasant experience surrounded by unbearable conditions. There was sickness, cramped quarters, and putrid stench of vomit, urine, and whatever else, with little ventilation.

But, even among the discomfort and sickness, the resilient Italians made the best of the situation, finding time for enjoyment and a bit of diversion. On occasion, they celebrated a marriage or birth. Then, there was always someone with a concertina to complement the immigrants' songfest and dancing. The Italian women passed time crocheting, while playing a bit of "briscola, tre sette or morro."

The journey to America was a long and harsh one. After days at sea, most immigrants landed at the infamous Ellis Island. As they walked into the cavernous dark halls, fearful and anxious, they were greeted by immigration officials shouting orders. The Italians, not understanding what they were saying, complained, "che diavolo hanno detto."

Their long, long day was about to begin. The primary concern was getting through the medical inspections. Chalk marks on the clothes of an immigrant identified his or her medical condition: H for heart problems, E for eye problems, L for lameness, and so forth, U.S. laws also required an intelligence exam to identify "the idiots, imbeciles, morons, or other mentally deficient persons." Those with minor illnesses are held in quarantine for a day or two; others with severe medical conditions were put aside, and likely deported.

For the anguish of it all, Italians dubbed Ellis Island, "l'isola delle lagrime," – the island of tears.

Having made landfalls, those without sponsorship of family, or fiends faced new concerns, like finding a place to live and work. They had no choice but to engage the services of "padrone" for assistance. The padrones were usually former immigrants themselves and were trustworthy and helpful; others were there to take advantage of the immigrants.

The Italians tended to settle and live together, forming communities often called "Little Italy." They organized fraternal societies providing them benefits, stability, social interaction, and a basic indoctrination into the American way of life.

Many Italian immigrants decided to stay and sent for family members, as many went back to Italy. For those who remained, life ahead would be no easy road.

The Italian immigrants contributed much to the success of this great nation; their legacy is a proud and generous one. And, for the sake of our descendants, the story of our ancestors must be told and never forgotten.

The successes of our ancestors are important occurrences in American history; they are undeniably part of our inheritance.

Early Italian Immigrants Were Second-Class Citizens

Italian immigrant woman arrives at Ellis Island in 1905. (Photo by Lewis W. Hine, Wikimedia.com, Google Art Project).

By Al Bruno
La Gazzetta Italiana
March 2020

Editor's Note in Italian (italicized):
Quella degli italo americani e la storia di un lungo percorso segnato da una forma di pregiudizio etnico che ha avuto picchi drammatici e momenti di tregua. L'immigrazione verso gli Stati Uniti, iniziata alla fine degli anni '70 dell'800, fu soggetta a condizioni particolarmente dure e mortificanti. Nei Paesi in cui emigrarono, gli italiani furono spesso oggetto di razzismo, pregiudizi ed astio radicati e diffuse che hanno purtroppo accompagnato i nostri compatrioti quasi ovunque e in ogni periodo della nostra emigrazione, a cui si aggiunsero le misere condizioni di lavoro nei campi, nelle miniere o nei cantieri, che rasentano vere e proprie forme di sfruttamento. Nonostante queste discriminazioni e maltrattamenti, gli immigrati italiani sono riusciti a guadagnarsi una reputazione come grandi lavoratori, sono diventati politici, imprenditori e artigiani di altissimo calibro.

THE PERILOUS JOURNEY to America in the late 1800s and into the first three decades of the 20th century was extremely difficult for Italian immigrant families, worn out and exhausted, toting an old foot locker and a couple of bags.

What they possessed in their hearts and hoped for was a lifetime opportunity to come to America to economically improve their family situations. Most arrived in stages, following Papa, who usually ventured first across-the-Atlantic to establish citizenship, securing full-time, employment opportunities.

"When the Italians began arriving in New York City in large surroundings around 1880, they faced fierce competition from the Irish who resented their working for less money and longer hours. And although they shared the same Catholic faith, Italians were viewed as superstitious because of their devotion to saints, which was expressed in the staging of elaborate feasts," insightfully writes Haydee Camacho, in "Reflections of Irish and Italian Immigration, Animosity, and Eventual Understanding."

"Irish pastors tried to accommodate their growing Italian communities by offering these Italian immigrants services in the basement of their churches, but pride would not have it. The stalemate led to the building of churches to serve Italians and other new immigrant groups, not only in New York but other major cities in America's mid and northeastern, major cities," writes Camacho.

Between 1876 and 1930, immigrants from Southern Italy, such regions as Calabria, Campania, Abruzzi, Molise, and Sicily, most of the five million Italian immigrants came to the United States as farm laborers and unskilled workers, known as 'cantadini.'

For the newly-arrived, Italian immigrants were confused and lost in America, but they were assisted by other Italian immigrants here, who introduced them to the 'padrone.' "The 'padrone' was a boss and middleman between the immigrants and the American employers.

"The 'padrone' was an immigrant from Italy who had been living in America for a while. He was useful for immigrants because he provided lodging, handled savings, and found work for the immigrants (acting as a translator often times out of necessity). All in all, he helped American employers by organizing a supply of labor," accurately depicts Alexandra Molnar, in "From Europe to America: Immigration Through Family Ties."

Molnar points out that "prejudices were especially aimed at Southern Italians who became the scabs during strikes in construction, railroad, mining, long shoring, and industry. Often times these Southern Italian workers were called derogatory names such as 'guineas' or 'dagoes' and were the only workers to work alongside black people,"

"So our desperate great- and great-great grandparents came in droves from Italy, spurred by the Industrial barons in need of cheap labor who welcomed them with open arms to America. Often dangerous jobs no one else wanted awaited them. Some, like my relatives, came here illegally, under false names or as stowaways. On one ship alone, 200 stowaways were found," by Helene Stapinski, "When America Barred Italians."

Before a United States congressional commission, a politician from Calabria testified that emigration from the South had gone too far, adding that he was sorry Columbus had ever discovered America. In fact, the United States government used the published views of native Italian, Cesare Lombroso, a 19th-century Northern Italian doctor, to stop his starving Italian countrymen and women from immigrating to America.

"Lombroso, a traitor to his own Italian people, was convinced that there was such a thing as a 'natural born criminal.' He measured the heads and body parts of thousands of fellow Italians – particularly Southerners – and came with a description that matched the description of most of the immigrants coming over at the time: short, dark, hairy, big noses, and ears," writes Stapinski. "Lambroso branded the Southern Italians savages and rapists, blaming them for the crime that was on the rise in the United States."

The United States Immigration Commission concluded in the infamous Dillingham report this way: "Certain kinds of criminality are inherent in the Italian race. In the popular mind, crimes of personal violence, robbery, blackmail and extortion are peculiar to the people of Italy."

The Immigration Act of 1924 barred most Italians from coming into the country, causing immigration from Italy to fall 90 percent, even though the vast majority of those coming to America were good, honest-working people and not criminals.

There was also growing anti-immigration sentiment that posited the idea that Italians and eastern Europeans were morally unfit to be Americans. Of course, the same argument was made with the Irish. Eventually, this attitude would result in a 1924 federal immigration law that blocked Italians and southern and eastern Europeans from coming to America.

Italian immigrants were chasing after the "American dream" and the "gold in the streets" they had heard so much of and hoped for when they were growing up and working on the farmlands and vineyards in sunny Italy. Like other immigrant groups, they had sons who honorably served their country in WWII.

Hall of famers Rocky Marciano, Lawrence "Yogi" Berra and Joe DiMaggio, all first-generation Italian Americans, served in the war. As a young child, heavyweight champion Rocky Marciano feared poverty most for his parents, and he wasn't going to let it happen, vividly remembering his younger brother, Louis.

Marciano felt pressured to make something special of himself and rescue his family. As the oldest good son, Marciano felt compelled to honorably lift them from their family's impoverished and limited lifestyle in their modest section of an old and immigrant-filled city of Brockton, Massachusetts. He had a burning desire to succeed and make his Italian parents proud: family first, the most important Italian mantra, honorably accepted by the oldest, first generation son.

Marciano did so remarkably, achieving a 49-0 record with 43 knockouts, and retiring as the only undefeated, heavyweight boxing champion in history. He is remembered and honored for his class as an individual and being a winner in everybody's book and recognized as Brockton's, all time, favorite son. The son of an Italian shoemaker from Abruzzi, Italy achieved the unthinkable and experienced the American dream.

Early Italians and Irish Clash in New York

By Al Bruno
La Gazzetta Italiana
May 2020

Editor's Note in Italian (italicized):
Quest'articolo parla della difficoltà che avevano gli immigrati irlandesi quando vennero negli stati uniti dopo la fame del 1840. Gli irlandesi riscontrano discriminazione, mancanza di lavorare e di un tetto, e molto sfortuna. Quando arrivarono gli italiani, riscontrano le stesse degli irlandesi. I due gruppi di immigrati hanno dovuto cambiare i loro cognomi per nascondere la loro etnia. Purtroppo, gli irlandesi e gli italiani ebbero molta competizione per il lavoro, nelle chiese per la religione per il potere nelle comunità. Allora c'erano dei problemi fra questi due gruppi perché non riuscivano a lavorare insieme. Piano piano, accorgendosi di avere gli stessi problemi e di poter lavorare insieme per migliorare le loro vite, collaborano per avere una grande influenza nelle città e affermare il potere su diverse strade.

Mass immigration changed the face of America forever. The tidal wave of immigrants coming to America from Europe (1880-1910) transformed an English-dominated, American culture into a melting pot of refugees and renegades in search of new opportunities and a new way of life.

"When Irish, German, Italian and other European immigrants came to the United States during a wave of immigration at the turn of the 20th century, captivated by the promise that all immigrants can be transformed into Americans, a new alloy forged in the crucible of democracy, freedom, and civic responsibility," writes Gary Marx in Sixteen Trends: Their Profound Impact on Our Future.

For the immigrant Italians and Irish from Europe, the massive surge into America's port cities was far from a welcoming experience, many hungry and homeless, leaving thousands of the early Irish wondering and asking themselves: Is America really the land of opportunity?

The treatment of Irish immigrants was especially detestable. Irish immigrants fought back and were resilient despite the common culture's efforts in 19th century America to shun and discriminate against the early Irish Americans, calling them savages and drunkards and reducing them to social outcasts. Likewise, the treatment of Italian immigrants was just as disturbing, in many cases, as Italians shunned and discriminated against and were callously called 'dagoes,' 'wops,' and 'guineas.'

By necessity, Italian and Irish immigrants became fighters for opportunity and fighters against oppression. There were no other options for the Italians and Irish in early America.

In particular, the story of Irish immigrants was a treacherously enduring one that would eventually become a triumphant one, but not without remembering the pains from the past. The Irish were the very first big wave of immigrants coming to America, after the potato famine in Ireland in the 1840s.

"No Irish need apply, a famous folk song of the common school period, referred to rental and employment signs telling Irish Americans they were not welcomed as residents and workers," writes Joel Spring, accurately depicting the malicious treatment of Irish immigrants in the late 1800s in The American School: A Global Context from the Puritans to the Obama Era.

The "Help Wanted" sign reads: "No Irish Need Apply." This is a painful reminder of the blatant, employment discrimination that once existed toward Irish Americans (Photo in public domain, Irish Immigration Video by Aidan Patterson).

Those were desperate times, requiring desperate measures, and survival meant everything. In fact, to gain desirable employment in a union shop, for example, many Irish Americans renamed themselves to English-sounding names, often omitting the "O or Mc" at the beginning of their names and consequently hoping to mask their Irish origins.

Many immigrant Italians changed their names too to mask their Italian identity to gain union jobs and membership. In one instance, at a Niagara Falls factory in 1959, an applicant with the last name of Benevenuto changed his name to Benton to secure union employment. This was an example of one of many deceptive tactics used back then: a commonplace practice.

When the Italians began arriving in New York City in large numbers around 1880, they faced fierce competition from the Irish who resented their working for less money and longer hours. In those days, they fought over jobs or turf, and when they jockeyed for power in the church, in politics, in unions, and in civil service.

"They clashed in parishes, workplaces, neighborhoods, and politics. But over time, these same arenas came to unite them. The Italians had no choice but to deal with the Irish, who were their union leaders, foremen, schoolteachers, cops, and ward heelers…

"The Irish had to deal with the Italians if they were to raise the status of the Catholic faith in Protestant America," writes Paul Moses in The Love-Hate Story of New York's Irish and Italians. After decades of literally rumbling and constantly competing, Italians and Irish began working together cooperatively as partners in community projects.

Irish growing numbers or demographics, as a group, helped as the early Irish gained eventual success in the workplace, especially in the labor and trade union movement. Large Irish populations in big cities like Boston, Chicago, and New York paved-the-way for the election of Irish candidates to public offices, launching the genesis of Irish political organizations in municipalities. Italian city planners, engineers, builders, and tradesmen benefitted in the remaking of a new America.

"Yet, in the years after World War II, the church played a key role in bringing the Irish and Italians together, and to the altar

This advertisement in the Buffalo Courier in 1907 clearly discriminates against the hiring of Italian workers.

in marriage. This is the very American story of the Irish and Italians: when people from once-warring tribes mingle and get to know each other as equals, the social barriers fall away," writes Moses.

"Following World War II, Italians who married a non-Italian partner nearly always married someone of Irish ancestry. And the Italians who married Irish spouses generally went to Catholic schools and were regular churchgoers." What a cultural transformation occurred between the Irish and Italians after World War II: Maybe it was a miracle from above.

After World War II, the changing, cultural attitudes are depicted in the Oscar-nominated film, Brooklyn, when in character, Tony Fiorello, an Italian kid, brings Ellis Lacey, a young man of Irish ancestry, to his home for dinner: This is a magically-produced, love-hate story of New York's Irish and Italians.

"We don't like Irish people," blurts out his little brother, Frankie. Frankie then offers a decades-old explanation about the Irish guys in the neighborhood beating up the Italians while Irish cops looked the other way.

Observably, the Irish displayed incredible organization and systemic delineation of tasks cultivated great political successes. "The Irish did not simply take over the conventional apparatus of politics. They transformed American municipal politics. They changed the class consumption of municipal government, putting the reins of power in the hands of men who had risen from the working class," writes Thomas Sowell, in his 1981 book, Ethnic America.

As ethnic groups, Irish and Italian Americans once detested each other and remarkably changed all that for the good of America: They deserve tremendous credit and recognition for their spirit and determination to succeed in a hostile new world that they believed from the onset was going to be the land of opportunity.

They (the early Italians and Irish) survived, adapted, and succeeded, and today's America was and continues to be better for it. Early Irish and Italians found the Catholic faith and intermarriage as the best blessed bridges, the conduits, to accepting and understanding each other better, curing all social maladies and for all groups and peoples to emulate.

Italian Americans in U.S. Were Targeted During World War II

Italian Americans rejoice in "Little Italy" borough in New York City as Japan surrenders, ending World War II on August 15, 1944. (Photo: Library of Congress)

By Al Bruno
La Gazzetta Italiana,
November 2020

Editor's note in Italian *(Italicized):*
Questo articolo tratta degli immigrati italiani che furono discriminate durante la Seconda Guerra Mondiale. Giacche l'America fu in Guerra con l'Italia, furono tanti gli italiani presi di mira dagli americani. Fu per colpa della discriminazione ricevuta che gil italiani non potettero mantenere le loro proprieta e le terre di confine in quanto vennero consfiscate. Dopo un periodo difficile per gil immigrati italiani, il Presidente Franklin Delano Roosevelt dichiaro che gli italiani non eranto piu nemici della nazione e diventaraono cittadini accollti.

During World War II, the U.S. saw Italian-Americans as a threat to homeland security: The executive order (#9066) that forced Japanese-Americans from their homes also put immigrants from Italy under the watchful eye of the government, day-and-night, it was reported.

It was 1941 when news broke out that Japan had just bombed Pearl Harbor in Hawaii, bringing the U.S. into war with the Axis Powers of Japan, Germany, and Italy. Italian immigrants were scared, confused, and dreaded the thought of deportation.

For people like Frank DiCara, now 92 years of age, whose parents came from Sicily three decades before, the news was doubly horrifying. Along with the anger and amazement that America had been attacked came the unbelievable news that Italy – their homeland – was suddenly the enemy. Overnight, the land his parents remember fondly from their youth – and where they still had family – could not be talked about with risking treason.

Poignantly, Italian Americans were the largest group of immigrants entering the United States and who passed through Ellis Island for much of the late 19th and early 20th century; between the years 1880 and 1930, 5 million Italians moved to the U.S. and not without a backlash.

"We took a lot of slur from people back then. Italian Americans were called 'guineas,' 'dagoes,' and 'wops,'" vividly recalls DiCara.

In addition to forcibly evacuating 120,000 Americans of Japanese ancestry from their homes on the West Coast to barbed-wire, encircled camps, the executive order called for the compulsory relocation of 10,000 Italian Americans and restricted the movements of more than 600,000 Italian Americans nationwide. As a result, a curfew was placed on Italians from 8 pm to 6 am each evening.

"Right after the Pearl Harbor attack, rumors were abound that the U.S. government was going to pass a law taking away all the property of all Italians who did not have citizenship papers. Italians living near defense factories would be forced to move; Italian homes would be searched and cameras, shortwave radios, and guns would be confiscated," writes David A. Taylor, an author for Smithsonian History.com.

"Even Joe DiMaggio's parents in Sausalito, California (near San Francisco), weren't spared. Though their son, the Yankee slugger, was the toast of New York, General John DeWitt, a leading officer in the Western Defense Command, pressed to arrest Joe's father, Guiseppe, who had lived in the U.S. for almost 40 years but never applied for citizenship papers..."

Guiseppe DiMaggio was not the only Italian immigrant processed at the turn of the 20th century at Ellis Island. In fact, "It varied from person to person, but for 80 percent, the process took a few hours, and those who passed through were on their way with no official paperwork. At the end of the day, less than 2 percent are rejected," writes Vincent Cannato in American Passage: The History of Ellis Island.

"Though the FBI stopped short of arresting Guiseppe, he and his wife had to carry 'enemy alien' photo ID booklets at all times, and he needed a permit to travel more than five miles from home. Guiseppe was barred from the waterfront, Fisherman's Wharf, where he had worked for decades and had his boat seized by the government," writes Taylor. Guiseppe was not the only Italian immigrant that was harassed during this wartime hysteria, affecting the American social landscape.

In a memorable instance, Lucetta Berizzi, a first-generation Italian American, was questioned by FBI agents and unfairly suspected of treason:

"Why did (Lucetta) speak such good Italian? Had her father engaged in suspicious activities? Was she a traitor? She was released without being charged, but soon thereafter suffered the consequences of the anti-Italian sentiment that had spread like wildfire since the United States entered World War II. After being seen speaking Italian with a customer, she was fired from her job as a salesperson at Saks Fifth Avenue," writes Erin Blakemore for History.Com.

"Her father wasn't a traitor, either. His only crime was being born in Italy. During the early years of World War II, however, that was enough to classify him as an 'enemy alien' and to justify freezing his assets, interrogating his family, and interning him for months," explains Blakemore. This and thousands of other harassing incidents were routinely performed during the war, chasing down innocent Italian Americans and penalizing them for being of Italian ancestry.

To help reconcile the irreparable harm to Italian Americans in the U.S., President Franklin D. Roosevelt delivered a memorable radio address in which he recognized Italian Americans as full and patriotic citizens, lifting the 'enemy alien' stigma forever.

In fact, on October 12, 1942, Attorney General Francis Biddle officially declared that Italians were no longer enemies of the state: "You have met the test. Your loyalty to democracy has given you this chance, you have proved and proven well…We have trusted you, you must prove worthy of that trust, so that it may never be said hereafter that there are disloyal groups of Italians." However, the FBI and other federal agencies continued to violate their rights behind the scenes.

Today, the persecution and internment of Italian Americans is a relatively unknown episode in the history of World War II, in part because of the humiliation and silence of the Italian Americans forced to live it.

"What happened to the Italians was based on wartime hysteria," Joanne Chiedi, a former U.S. justice official and daughter of Italian immigrants who helped write the report, told the San Francisco Chronicle in 2001: "We are trying to educate people so it won't happen again. This story needs to be told."

Also in 2001, the US Attorney General reported to Congress on a review of the treatment by the Department of Justice of Italian Americans during World War II. In 2010, the California Legislature passed a resolution apologizing for the US mistreatment of Italian residents during World War II.

First Generation Italian Greats Refused to Follow Their Fathers' Footsteps

President Dwight D. Eisenhower meets with retired baseball great Joe DiMaggio and the current heavyweight boxing champion Rocky Marciano in 1953 at the White House. Rocky Marciano confidently brandishes his knock-out power in his right hand, as Joe DiMaggio looks on with approval. (Wikimedia.com, Google Art Project and permission from Rocky Marciano, Jr.).

By Al Bruno
La Gazzetta Italiana
May 2019

Editor's Note in Italian (italicized):
I primi anni del 1900 hanno visto l'America aprire le porte ad immigrati provenienti da molte parti dell'Europa e dell'Asia, che arrivano condividendo il sogno comune di un'opportunità per migliorare le impossibili condizioni di vita lasciatisi alle spalle. In cambio, i loro figli servirono onorevolmente la nuova patria durante la seconda guerra mondiale. Rocky Marciano, Vince Lombardi, Yogi Berra, e Joe DiMaggio, tutti italoamericani di prima generazione, inizialmente seguirono anche le impronte partner nella professione, per poi intraprendere una strada completamente diversa che li ha portati a l'agognato successo.

The early 1900s saw America open its doors to immigrants from all parts of Europe and Asia. These pioneering immigrants arrived at New York Harbor, undoubtedly worn out and exhausted, toting an old foot locker and a couple of bags.

What all these immigrants possessed in their hearts, they earnestly believed, was a lifetime opportunity here to economically improve their family situations. In fact, most arrived in stages, following Papa, who usually came first for most Italian immigrants, to establish citizenship and secure gainful employment.

These Italian immigrants were chasing after the "American dream" and "gold in the streets" they had heard so much of and hoped for when they were growing up and working on the farmlands and vineyards in sunny Italy. Like other immigrant groups, they had sons who honorably served their country in World War II.

Hall of famers Rocky Marciano, Lawrence "Yogi" Berra, and Joe DiMaggio, all first-generation, Italian-Americans, served in World War II. Vince Lombardi, the venerable hall of fame NFL coach and a first-generation son, received a waiver because he was married, had an infant son, and was a full-time student at Fordham University in NYC.

At first, these first generation greats obeyed and followed their Italian fathers into the trades, working side-by-side with them at first, realizing this was not the end game and success they wanted for themselves.

Marciano dropped out of high school in 10th grade and worked with his father, Pierino, at a shoe factory, and he drove a coal truck in Brocton, Massachusetts. Berra dropped out of school in the 8th grade to help support his family, working with his father, Lawrence, in a brick yard in St. Louis, Missouri.

DiMaggio worked with his father, Guiseppe, a successful fisherman for decades, in San Francisco. DiMaggio would do anything to get out of cleaning his father's boat: The smell nauseated him. Guiseppe called him "lazy" and "good for nothing." DiMaggio dropped out of high school and instead worked odd jobs, hawking newspapers and working at a warehouse.

Lombardi worked with his father, En-

Yogi Berra is pictured here in 1956 during the New York Yankee dynasty run. His remarkable life making his one of the all-time, Italian American greats in baseball. He earned a Purple Heart for courageous service in World War II. (Wikimedia.com, Google Art Project)

rico, in the butchering and meat distribution business in Brooklyn. Enrico worked tirelessly and Vince followed, knowing full well, that hauling 200 lb. sides-of-beef into walk-in coolers everyday was not the work he wanted to do for the rest of his life. Of these four great Italian sons, Lombardi was the only one to graduate from high school and college.

Marciano, Berra, DiMaggio, and Lombardi worked those grueling, physical jobs with their fathers, appreciating them simultaneously as the fathers appropriately imparted and displayed those intangible qualities that would eventually translate into their great efforts on the playing fields.

The Italian fathers led the way with exemplary work habits, modeling vocational readiness and applications, while always striving for perfection; no shortcuts were ever allowed, and they were reminded with a warning: "You don't do things right once in a while. You do them right all the time," Papa Ernie Lombardi would shout at a young, aspiring Vincent. This was a commonplace mantra articulated in most Italian households during that time.

Coach Vince Lombardi is pictured in this portrait in the late 1960s. He very much wanted to be a head football coach, not a butcher or meat distributor like his father. (Permission from Vince Lombardi, Jr).

Outwardly, these fathers were culturally prideful and absolutely detested those accepting handouts, food, and generosity from government agencies.

As a positive result, the sons learned all about hard work, toughness, commitment, and perseverance from their fathers.

These first-generation sons were very special and they were encouraged to be trailblazers because they believed they could achieve much more as a prize athlete in competitive, physically-demanding sports like football, baseball, boxing, wrestling, and even weightlifting: They intuitively knew they possessed the physical skills for sports but lacked the academic abilities to go farther in life in the white-collar professions.

The Italian mothers had a special place in their hearts for their ambitious sons, and their motherly care and concern would not go unattended: They would always find a quiet moment alone with their sons, usually in the kitchen, while stirring the tomato sauce for Sunday's dinner.

Reminding them about the importance of focus and achievement, the Italian mothers would privately and emphatically affirm this Italian mantra: "Poche parole e fai i fatti, figlio mio." Literally translated, it meant: 'use few words and make it happen, my son.' Culturally, native Italians frowned on bragging and showboating; therefore, demonstrating humility meant quiet respect for achievement and class as an individual.

Socially and for future achievements, Italian mothers would remind them of this Italian mantra: "Vai con chi meglio di tu e fai i spessi," which meant 'befriend those that are better and more accomplished than you and even pay their expenses' to ensure your future successes.

Italian cultural, vocational, and religious traditions guided their sons' ambitious footsteps into a hopeful future, and they wanted to make their families feel the proudness of being an accomplished, Italian son: What they were given and prepared with by their Italian parents, using their best of old-country values to interpret, teach, and arm them for success in a progressive and future America.

The Italian sons very much wanted to forge their own distinct identity, helping their families see, experience, and benefit from the "American dream." And they succeeded in unimaginable ways for all to appreciate.

First-Generation Italian Americans Trailblaze Paths and Opportunities for the Professions

Joe DiMaggio, honorably remembered as the Yankee Clipper and Joltin' Joe, fulfilled a lifelong dream to become the symbol of American baseball, (The Official Site of Joe DiMaggio, joedimaggio.com).

By Al Bruno

After World War II, the confidence of Americans grew incredibly as young people of all cultures entered the job forces and looked for opportunities to succeed. For the early Italians entering New York Harbor via Ellis Island, the pressure fiercely mounted on their children: Those first generation Italian Americans eagerly and opportunistically yearned to make their mark and enter the professions.

Hall of Famers Joe DiMaggio, Yogi Berra, Rocky Marciano, all first-generation Italian Americans honorably served in World War II. Yogi Berra, most notably, courageously participated as a Navy gunner at the D-Day conflict in Europe, earning him the distinguished, Purple Heart. Vince Lombardi, the venerable NFL hall of fame coach and a first generation Italian son, received a waiver because he was married, had an infant son, and was a full-time student at Fordham University in New York City.

At first, these unknown and eventual, first generation Italian greats in sports, obeyed and followed their fathers into the trades, working side-by-side with them realizing this was not the end game they nervously wanted for themselves and their parents. Their fathers led the way with exemplary work habits, modeling vocational readiness and applications while striving for perfection; no shortcuts were allowed by their Italian fathers, working 15 to 16 hours a day, paving the way for their children's futures.

Obediently, these Italian sons did those grueling jobs while their fathers imparted the intangible qualities that would eventually translate into their great athletic efforts on the playing fields and arenas, as they would later fortunately experience in life: DiMaggio hated cleaning his father's boat, saying it nauseated him; Marciano hated the oppressive conditions of factory work; Berra did not want to work in a brick-and-cement yard; and Lombardi had a huge disdain for hauling around 200 lb. slabs in and out of walk-in freezers. They accepted the grind and did the work, commendably, like first generation Italian sons were supposed to do, tough and enduring, like their papas.

Fortunately for those first generation Italian sons, they made it big and gained enduring notoriety, and they were the first great pioneers and trailblazers: They were special, incredibly hard-working, and talented in competitive, physically-demanding sports like football, baseball, boxing, wrestling, and even weightlifting. They intuitively knew they possessed the physical skills but

Rocky Marciano is pictured here in his heyday with his championship belt, retiring as the only undefeated heavyweight champion in boxing history with a perfect record of 49 and 0. (Wikimedia.com, Google Art Project and permission from Rocky Marciano, Jr.).

lacked the academic abilities to go farther in music and the arts and the white-collar professions.

Their lack of formal education-and-training was a culturally-damning perception that weighed down their progress for decades, and this would all miraculously change for first generation Italian Americans in the 1960s, 70s, and 80s in music, acting and the arts, law, public service, and in professional coaching.

A storied legacy of Italian resilience would ensue, and the new boundless opportunities would become realities that were closed off to their fathers and uncles in the 1920s, 30s, and 40s, remembering their pitfalls and despair. Fortunately, they somehow perseveringly overcame the obstacles, fiercely competed, won championships, and garnered deserving awards in the performing arts, experiencing unimaginable success and achieving the American Dream: an invigorating saga of Italian American contributions in courage and determination.

First generation Italian American Frank Sinatra enjoyed great success as one of the most popular musical artists of the 20th century.

Yogi Berra was the best "bad-ball" hitter of all-time for the New York Yankees. Berra and the Yankees won 10 World Series championships together, and he was named American League MVP three times in a memorable baseball career. (Wikimedia.com, Google Art Project and the Yogi Berra Museum and Learning Center in Little Falls, NJ).

Sinatra was born in 1915 in Hoboken, New Jersey, to Italian immigrants Natalina "Dolly" Garaventa and Antonio Martino "Marty" Sinatra, and he passed away in 1998. His great musical career began in the swing era with bandleaders Harry James and Tommy Dorsey.

Some of Sinatra's greatest and most memorable hits include "New York, New York"

(1977), "My Way" (1969), "Strangers in the Night" (1966), Luck Be a Lady" (1966), and "My Kind of Town (Chicago is)" (1964). Sinatra's musical success in the 1960s, 70s, 80s, and beyond ranks him as one of the best music and arts talents of all time, amazingly spanning the second half of the 20th century.

Young and thriving Frank Sinatra is pictured in his early years. Sinatra opened music and acting, career opportunities for all Italian Americans in the 1960s, 70s, and 80s, like no other pioneer and trailblazer. (Wikimedia.com, Google Art Project)

He has sold more than 150 million records worldwide, and his earnings are in the mega millions and Sinatra's artistry and his span of influence continue to be an immeasurable contribution on American society. In addition to his incredible earnings in singing, Sinatra had great success as an actor and producer, appearing in "Guys and Dolls" (1955), "High Society" (1956), and Tony Rome (1967).

Sinatra was politically active and campaigned for future Presidents John F. Kennedy and Ronald Reagan. "Old Blue Eyes," he was soon called, and he was respectfully revered as the "Chairman of the Board." Because of his public association with Italian celebrities and businessmen, he was targeted and investigated several times for his alleged ties to the Mafia; he was never convicted of any criminal wrongdoing.

Sinatra was a musical perfectionist and insisted on recording live with his band because of his impeccable attire, tailored suits, and a commanding persona and presence, delighting audiences everywhere, a musical "virtuoso" in every sense. He was honored at the Kennedy Center Honors and the Presidential Medal of Honor, both in 1983, the Presidential Medal of Freedom by President Ronald Reagan in 1985, and the Congressional Gold Medal in 1997. Time magazine named him as one the 20th century's 100 most influential people.

A young Sophia Loren is pictured here at age 21 in 1955 and on her way to international stardom in theater. (Wikimedia.com, Google Art Project).

The 1950s and 1950s saw the sudden emergence of the beautiful actress Sophia Loren from Italy, an international movie star. Sophia Loren was born as Sofia Scicolone at the Clinica Regina Margherita in Rome on September 20, 1934. Growing up in the slums of Pozzuoli during the second World War without any support from her father, she experienced great sadness in her childhood. Her life took an unexpected turn for the best when, at age 14, she entered into a beauty contest and placed as one of the finalists. It was there that Sophia caught the attention of film producer Carlo Ponti, some 22 years her senior, who later married, spurring a great international career as a movie star in Italy and America.

By her late teens, Sophia was playing lead roles in many Italian features such as La Favorita (1952) and Aida (1953). In 1957, she embarked on a successful acting career in the United States, starring in Boy on a Dolphin (1957), Legend of the Last (1957), and The Pride and the Passion (1957): a phenomenal year for Sophia.

While under contract to Paramount, Sophia starred in Desire Under the Elms (1958), The Key (1958), The Black Orchid (1958), It Started in Naples (1960), Heller in Pink Tights (1960), A Breadth of Scandal (1960), and The Millionaires (1960) before returning to Italy to star in Two Women (1960). This performance received International acclaim and was honored with an Academy Award for Best Actress.

Sophia remained a bona fide international movie star throughout the sixties and seventies, making films on both sides of the Atlantic, and starring opposite such leading stars as Paul Neuman, Marlon Brando, Gegory Peck and Charlton Heston. Sophia's English-language films included El Cid (1961), The Fall of the Roman Empire (1964), Arabesque (1966), Man of La Mancha (1972), and The Cassandra Crossing (1976). She gained wide respect with Italian films, Marriage Italian Style (1964) and a Special Day (1977), both of which co-starred Marcelo Mastroianni. During these years, Sophia received a second Oscar nomination and won five Golden Globe Awards.

From the eighties onward, Sophia's appearance on the big screen came few and far between. She preferred to spend the majority of her time raising sons Carlo Ponti, Jr. and Edoardo Ponti.

A young Al Pacino is pictured in the play, The Basic Training of Paulo Hummel in 1971. (Wikimedia.com, Google Art Project).

First generation Italian American icon and movie great, Al Pacino, had an enormous widespread effect and paved acting opportunities for all Italian Americans in the early 1970s with the memorable roles in blockbuster movies like "The Godfather and Godfather II" (1972 and 1974), "Serpico" (1973), and "Dog Day Afternoon" (1975). He went on to flourish in greatness as well in "Scarface" (1983), "Heat" (1995), "Godfather III" (1990), Donnie Brasco" (1997), and "Any Given Sunday" (1999), just to name several more of the exhausting list of award-winning, dramatic performances in his hall of fame, acting career.

In retrospect as a youngster, Pacino was bored with living out his life in regular high school, dropping out as a teenager and determined to make acting his lifetime career. He then auditioned and was admitted to the prestigious, High School of the Performing Arts in New York City, then opting to study theater at the Herbert Berghof Studio in New York City. His acting talents were discovered, and phenomenal success ensued for this first generation Italian American, born in 1940 in East Harlem, in New York City. He is the son of Rose and Salvatore Pacino, both Italian immigrants from San Fratello, Sicily.

Shifting to New York City (NYC) and national politics, no first-generation, Italian-Jewish American has shaped the lives of Italian immigrants (and all immigrants, in effect) and their first-generation children like Fiorello Enrico La Guardia, widely considered one of the greatest NYC mayors.

Fiorello La Guardia is heralded as one of the greatest NYC mayors and a champion and ambassador for all immigrants. (Wikimedia.com, Google Art Project).

Born of mixed Catholic and Jewish parentage, La Guardia has been called "the most remarkable hybrid in the history of New York City." Early in his life in 1900 to his credit, at age 18, La Guardia began working for the American Consulate in Hungary where he remarkably learned six languages (English, Italian, Yiddish, German, Croatian, and Hungarian), improving the medical inspection system for immigrants.

In 1906, La Guardia left for NYC and was appointed as an interpreter and in night court at Ellis Island, specializing on the rights of Italian and Jewish immigrants employed in the garment industry. Painfully, he recalled: "I never managed to become callous to the mental anguish, the disappointment, and the despair I witnessed daily." These experiences confirmed his compassion for the powerless and oppressed, motivating him to obtain a law degree from New York University at night, while working during the day.

Mayor La Guardia's leadership style was hands-on and personal, temperamental, and even abrasive. Yet his dramatic style reflected a desire to inspire public interest in and win support for his fight against crime, corruption, and the callous disregard for human suffering.

"La Guardia supervised everybody and cared about everybody, perhaps to a fault. When he wasn't rushing to fires, conducting orchestras, giving advice over the radio, he was berating his commissioners, firing incompetent city workers, taking over court cases, smashing slot machines, and chastising reporters," (excerpted from La Guardia's archives at lagcc.cuny.edu).

Escalating racial riots in Harlem in 1943 were horrific for NYC residents, making news headlines nationally; six died with another 185 wounded and millions of dollars in property damages were incurred as a result.

La Guardia promised to meet Harlem's immediate needs and quell the uprisings, exuding an uncommon understanding and sensitivity of the real causes.

"La Guardia gave radio addresses to reduce racial tension and recommended that schools use racially-progressive curriculum materials. He official opposed discriminatory rental polices like those used at Stuyvesant Town and, the City Council adopted the nation's first anti-discriminatory housing policy in 1944. La Guardia not only attend an Interracial Unity Conference at Hunter College, but also reopened the Savoy Ballroom. Addressing slum conditions, La Guardia planned several new public housing projects while moving to control rents and food prices. He established a biracial committee on race relations," (excerpted from La Guardia's archives at lagcc.cuny.edu).

Instinctively, he was highly-effective in positioning NYC as a model city during the Great Depression, thereby creating a laboratory for national reform and configuring an incubator of modern political liberalism: La Guardia fostered a close relationship with President Franklin Delano Roosevelt and Secretary of the Interior Harold Ickes, who ran the New Deal programs.

As a positive political result, NYC received a huge infusion of money for capital improvements that provided desperately-needed jobs: new sewage treatment plants, an extended subway, enclosed retail markets, docks, bridges, parks, playgrounds, parkways, public housing, schools, swimming pools, hospitals, and health stations.

Deservingly, La Guardia is remembered for his game-changing leadership, and most earnestly, for dedicating himself to champion the rights of all immigrants arriving at Ellis Island.

First generation Italian American Rudolf "Rudy" Giuliani was a trailblazer for all Italians in the 1980s and 1990s because of his commendable work as a proven prosecutor of all criminals and Italian, organized-crime machine in New York, in particular.

In the Mafia Commission Trial in 1985 and 1986, Giuliani's pressing prosecutorial stance rose immeasurably when he indicted 11 organized crime figures, including the heads of New York City's "Five Families," under the RICO Act on charges of extortion, labor racketeering, and murder for hire.

Time magazine called this the "Case of Cases," and possibly, "The most significant assault on the infrastructure of organized crime since the high command of the Chicago Mafia was swept away in 1943," and quoted Giuliani's motivation: "Our approach is to wipe out the five families."

His life was threatened by mobsters several times, and his courage was admirable, influencing, and revered as a tough-yet-fair champion for justice. Giuliani's, "get-tough" reputation and resolve, aggressively targeting virulent crime, would help ascend him to becoming the heralded, NYC Mayor.

Elected NYS Mayor in 1993, Giuliani is credited for reducing the crime rate in the city. Giuliani advocated the privatization of the city's public schools and initiated the reduction of state funding for them. He proposed a voucher system to promote private schooling. Giuliani continued to support protection for illegal immigrants such as sending their children to school or reporting crimes to the police without fear of deportation.

Importantly, Giuliani is credited for his outstanding governing principles and practices in quelling and remarkably stabilizing the New York City community which fell into complete disarray, after an unforeseen, historical attack and destruction of the World Trade Center Twin Towers in the September 11, 2001 atrocity, devastating Manhattan and killing 2,977 New Yorkers that most dreadful day in recent American history.

His hard-working, Italian immigrant parents were from Montecatini Terme in Tuscany, Italy. Giuliani was born in 1944 and grew up in Brooklyn, and he graduated from Manhattan College and later the New York University School of Law; he is currently an advisor and personal attorney for President Donald Trump.

Rudy Giuliani is a New York legacy in government as NYC mayor and federal prosecutor. (Wikimedia.com, Google Art Project).

First generation Italian American Mario Cuomo virtually rewrote modern-day gubernatorial leadership and achievement in New York. Cuomo was a three-term governor and pioneer for all Italian Americans in public service and statecraft.

He was the son of Italian immigrants, Andrea and Immaculata Cuomo, both from the Campania region of Italy. The Cuomo family ran Kessler's Grocery in South Jamaica, Queens, New York; he graduated from St. John's University, earning a bachelor's degree and then from the St. John's University School of Law with co-valedictorian honors in 1956. Cuomo is honorably remembered, especially in New York and New Jersey, his home base.

Many historians point to his memorable speech in 1984 at the Democratic National Convention in San Francisco, addressing the nation and declaring the inequities and the fallacy of "the shining city on a hill," as portrayed by then President Ronald Reagan.

For posterity, Cuomo eloquently stated: "There are ghettos where thousands of young people, without a job or an education, give their lives away to drug dealers every day. There is despair Mr. President, in the faces that you don't see, in the places you don't visit in your shining city."

Cuomo brought the convention to its feet in resounding applause in his concluding remarks about his own life and what he saw and lived by each day, the son of Italian immigrants, working in Queens as a grocer; he stated with fervor:

"I watched a small man with thick calluses on both his hands work 15 and 16 hour days. I saw him literally bleed from the bottoms of his feet, a man who came here uneducated, alone, unable to speak the language, who taught me all I needed to know about faith and hard work by the simple eloquence of his example. They asked only for a chance to work and to make the lives of their children. This nation and this nation's government did that for them…"

Cuomo concluded resoundingly and proudly, stating: "They were able to build a family and live in dignity in South Jamaica on the other side of the tracks where he (Mario Cuomo) was born to occupy the

NYS Governor Mario Cuomo is pictured here in 1987 at a rally. He lived the humble life of a grocer, rising up to become an Italian-American legacy in public service. (Wikimedia.com, Google Art Project).

highest seat, in the greatest state, in the greatest nation, in the only world we would know. This is an ineffably beautiful tribute to the democratic process." A standing ovation enthusiastically ensued for the proud Mario Cuomo, New York's standing governor and a first generation Italian American who beat the steep odds against him and did the unimaginable, capturing the hearts and affections of New Yorkers for the ages.

First generation Italian American Geraldine Ferraro was a pioneer and advocate for Italian Americans and women's rights, serving as a public attorney and member of the U.S. House of Representatives, and the first woman to be chosen to run as the 1984 Democratic Vice-Presidential nominee, accompanying Presidential nominee Walter Mondale.

A licensed teacher and then attorney, Ferraro worked in the Queens New York District Attorney's office, where she started the Special Victims Bureau.

As part of the District Attorney's office, Ferraro worked long hours and gained a reputation for being a tough prosecutor but fair in plea negotiations. To her credit, Ferraro's proactive approach allowed her to try cases that were destined to other divisions for prosecution; juries were impressively persuaded by Ferraro's summations, gaining public recognition in NYC.

Ferraro ran successfully for Congress from New York City's 9th District in Queens in 1978. Her main focuses were law and order, support for the elderly and neighborhood preservation. Ferraro's Italian heritage strongly appealed to ethnic residents of the Queens district. In 1983, Ferraro was named to the powerful, House Budget Committee. She also served on the Public Works and Transportation Committee, both of whom allowed Ferraro to push projects to benefit her district.

In 1984, Ferraro was picked to run as the Vice President of the United States on the Democratic Party ticket with former Vice President Walter Mondale. In her acceptance speech, memorably Ferraro spoke from her heart about realizing the American Dream:

"Tonight, the daughter of an immigrant from Italy, has been chosen to run for vice president in the new land my father came to love…" Unfortunately, the ticket lost, but Ferraro's candidacy forever shaped the American political and social landscape and its place in great American lore.

Ferraro's mother, Antonetta, was a first generation Italian American, and her father, Dominic, was a restaurateur and an Italian immigrant from Marcianise, Campania, Italy. Ferraro graduated from Iona College and later Fordham University Law School with honors.

In 1973, few in college basketball knew of Coach Dick Vitale outside of those residing in the tri-state region; he is a first generation Italian American, who was born in Passaic, New Jersey, to John and Mae Vitale, Italian immigrants, both working tirelessly in the clothing industry to give him a better life in America, indeed.

"I am living the American dream," Vitale passionately emphasizes. "I watched as my

Geraldine Ferraro actively campaigns in 1984 as the Democratic Vice Presidential nominee. (Wikimedia.com, Google Art Project)

dad pressed coats in a factory. He told me that I needed an education so that I could do other things in life."

Now in 2022, Vitale is known almost everywhere in "Sports America" where he enjoys his legendary status as a hall of fame basketball coach and active ESPN broadcaster: all in one, storied, ambitious lifetime.

Vitale's roots are in teaching the game he has loved since childhood: basketball. Following graduation from college, he got a job teaching at Mark Twain Elementary School (Garfield, NJ) and coaching junior high football and basketball. He began coaching at the high school level at Garfield High School, where he coached for one season (1963-64).

Vitale then earned four state sectional championships, two consecutive state championships, and 35 consecutive victories during his seven years at his alma mater, East Rutherford NJ High School; he joined Rutgers University for two years (1970-72) as an assistant coach, helping Phil Settlers and Mike Dabney, two cornerstones on an eventual NCAA Final Four Team in 1976.

Young Vitale got his break in 1973 and was named the head basketball coach of the University of Detroit, compiling a winning percentage of .722 (78-30), which included a 21-game winning streak during the 1976-77 season when the team participated in the NCAA Tournament. As a positive result, Vitale gained basketball coaching notoriety and became celebrated nationally.

In April 1977, Vitale was named Athletic Director at the University of Detroit and later that year was named the United Fund's Detroit Man of the Year. The next year in May 1978, he was named head coach of the NBA's Detroit Pistons, which he coached during the 1978-79 season prior to joining the ESPN broadcast team.

In 1979, Vitale began working with ESPN as a college basketball broadcaster and has been contributing as an analyst ever since. His thorough knowledge of the game is presented in an enthusiastic, passionate, sometimes controversial, but never boring style. Vitale has distinguished himself with ESPN by spontaneously spewing his riveting and conjured, basketball insights and memorable quips. Vitale makes an indelible impression on audiences. He is that vivacious personality that there is no substitute for.

Coach Dick Vitale is pictured here at a press conference. (Wikimedia.com, Google Art Project).

Deservingly, Vitale has been selected to nine sports halls of fame, including the National Italian Sports Hall of Fame.

First generation Italian American Jimmy Valvano followed up on the Italian pioneering that Dick Vitale did in the 1970s for men's college basketball.

Valvano is remembered most, competitively, for coaching the North Carolina State University's Wolfpack to the unlikely and miraculous garnering of the NCAA Division 1 Men's Basketball Championship from the highly-favored University of Houston Cougars, dramatically beating Houston at the buzzer with a dunk by Lorenzo Charles, 54 to 52, and ecstatically running around the center of the basketball court, looking for someone to hug and celebrate with. This was a candid and spontaneous moment of total human elation in climbing the mountain of success and finally reaching the pinnacle of college basketball in D-1 championship competition.

Valvano demonstrated his remarkable winning ways as head coach of NC State from 1980 to 1990. He led the Wolfpack in one of the greatest Cinderella stories in college basketball history, culminating as winners of the 1983 NCAA championship. During his 10 seasons at NC State, Valvano's teams were the ACC's tournament champions in 1983 and 1987, and they were regular season champions in 1985 and 1989. In addition to gloriously winning the 1983 NCAA championship, the Wolfpack then advanced to the NCAA Elite 8 in 1985 and 1986.

Coach Jim Valvano became the symbol of a "Never Quit" American legacy in sports. (Wikimedia.com, Google Art Project)

Valvano is remembered, too, for his sustained and courageous fight against cancer and his memorable address to the nation at the 1993 ESPY Awards. Remarkably and from the heart, Valvano told the viewing audience for posterity: "Keep your dreams alive in spite of problems, whatever you have. Work hard for your dreams to come true…"

And then again, spontaneously and passionately, he declared: "Don't ever give up. That's what I am going to do with every minute left. I will thank God for the day and moment I have." Great applause ensued, and the tears flowed from the faces of those sports celebrities and media personnel in attendance, demonstrating an outpouring of love and appreciation for Jimmy Valvano's courage and his passion for coaching.

Less than two months after that most memorable at the ESPY awards, Valvano died at age 47. Coach Mike Krzyewski, the legendary head coach of Duke University's Men Basketball, reflected in a deep heartfelt commentary on Coach Valvano: "Jimmy formed the V Foundation during the last couple of months of his life. We would joke, and cry at the hospital together. One night he said. 'I want you to try to fund researchers to attack cancer. I want you to be on my team. He recruited me during that time. His wisdom and his ability to think beyond his life was incredible."

He is a first generation Italian American and the son of Rocco and Angelina Valvano, both Italian immigrants; Valvano's father, Rocco, was born and raised in Guardio Lombardi, Avellini, Campania, Italy.

Valvano was born and grew up in Queens, New York, in 1946. He excelled in basketball, playing and studying at Rutgers University; he was named player of the year as a senior, graduating with a bachelor's degree in English in 1967. In his honor after his early and tragic passing in 1993, the V Foundation was established and flourished with millions of dollars raised in charitable donations as a cancer research center, assisting cancer patients nationwide, in his name and creating a long-lasting legacy in American sports.

This Italian immigrant kid, Geno Auriemma, arrived in Norristown, Pennsylvania, at age seven in 1961 from Montella, Italy, and he was unable to speak English, not knowing how to dress right, feeling out of place, and constantly feeling unsure of himself.

From birth on, Geno Auriemma assumed the role of natural leader out of necessity for his family, in pursuit of perfection, and this mantra was firmly ingrained in his physical being and in his DNA. When his family immigrated to the United States in 1961, it was not uncommon for this seven-year-old, Geno, to help his parents, Donato and Marcella, interpret, negotiate, and often remedy English language issues.

Coach Geno Auriemma is pictured here speaking at the Pentagon in 2014. (Wikimedia.com, Google Art Project).

Auriemma was the oldest son and much was expected; he instinctively guided and taught his younger brother, Ferrucci, and young sister, Anna, the English language and the American ways. This was an incredible display of leadership and initiative for this treasured gem, the oldest son of the Auriemma family, placing the family's needs first: the most important Italian mantra instilled in Geno by his parents. God blessed Geno and his family, and phenomenal, record-breaking success ensued in women's college basketball and American sports lore for the ages.

Auriemma continues to contribute and transform women's college basketball into what it is today as the nation's, most winningest and most celebrated women's coach in history, building a losing University of Connecticut women's college basketball team that he inherited in 1985 into perennial winners, a model of excellence, emulated by women's coaches in the United States and around the world. That is truly earned respect and an enduring legacy.

Since Auriemma's arrival to the University of Connecticut (UConn) Huskies in 1985, the UConn women basketball team achieved 43 regular season tournament titles, advanced to 17 Final Fours, posted an astounding, six perfect seasons - perfection, the ideal, and won 11 national, D-1 championships. He is an eight-time, AP College Basketball Coach of the Year and a three-time, American Athletic Coach of the Year.

Auriemma was the head coach of the United States women's national basketball teams from 2009 through 2016, during which time his team won the 2010 and 2014 World Championships; he garnered gold medals at the 2012 and 2016 Summer Olympics, going undefeated in all four tournaments.

"We have won 11 national championships, and we've never taken any of them for granted. Every one of those championships is special," emphasizes Auriemma. Coach Auriemma's incredible coaching achievements have built bridges of success and opportunity for Italian Americans and all who venture to coach women's college basketball.

And in Buffalo, New York, most recently and sadly, beloved Buffalonian Joey Giambra succumbed to Covid-19. He was hospitalized at the Buffalo General Medical Center since April 25, and he passed on May 14, 2020; he was 86 years young, creatively sharp, congenially engaging, and will be sorely missed by the Buffalo community and beyond.

Buffalo's Joey Giambra is one of the city's favorite sons and a first generation Italian American, connecting the past from the Lower West Side into our present and future living contexts through his music, drama, poetry, and writing. Giambra was an Italian icon, an ambassador of understanding, and his flourishing artistry had no end to his talents and so did his affection for all peoples, a caring people person: a rare, spiritual quality that few possess.

Buffalo's Joey Giambra is an Italian icon in Buffalo, contributing as musician, playwright, author, and poet in his remarkable life. (Permission from Joey Giambra family).

Giambra had an inviting and contagious smile, and he somehow magically wove it into an incredible sensitivity and a literary love for culture and the goodness in people.

To his greatness, Giambra envisioned and ambitiously lived out five careers in one remarkable lifetime, as the chronicles affirm, in addition to the important roles of dedicated father and husband which he did, expertly, as everything else he endeavored.

In 1963, he joined the Buffalo Police Department and served for 20 years as a police officer and sergeant before retiring as a detective. At 44, Giambra would earn a bachelor's degree in criminal justice from SUNY Buffalo State. He was a self-taught trumpeter, a pianist, an actor, a singer and songwriter, a former restaurant owner, a filmmaker, a poet, an Italian chef, the author of four books, a historian, and a one-time candidate for mayor of Buffalo; he spoke fluent Sicilian, and he possessed endless bundles of creative energy to expend.

His recorded and published works, his beautiful words, provide cultural clarity and a bridge to understanding the Lower West Side the way Giambra vividly and eloquently describes it: His great literary works are part of the city's annals and libraries for appreciation now and for posterity.

"I am saddened to hear of Joey Giambra's passing. His contributions to Buffalo's music and theater will be felt for years to come," announced Buffalo Mayor Byron Brown.

"We, the many, many people he loved and touched, are left with a big hole in our lives. For me, there will always be something missing," painfully writes Tom Naples, his old friend, a guitarist who often worked with Giambra.

Joey Giambra was and will always be a good friend and a cultural inspiration to me personally, mentoring and encouraging: "Keep writing insightfully about what you experienced firsthand on the Lower West Side, Al, as a first generation Italian American." His inspiring words were instructive and a heart-felt plea, awakening one's spirit and drive to achieve new heights.

Joey Giambra magically touched and moved everyone in a special way: What a boundless gift he possessed and passionately shared. He will be sorely missed but never forgotten, Buffalo's best in the arts.

Giambra wrote four books, but the one he wrote about his longtime Italian friend, Russell Salvatore, the great Buffalo restaurateur and community benefactor, informing readers of the resilience, ingenuity, and greatness of first generation, Italian Americans who quickly adapted and were determined to be the difference-makers and game-changers. It is an insightfully-touching work about one of Buffalo's Italian pioneers, entitled: "Well Done, From Skipping Class to First Class: The Life and Times of Russell J. Salvatore" (2013).

Salvatore's philanthropic contributions are unbelievably numerous into the millions, but here is the short list: In 2008, he donated the land and building for the Trocaire College Extension Center, now known as the Russell J. Salvatore School of Hospitality and Business; he created the Russell J. Salvatore Foundations, totaling more than $4 million in grants to date; and in 2017, he donated $1 million to Erie County Medical Center's Campaign.

Importantly and for posterity, Salvatore has also created "Patriots and Heroes Park" on Transit Road right of Russell's Steaks; he purchased the land with thoughts of building a shopping plaza but donated it and $3 million, instead, to all the servicemen and the victims of Flight 3407 and 9/11 in New York City, beautifully stating: "It's dedicated to all those people from the bottom of my heart. This is not my park. This is your park."

Salvatore was openly asked about his charitable contributions and what motivates him to do so; he responded this way: "I don't want to die with a bushel full of money, so I'm giving it to those who need it. I was born in Buffalo and the people of Buffalo have been good to me. So why not give it back to the people who made me the success that I am?"

Philanthropist Russell J. Salvatore has donated millions to Buffalo hospitals and education. (Permission from Russell Salvatore).

The great restaurateur and community benefactor to Buffalo explained further: "When I pass away, I'll take as little as I can. I hope there's a cocktail lounge in heaven, but I'll need someone to buy me drinks; I will have left all my money here, and I'll be broke."

Salvatore was born in Buffalo in 1933 to Italian immigrants, the youngest of three children, and lived to see and build a great restaurant and tradition, "Mr. Steak," becoming a multi-millionaire in the process, and most importantly to him, a beloved, Buffalo community benefactor, that will be remembered for donating most of his life's incredible earnings to the community he so loves. What a remarkable life: Salvatore continues to live the American Dream at the young age of 87.

These first generation, Italian Americans were the first great wave of pioneers and trailblazers that opened boundless opportunities for all Italian Americans.

They wanted to make their parents and families feel the proudness of being an accomplished, Italian son or daughter in the professions and not back in the vineyards of Italy, endlessly working from sun-up to sundown (with worn-out pitchforks, pics, and shovels) for small, daily gains: Their great accomplishments were realized because of what they were imparted and modeled by their Italian parents, always exuding their devoted source of faith and enduring values for hard-work that guided, interpreted, and armed them for imminent success in a progressive and future America.

These first generation Italian sons and daughters very much wanted to forge their own distinct identity, their merited and rightful place in the professions, helping their parents see, feel, and benefit from the American Dream. And they seized the opportunities, carpe diem in effect, transforming the landscape of occupations, remarkably, and imprinting their pervasively perilous passage into the annals and halls of fame forever: They triumphantly succeeded in unimaginable ways for all to appreciate now and for future generations in America.

The Memorable 1960 Rome Olympics Catapulted Athletic Competition Worldwide Like Never Before

By Al Bruno
La Gazzetta Italiana,
May 2022

Editor's Note in Italian (italicized):
Nel 1960, Roma ospitò gli Olimpici Estivi. Furono 5,338 atleti da 83 paesi. Il corridor di pita, Giancarlo Peris, accese la torcia. Gli spettatori ancora ricordano le grida e l'applauso di quando gli atleti italiani entrarono nello stadio con le giacche azzurre, I pantaloni bianchi, e con I berretti bianchi. Fu la prima volta che gli Olimpici furono trasmessi. Giacche erano tanti gli immigrati negli Stati Uniti, ebbero l'opportunità di guardarli e celebrare la loro nazione. Gli italiani vinsero 36 medaglie totali.

The 1960 Rome Olympic Games, also known as the SVII Olympiad in Rome, Italy, were spectacular, moving, and historically memorable: Immeasurably, the 1960 Rome Olympics catapulted athletic competition worldwide like never before, held from August 25 to September 11, 1960.

The Games hosted 83 countries and 5,338 athletes (4,727 men and 611 women) from around-the-world that competed in 150 individual events.

Importantly, holding the Olympics in Rome, Italy, did bring together the mixture of ancient times and the modern era. The Basilica of Maxentius and the Baths of Caracalla were restored to host the wrestling and gymnastics events respectively, while an Olympic Stadium and a Sports Palace were built for the Games.

The opening ceremonies were riveting and colorfully assembled, distinctly configured, nation-by-nation in Olympic Stadium: "Here came the Italians, looking molto bello in their light blue jackets, white slacks, and white hats. The Italian hosts entered in full force, 300 strong, and the roar for the home team was deafening," recalls author David Maraniss in his book, Rome 1960: The Summer Olympics That Stirred The World (2008).

"Livio Berruti, the fleet sprinter from Torino, felt overwhelmed by a spirit of equality and fraternity. As he marched around the stadium, warmed by the shimmering rays of the early evening sun, Berruti said later, it seemed as though all of Europe was walking with him, out of the shadows, away from the past," writes Maraniss.

Italian track athlete Giancarlo Peris lit the Olympic flame, a touching moment for all those in attendance and millions watching on television worldwide. For posterity, Italian President Giovanni Gronchi declared the Summer Olympics open on August 27, 1960, by stating in Italian, which translated into English as: "I proclaim the opening of the Games of Rome, celebrating the XVII Olympiad of the modern era."

Remarkably, there were many firsts at these Olympics, including the first commercially-televised Summer Games, the first doping scandal by athletes, the first time the newly-chosen Olympic Anthem, composed by Spiros Samaras, was played in the opening day ceremony, and Abebe Bikila of Ethiopia surprisingly won the gold medal with bare feet for the first time; also, Bikila was the first Black African to become an Olympic champion.

Rome waited 54 years to finally host the Summer Olympics. Looking back, the International Olympic Committee (IOC) agreed and chose Rome to host the 1908 Summer Olympics. Unpredictably and tragically, when Mt. Vesuvius erupted on April 7,

1906, killing 100 people and burying nearby towns, Rome painfully passed on hosting the Olympics to London for 1908.

The Cold War between the United States of America (USA) and Russia was ramping up and reeling still from the shock of the Soviet launch of Sputnik in 1957, reinforcing Soviet leader Nikita Khrushchev's boast the year before by saying to the USA, "We will bury you." Presidential candidate John F. Kennedy pledged in his campaign to get America moving again and compete against Russian technological advancements because "We are losing the respect of the peoples of the world."

"One week before the Opening Ceremony (in Rome) a Moscow trial brought the conviction of an American pilot, Francis Gary Powers, on espionage charges after his high-altitude, U-2 Reconnaissance plane was shot down over Soviet territory," writes Maraniss .

This was Cold War propaganda between the USA and Russia, heightening the competitive atmosphere that the US Olympic team felt as they assembled in Rome in 1960. American athletic prospects were bright: "We don't feel at all abashed about urging our boys in Rome to go out and beat the pants off the Russians and everyone else," Sports Illustrated editorialized.

"Soviet Premier Nikita Khrushchev set sail for New York for a dramatic appearance at the U.N. General Assembly, where he pounded his fist and rallied against America and the West...Officials in East Berlin closed their border temporarily, laying the first metaphorical bricks for what months later would become the all-too-real Berlin Wall," writes Maraniss.

"The contests in Rome shimmered with performances that remain among the most golden in athletic history...Interwoven in so many ways – one could see an older order dying and a new one being born. With all its promise and trouble, the world as we see it today was coming into view," writes David Maraniss.

Back in the United States, millions of immigrant Italians and their children, now first-generation Italian Americans, were loyal American citizens and proudly watching the 1960 Rome Olympics on television for the first time, cheering on both the American and Italian teams: They certainly felt an unsettling ambivalence between their native Italian countrymen and their newly-adopted USA countrymen.

Important to note, thousands of first-generation Italian Americans honorably served in World War II as American soldiers either in the army, navy, air force, or marines, including Yogi Berra, Joe DiMaggio, and Rocky Marciano, for examples: All three are American sports hall of famers who earnestly accepted their duty-to-country, refusing to file for a pardon, as was their right to do so during wartime.

As a result, the hearts of immigrant Italians and first-generation Italian Americans were still with their native Italians, but they never voiced that preference publicly for fear of retaliation and being repatriated back to Italy by the American government's immigration service, like they and other Italians horrifically experienced here in America during World War II. One of those unfortunate immigrant Italians from Sicily was DiMaggio's father, Joe DiMaggio, Sr., a successful fisherman in San Francisco, whose background was being investigated and was made an example of for the public to witness, resulting in his fishing boat being seized, unexplainably, by the American government during the War.

As most predicted, the Soviet Union would prevail and won the total medal count with 103 medals (43 gold, 29 silver, and 31 bronze).

Record-breaking, Russian gymnasts Boris Shakhlin (all-round, parallel bars, pommel horse, and vault) and Larisa Latynina (all-

Livio Berruti (center) of Italy proudly won the gold medal in the 200-meter dash at the 1960 Rome Olympics before his Italian countrymen. Lester Carney (right) of the USA garnered the silver medal, and Abuloulaye Seye (left) of France garnered the bronze medal. (Wikimedia.com, Google Art Project).

round, floor exercise, and women's team) amazingly won a total of seven gold medals for the Russian Team at the Rome Olympics. Weightlifters Yury Vlasov (heavyweight), Yevgeni Minaev (featherweight), Viktor Georgiyevitch Bushuyev (lightweight), Aleksander Kurynov (middleweight), and Arkady Vorobyoc (middle-heavyweight) won gold medals (five in all). Wrestlers Ivan Bogdan (super-heavyweight), Oleg Karavaev (bantamweight), and Avtandil Koridze (lightweight) won gold medals (three in all).

The United States finished second and provided some great Olympic memories, totaling 71 medals (34 gold, 21 silver, and 16 bronze).

Most recognizably, Wilma Randolph won the hearts of Americans by winning three gold medals in the 100-meter, 200-meter, and in the 4 X 100-meter track events; Rudolph is the first American woman to do so in a single Olympic Games. A young Cassius Clay, later known as Muhammad Ali, flashed his early brilliance by winning the gold medal in boxing's, light-heavyweight division. Rafer Johnson won the gold medal in the decathlon, having won silver in 1956; he was the USA's flag bearer at the Rome Olympics.

For the all-time Olympic records, the USA men's basketball team, led by Oscar Robertson and Jerry West, the USA co-captains and future NBA hall of famers, captured the USA Team a fifth, straight Olympic gold medal.

The Italian Team showed its nationalistic pride and showed well, finishing a very respectable third in the XVII in Rome with 36 total medals (13 gold, 10 silver, and 13 bronze).

Livio Berruti was a surprise Olympic gold medalist in track, winning the 200-meter dash. Boxers Giovanni "Nino" Benvenuti, Francesco Musso, and Francesco De Piccoli all won gold medals and so did the track cyclist team of Luigi Arienti, Franco Testa, Mario Vallotto, and Marino Vigna. Impressively as well was the cycling team TTT of Antonio Bailetti, Ottavio Cogliati, Giacomo Fornoni, and Livio Trape, garnering a gold medal. The fencing team of Giuseppe Delfino, Alberto Pellegrino, Carlo Pavesi, Edoardo Mangiarotti, Fiorenzo Marini, and Gianluigi Saccaro also garnered a gold medal.

A complete breakdown of Italian gold, silver, and bronze medalists at the 1960 Rome Olympics is as follows:

Italian Gold Medalists

Livio Berruti (200-meter). Luigi Arienti, Franco Testa, Mario Vallotto, and Marino Vigna (track cycling, team pursuit, 4,000-meter). Sante Gaiardoni (track cycling, sprint). Sergio Bianchetto and Giuseppe Beghetto (track cycling, tandem, 2000-meter). Sante Gaiardoni (track cycling, 1,000-meter). Francesco Musso (boxing, featherweight). Giovanni "Nino" Benvenuti (boxing, welterweight). Francesco De Piccoli (boxing, heavyweight). Raimondo D'Inzeo (equestrian, jumping, individual). Giuseppe Delfino (screens, epee). Guiseppe Delfino, Alberto Pellegrino, Carlo Pavesi, Edoardo Mangiarotti, Fiorenzo Marini, and Gianluigi Saccaro (fencing, sword, team). Danio Bardi, Guiseppe D'Altrui, Franco Lavoratori, Gianni Lonzi, Rosario Parmegiani, Eraldo Pizzo, Dante Rossi, Amedeo Ambron, Salvatore Gionta, Luigi Mannelli, Brunello Spinelli, and Giancarlo Guerrini (waterpolo, team). Antonio Bailetti, Ottavio Cogliati, Giacomo Fornoni, and Livio Trape (cycling, TTT).

Italian Silver Medalists

Primo Zamparini (boxing, bantamweight). Carmelo Bossi (boxing, half-middleweight). Alessandro Lopopolo (boxing, lightweight). Aldo Dezi and Francesco LaMacchia (canoeing, C-2, 1,000-meter). Piero D'Inzeo (equestrian, jumping, individual). Tullio Baraglia, Renato Bosatta, Giancarlo Crosta, and Giuseppe Galante (rowing, four-without-mate). Alberto Pellegrino, Luigi Arturo Carpaneda, Mario Curletto, Aldo Aureggi, and Edoardo Mangiarotti (screens, foil, team). Galliano Rossini (shooting, stairway, 125 targets). Giovanni Carminucci (gymnastics, bridge). Livio Trape (cycling, road race).

Italian Bronze Medalists

Giuseppina Leone (track, 100-meter). Abdon Pamich (track, 50 km walk). Valentino Gasparella (track cycling, sprint). Giulio

Franco De Piccoli, gold medalist in heavyweight division. Wikimedia.com, Google Art Project)

Saraudi (boxing, light heavyweight). Sebastiano Mannironi (weightlifting, featherweight). Raimondo D'Inzeo, Piero D'Inzeo, and Antonio Oppes (equestrian, jumping, team). Fulvio Balatti, Romano Sgheiz, Franco Trincavelli, Giovanni Zucchi, and Ivo Stefanoni (rowing, four-with-mate). Bruna Colombetti, Velleda Cesari, Claudia Pasini, Irene Camber, and Antonella Ragno-Lonzi (fencing, foil, team, women). Wladimiro Calabrese (fencing, saber, individual). Wladimiro Calabrese, Giampaolo Calanchini, Pierluigi Chicca, Roberto Ferrari, and Mario Ravagnan (fencing, saber, team). Giovanni Carminucci, Pasquale Carminucci, Gianfranco Marzolla, Franco Menichelli, Orlando Polmonari, and Angelo Vicardi (gymnastics, team). Franco Menichelli (gymnastics, floor exercise). Antonio Cosentino, Antonio Ciciliano, and Giulio De Stefano (sailing, dragon class).

The closing ceremonies were less spectacular than the opening ceremonies because most of the winning participants had departed from the city of Rome, leaving the nations of the world with lone flag bearers. After the stadium emptied, the black lit sky lit up, this time with a midnight fireworks celebration.

Afterwards, New York Times reporter Arthur Daley assessed the 1960 Rome Olympics this way: "Maybe it was the best ever. It's impossible to visualize or recollect any Olympic Games that match the tone these noble Romans threw. The entire production was conducted with totally un-Italian efficiency but with typical Italian flair for drama and beauty."

Daley was haunted with thoughts of Soviet prominence and of a world catching up to the United States, candidly stating: "The world is stirring not only politically but athletically, too. The U.S. scares not a soul any more. Once, the Americans dominated the show. They don't any more, nor are they likely to do so again."

Bluntly, Daley was disappointed, admitting that this was a crushing American defeat to the Soviets, stating: "The Rome Olympics represented a resounding victory for Soviet Russia. The Red brothers beat us in total medals and in unofficial total points."

Final Thoughts on the 1960 Rome Olympics

The 1960 Rome Olympics were witnessed and copiously recorded almost 62 years ago on the world stage, and those moments of athletic glory continue to be retold into perpetuity as precious, penetrating Olympic lore: Those 1960 Games were memorable because the city of Rome played an instrumental role in magically transforming and catapulting athletic competition worldwide from ancient times into the modern era with unifying grace, style, and purpose, despite the Cold War antics and posturing between the United States and Russia over global superiority and might.

In reflection, the contributions of the 1960 Rome Olympics should never be diminished or overlooked in importance because Rome, the seat of the Roman Empire and the cradle of Christianity, again became the golden center of multinational intersection and sharing, the crossroads this time, for advancing athletic competition worldwide, like never before. Long live the enduring legacy of Rome and the progressive and determined will of Italian peoples, earnestly endeavoring to envision, build, and sustain a more competitive and greater, global society for all to emulate.

Bravo per la bella città di Roma, il nostro centro di oro, di grazia e risultati.

Part Three

GREAT BUFFALO ITALIANS, IMAGES, AND LESSONS LEARNED

BUFFALO WRESTLING HALL OF FAMER ILIO DiPAOLO HONORED IN ITALY

Introdacquan officials graciously greet Buffalo's Dennis and Michael DiPaolo at the DiPaolo Education Scholarship presentation on August 18, 2023, celebrating the great legacy of native Ilio DiPaolo, Introdacqua's favorite son. (Permission from Dennis DiPaolo).

By Al Bruno
La Gazzetta Italiana
October 2023

Buffalo's wrestling hall of famer Ilio DiPaolo was honored at La Piazza Cavour in an all-day festival in his hometown of Introdacqua in the Abruzzo region of Italy on August 18. 2023. Mayor Christian Colasante and Carla DeBenedetto scheduled this day as part of a week-long feast honoring St. Antonio and St. Feliciano.

Over 3,000 locals were in attendance to celebrate the great legacy of Ilio DiPaolo, Introdacqua's favorite son and the highly-successful, American wrestler and community benefactor from the Buffalo, New York area. In 1997, Introdacqua presented the DiPaolo family with a beautiful bronze bust of Ilio DiPaolo which is now permanently housed in City Hall for public display. Also, a museum honoring Ilio DiPaolo with many artifacts, posters, pictures, articles and books, was dedicated in 2017. The museum housed in the D'Angelo House is the work of Panifila Colangelo and Massimo Tardio.

DiPaolo was inducted into the Greater Buffalo Sports Hall of Fame, Professional Wrestling Hall of Fame and Museum, and Canadian Wrestling Hall of Fame. He was a

Introdacqua town officials present Buffalo's Dennis DiPaolo and Aunt Joanna Phelan in 2019 with a beautifully-detailed bronze bust of Ilio DiPaolo, heralded hall of fame wrestler in America, who was born and raised in Introdacqua, Italy. The Ilio DiPaolo bust is now permanently housed and on public display at City Hall in Introdacqua. The legacy of the great and immortal Ilio DiPaolo is now celebrated in the two continents of North America and Europe. (Permission from Dennis DiPaolo).

member of the Worldwide Wrestling Association, Midwest Wrestling Association, and Stampede Wrestling Association as well.

Importantly, DiPaolo's community involvement was recognized by outstanding citizen's awards from many community organizations, including Hilbert College, Southdowns' Rotary Club, Lions Club of Blaisdell, Boys Town of Italy, St. Francis High School, and Western New York Italian-American Association. DiPaolo campaigned vigorously for a variety of causes including the Leukemia Society, Children's Hospital, Cystic Fibrosis, People Incorporated, and Camp Good Days and Special Times. Hunter's Hope was added after DiPaolo's passing in 1995. In 2019, the Scholarship Fund started a scholarship in the name of Ilio DiPaolo as a show of gratitude to the People of Introdacqua. A selection committee consisting of Panfilia Colangelo, Massimo Tardio, Giannina Restano, and Carla De Benedetto put on a marvelous presentation for the students of Introdacqua.

The gala event was simply "spectacular," and the Abruzzo Centro News was on hand to cover the Ilio DiPaolo celebration,"Premiazione: Borsa di Studio 'Ilio DiPaolo' 2023." The Abruzzo Centro News affirmed and complimented the talents of this year's scholarship recipient, Cecilia Bonaventura: "She is an extraordinary flutist, a true talent that carries the name of Introdacqua, Citta Musicale, in Italy and in Europe." Cecilia Bonaventura performed at the Ilio DiPaolo celebration with flutist Micaela Faiella and pianist Frederico Laudadio, who played pieces by W.A. Mozart, A. Vivaldi, and F. Borne.

Ten overflowing tables of delicious Italian pasta dishes, meatballs and sausage, assorted salads, Italian pastries and delicacies, and fresh fruit were offered to all in attendance. The memorable event was sponsored by the municipality of Introdacqua as well as Panfilia and Massimo, in conjunction with the D'Angelo House of Introdacqua.

Oldest son Dennis DiPaolo eloquently and graciously addressed the townspeople of Introdacqua in Italian for posterity; his important message was recorded in the annals and translated into English as follows:

"I would like to express my sincere gratitude to Panfilia Colangelo, Massimo Tardio, Giannina Restano, and the entire scholarship committee for their hard work and dedication in making this a wonderful and memorable event. Mayor Christian Colasante and Carla DeBenedetto, thank you, for your support and for helping in this week of celebrations. Special thanks to Anna Marie and Carlo DeCellis of Pacento for all you do for our family, and to Ron Corbo, of New York, for his generous donation to help Fund the scholarship on behalf of my father, Ilio DiPaolo."

Dennis DiPaolo continued with the announcement of this year's scholarship winner, "We are proud to recognize the young people of Introdacqua and support them in their future endeavors. This year's winner of the Ilio DiPaolo Scholarship Fund is Cecilia Bonaventura, flutist. She began studying the flute at the age of seven and continued to improve at the Luisa D'Annunzio Conservatory of Music in Pescara. We wish her much success in the years to come. On behalf of my Aunt Giovanna, Uncle Tomasso Phelan and our entire family, we will forever be grateful to all of you at Introdacqua."

In La Piazza Cavour in Introdacqua, an authentic and artistically-designed cement staircase has the following Italian words inscribed on each of the stairs, describing the magnificence of the great town of Introdacqua and its legendary wrestling hero, Ilio DiPaolo, "The Giant Wrestler from Abruzzo." The Italian inscription is translated into English as follows:

"Between two green pine forests, is he hiding in the middle of one? Our beautiful country is in the valley. When you arrive, you see it, and you can't resist! If you sow onions here, bandits are born! This little village is enchanted, timeless, where fountains gush, and there is excellent wine. As in a fairy tale, the notes fly here, and the bells hang from the twigs. It is a magical village, full of art and love where the poet D'Angelo and the wrestler DiPaolo were born. My Introdacqua, beautiful Introdacqua. 'Mignorinella' overlooks the balcony. Splendid country of musicians and choirs. The more you live it, the more you fall in love."

To fully clarify the inception of the scholarship, after DiPaolo's, unforeseen tragic passing in 1995, friends and family members organized a scholarship fund in DiPaolo's name, the Ilio DiPaolo Scholarship Fund. It was led by Bud Carpenter, Jim Kelly, and Randy Ribbeck of the Buffalo Bills. Today the fund has awarded close to $1.3 million in scholarships and donations for the less fortunate in the community.

Bud Carpenter, president of the Ilio DiPaolo Scholarship Fund and a member of the Greater Buffalo Sports Hall of Fame, continues to lead the organization to support such groups as Greater Adaptive Sports and the Center for Handicapped Children, expanding the scholarship to include women's wrestling as well as Ilio's hometown in Italy, Introdacqua. The Ilio DiPaolo Scholarship Fund has been honored by the NYS Section VI Hall of Fame, WNY Wrestling Coaches Hall of Fame, and numerous other organizations, thanking them for their contributions.

FINAL THOUGHTS ON ILIO DI-PAOLO'S TRANSCONTINENTAL GREATNESS

The great legacy of Ilio DiPaolo now joins a very elite group of native-born, Italian sports greats and hall of famers like Leo Nomellini, Bruno Sammartino, Mario Andretti, and Geno Auriemma, all of whom deservingly had statues and busts constructed in his own image and piazza gala events were held, honoring and celebrating these hometown Italian heroes for their enduring sports achievements, living the American Dream, for all to appreciate and emulate into perpetuity. These Italian sports legends are established and fortified transcontinental giants on two continents: North America and Europe. They are awesome, all-encompassing Italian sports legends that we must always fondly recognize, remembering and retelling their numerous monumental achievements that were recorded on both continents.

In fact, consider this: Nomellini, Sammartino, Andretti, and Auriemma have all set remarkable world records, won multiple championships, and were the undisputable goats in their respective sports eras. However, only one Italian-born, wrestling hall of famer and champion, Ilio DiPaolo, remains the fluid funding gift that just keeps on giving in America and in Italy: No one else can best that philanthropic contribution-to-community, really.

Bravissimo, Ilio DiPaolo, molto ben fatto. Sei un uomo incredibile e sei una borsa robusta di studio in istruzione in America e in Italia.

BELOVED BUFFALONIAN JOEY GIAMBRA SUCCUMBS TO COVID-19

Beloved Buffalonian Joey Giambra lost his fight to Covid-19 on May 14, 2020. Giambra is one of Buffalo's favorite sons and an Italian icon, contributing as a musician, actor, playwright, author, and poet in his remarkable life. He will be sorely missed but will never be forgotten. (Permission from Joey Giambra family)

By Al Bruno
La Gazzetta Italiana
September 2020

Editor's Note in Italian (italicized):
Joey Giambra, un italo-americano che abitava in Buffalo, e morto per il COVID in Maggio. Giambra era un uomo rispettato nella città per molte ragioni. Lui era era poliziotto, uno scrittore, un poeta, un drammaturgo, e un musicista. Era un'icona in Buffalo, dopo aver lavorato vent'anni nella polizia, ha cominciato il libro e "La terra promessa" che parla dell'esperienza di immigrati italiani. Lui aveva anche inciso un CD della musica chiamata "I love you Buffalo." La sua musica era popolare tra I suoi amanti. Il suo capolavoro e un libro intitolato "The hooks." In questo libro, parla delle vita difficile per gli immigrati italiani, dovevano lavorare duramente ma che non hanno mai dimenticato mai di onorare le feste italiane, specialmente la festa di San Antonio. Per queste ragioni, nella comunità di Buffalo sono molto triste per la morta di Giambra perché era un uomo molto bravo.

Beloved Buffalonian Joey Giambra recently succumbed to Covid-19. He was hospitalized at the Buffalo General Medical Center since April 25, and sadly, he passed on May 14, 2020; he was 86 years young, creatively sharp, congenially engaging, and will be sorely missed by the Buffalo community and beyond.

Buffalo's Joey Giambra is one of the city's favorite sons and a first-generation Italian American, connecting the past from the Lower West Side into our present and future living contexts through his music, drama, poetry, and writing. Giambra was an Italian icon, an ambassador of understanding, and his flourishing artistry had no end to his talents and so did his affection for all peoples, a caring people person: a rare, spiritual quality that few possess.

Giambra had an inviting and contagious smile, and he somehow magically wove it into an incredible sensitivity and a literary love for culture and the goodness in people: He made an indelible impression, stirring and inspiring you with energy, spirit, and the promise to do better.

"I am saddened to hear of Joey Giambra's passing. His contributions to Buffalo's music and theater community will be felt for years to come," announced Buffalo Mayor Byron Brown.

To his greatness, Giambra envisioned and ambitiously lived out five careers in one remarkable lifetime, it seems, in addition to the important roles of dedicated father and husband which he did, expertly, as everything else he endeavored.

In 1963, he joined the Buffalo Police Department and served for 20 years as a police officer and sergeant before retiring as a detective. At 44, Giambra would earn a bachelor's degree in criminal justice from SUNY Buffalo State. He was a self-taught jazz trumpeter, a pianist, an actor, a singer and songwriter, a former restaurant owner, a filmmaker, a poet, an Italian chef, and the author of four books, a historian, a one-time candidate for mayor of Buffalo, he spoke fluent Sicilian, and he possessed endless bundles of creative energy to expend.

Giambra briefly spoke about his 20-year service as a member of the Buffalo Police Department in an interview with Maria Scrivani, a writer for the Buffalo Spree magazine, recalling this: "When I became a detective in plainclothes, they wanted me to keep tabs on the Mafia. I never framed anybody. That would have been easy to do in narcotics where I was working, then. I never took money. I only fired a gun three times, and they were warning shots."

Giambra's long writing career included "La Terra Promessa," a documentary that insightfully chronicles the Italian-America immigrant experiences in Western New York in the early 1900s. His earlier work entitled, "Bread and Onions," published, in part, by the Per Niente magazine of Buffalo, edited by Joe DiLeo and Giambra, did inspire him to produce "La Terra Promessa."

His many movie appearances included such films as "Hide in Plain Sight," "Buffalo '66," and "Marshall." In 1978, Giambra recalls: "When Hide in Plain Sight was being shot in Buffalo, I had a chance to read for the producers. Then, they had me read for James Caan. They cast me as a cook in my own restaurant," as quoted by Maria Scrivani.

In 2017, Giambra looked to the future with optimism about his future artistry as a playwright and actor, announcing, "What I want to do next is to direct my play, 'No One Is Us,' on stage right here in Buffalo. And cook and bake. It kills me to pay three dollars for a loaf at Wegman's when I can bake it for thirty-three cents. Whatever I've done in life, I have trusted my art – that's what keeps me going," as quoted by Maria Scrivani in conclusion.

Giambra also produced a recorded CD, entitled, "I Love You, Buffalo," and he debuted as a vocalist. Mayor Brown noted that the work is now part of the city's, sesquicentennial time capsule at Buffalo's City Court plaza, remarking, "This is a lasting legacy and remembrance of Joey Giambra for future generations," a deserving honor to the greatness of Joey Giambra, Buffalo's own.

Poignantly, Giambra writes about "The Hooks," a waterfront ghetto where Italians arrived and lived in downtown Buffalo in the early 1900s. Giambra writes in Per Niente magazine, excerpting from his work, "Bread and Onions," this horrible and despairing depiction: "To escape stigmatic welfare, men shoveled snow and concrete and dug ditches. They ate bread and onions, pasta and lentils, drank wine, got old, and waited to die…

"The Hooks were old, ghostly and dilapidated, and would soon perish. Politicians promised renewal but none came. As the Depression ended, businesses closed or moved, as did many families."

Despite the pain of the times, the arriving Italians still had the Feast of Saint Anthony to look forward to in the summer. Giambra's accurate descriptions still live on and are retold from generation to generation; he writes:

"A marching band played to great applause, no emotional restraint, Sicilian veneration. Men, women, and children: Americans of the first generation carried banners and a huge statue of Saint Anthony past wooden-framed homes. Multi-colored lanterns adorned windows and front porches…They were transformed into stunning, candle-lit altars. Hanging in a backdrop of embroidered linen were the flags of America and Italy."

The Italians then moved to congregate on the sidewalk in front of Saint Anthony's Church, recalls Giambra, "Spiritually unified people knelt in prayer. Devotion was the rule, the highest example…Fireworks lit up the sky, a pyrotechnic blizzard, the last night of the feast, the final goodbye."

Giambra was born in 1933 on Georgia Street on Buffalo's Lower West Side; that is his reference point that informs his writing. The cultural and colorful descriptions of the early, Lower West Side were insightfully created through the cultural and environmental lens from his Georgia Street home and neighborhood. Those beautiful words provide cultural clarity and a bridge to understanding the Lower West Side the way Giambra vividly and eloquently describes it: His great literary works are part of the city's annals for appreciation now and for posterity.

"His family recalls that he received his early passion for music and drama from Anne Rodenhoffer, an elementary school teacher at the old Public School No. 2. He went on to Hutchinson Central High School, where he formed a band that maintained a steady business at weddings, parties, and other events," writes Sean Kirst in the Buffalo News.

"We, the many, many people he loved and touched, are left with a big hole in our lives. For me, there will always be something missing," painfully writes Tom Naples, his old friend, a guitarist who often worked with Giambra.

Giambra is survived by his wife of 66 years, Shirley; a son and grandson, Gregory Sr. and Gregory Jr.; and he was predeceased by a daughter, Michele.

Restaurateur Russell J. Salvatore Has Generously Gifted Millions to Buffalo and WNY Projects

Philanthropist Russell J. Salvatore has donated millions to Buffalo hospitals and education (Permission from Russell J. Salvatore).

By Al Bruno
La Gazzetta Italiana,
April 2022

Editor's Note in Italian (italicized):
L'articolo descrive la vita di Russell J. Salvatore, un cuoco e proprietario del famoso ristorante, Salvatore's Italian Gardens. Salvatore ha ingrandito il ristorante da una piccola trattoria che era ad un grande ristorante con una presenza forte nella comunità di Buffalo. Il ristorante è decorato per assomigliare al Vaticano. Nelle sue parole, lui spiega come il suo menù ha dei diversi piatti e che ad un bambino di 8 anni o un vecchietto di 80 anni può trovare qualcosa che gli piaccia la mangiare. Più importante, Salvatore ha donato milioni di dollari alla sua comunità. Ha detto che non vuole morire con i soldi della banca ma vorrebbe donare i suoi soldi a diverse cause per la città di Buffalo. Lui vuole migliorare la sua città perché sono proprio i suoi vicini e la sua comunità che gli hanno dato sostegno negli anni.

Restaurateur Russell J. Salvatore has become synonymous with everything for a greater and progressive Buffalo, one of Buffalo's greatest community benefactors. Salvatore has generously gifted millions to Buffalo and WNY projects.

Born in 1933 to Italian immigrants, a first-generation Italian American, and the youngest of three children, Salvatore lived to build and realize a great restaurant and tradition, "Mr. Steak," in Buffalo and WNY, becoming a multi-millionaire in the process and most importantly to him, a beloved philanthropist that will be remembered for donating most of his life's earnings to the community (Buffalo) he dearly loves. What a remarkable life: Salvatore continues to live the American Dream at the young age of 89.

While still in grammar school, Salvatore worked at his father's tavern on Delevan Avenue on the East Side of Buffalo: It was a modest business where Chevy plant employees would cash their checks and stay for a shot and a beer. Young Salvatore would often skip classes at his high school to work side-by-side with his father at the tavern.

He loved working more than doing classwork, he readily admits in his book, Well Done: From Skipping Class to First Class (The Life and Times of Russell J. Salvatore, 2013) by Joey Giambra, his longtime West Side friend, informing readers about Salvatore's arduous journey to become one of Buffalo's great restaurateurs and pioneers by incorporating those enduring qualities of resilience and ingenuity, initiated by those early first-generation Italian Americans, who then quickly adapted and became the difference-makers and game-changers.

Then in 1967, Salvatore opened his own restaurant, Salvatore's Italian Gardens, near the corner of Genesee and Transit Road. Over the next 40 years, Salvatore's Italian Gardens became one of the largest and most successful restaurants in the country.

"I bought the whole property, eight acres, for $40,000," Salvatore recalls. "Then we started growing. We put on an addition every year."

Slowly and artistically, Salvatore's Italian Gardens was constructed to showcase a decorative, Italian-style architectural elegance, and some people thought it had a Vatican theme: Customers could gaze on a three-dimensional panorama of Rome by moonlight. The St. Peter's Dome there was impressive and memorable to onlookers.

"I used to go to different auction and antique shops and buy things," Salvatore said. "I was down in Florida, and I went to this place that sold cement statues. I bought thousands of them there, and they ended up lining the driveway," Salvatore said.

Salvatore then tried retirement, but being away from what he loved was too tough to take.

"I look forward to going to work. What are you going to do, sit home and watch television? You get bored. You get depressed," Salvatore said.

"I go to work because I shake hands with people, meet new people, and it's a good feeling to make people feel good, and in the restaurant business, if you serve a decent meal and give good service, you get the pats on the back and that makes you want to come back to work every day."

In 2008, Salvatore opened Russell's Steaks, Chops, and More along with Salvatore's Grand Hotel. Today Russell's is known as one of the premier steaks houses in the entire country.

Salvatore's philanthropic contributions are unbelievably numerous into the millions. In 2008, he donated the land and building for the Trocaire College Extension Center, now known as the Russell J. Salvatore School of Hospitality and Business; he created the Russell J. Salvatore Foundations, totaling more than $4 million in grants to date; and in 2017, he donated $1 million to Erie County Medical Center's Campaign.

Importantly and for posterity, Salvatore has also created Patriots and Heroes Park on Transit Road, right of Russell's Steaks; he purchased the land with thoughts of building a shopping plaza but donated it and $3 million, instead, to all the servicemen and the victims of Flight 3407 and 9/11 in New York City, beautifully stating: "It's dedicated to all those people from the bottom of my heart. This is not my park. This is your park."

Since building Patriots and Heroes Park, Salvatore has added a statue of St. Michael Archangel, the patron saint of law enforcement and World War II monument dedicated to the men who fought in the Battle of the Bulge.

Salvatore has also had a long relationship with the fans of the Buffalo Bills. More than once Salvatore has bought out the remaining tickets for a Bills home game so that it could be shown on local and television and not be blacked out. In December 2012, Salvatore purchased the remaining 10,000 tickets for the Bills/St. Louis Rams home game which was not shown in the Buffalo market.

During the 1990s and the Bills' Super Bowl years, Salvatore was one of the biggest supporters of the team as any business owner in the region, but he did not stop there. Salvatore has sponsored countless events that have benefitted sports at all levels.

"The participants and fans of WNY sports cross every possible demographic from little league, high school, college, and the pros. Whether you are 8 or 81, a man or a woman, there is something for everyone. Next, to our great independent restaurants, sports means Buffalo to me!" said Russell.

While Salvatore has enjoyed remarkable

success as a restaurateur, he also learned at an early age "giving back" is important.

"I can remember as a young boy my dad having delivered Christmas gifts to neighbors and friends. He was so appreciative of his customers," said Salvatore, "My dad would always have holiday parties for all the customers; he would arrange trips and alike to back what he could. I guess this instilled in me to never take customers for granted and by giving back to your community, and you can help make it stronger."

Salvatore was openly asked about his charitable contributions and what motivates him to do so; he put it this way: "I don't want to die with a bushel full of money, so I'm giving it to those who need it. I was born in Buffalo and the people of Buffalo have been good to me. So why not give it back to the people who made me the success that I am?"

The great restaurateur and community benefactor to Buffalo explained further: "When I pass away, I'll take as little as I can. I hope there's a cocktail lounge in heaven, but I'll need someone to buy me drinks; I will have left all my money here, and I'll be broke."

Buffalonians are very fortunate to have been graced by Salvatore's incredible generosity and philanthropy, now, and into perpetuity. Salvatore is indelibly inscribed into the annals as a living Buffalo legend; importantly, Salvatore is that fluid gift that just keeps on giving. Bravo, very well done, and thank you, Russell J. Salvatore: A resilient, first-generation Italian American, a successful Buffalo restaurateur, and a trailblazer for monumental civic progress.

My Father, Joseph Salvatore

The Salvatores: Mary, Anthony, Russell, and parents Gaetana and Joseph (Permission from Russell J. Salvatore).

By Russell Salvatore, son
Per Niente
Winter 2015

My father, Joseph Salvatore, was born in Accadia, Italy, in 1886. At age 18, he immigrated to America and arrived in New York City on May 18, 1904. Soon, after a series of menial jobs there, he came to Buffalo, NY, to live with his sister, Jenny, on South Division Street on the lower East Side and worked as a water boy, paint sprayer, and laborer on the Erie Canal.

In 1918, my father opened a grocery store on Seneca Street near DiTondo's and other buildings that would soon house Santora's, Buffalo's original pizzeria and a small Italian restaurant called, Chef's.

In the mid-1920s, my father met my mother, Gaetana Martorana, an immigrant from Agrigento, Sicily, who lived in Rochester, NY, but who was in Buffalo visiting her sister who lived on Swan Street. After the reception, my parents came to Buffalo and lived on Harriet Street in the humble surroundings of the Bailey, East Delevan corridor where they produced three children: Mary, Anthony, and me.

It was then that my father moved his Seneca Street grocery store business to 1448 East Delavan Avenue, an address that would later become Salvatore's Restaurant. My mother and father were the strictest parents in the world. Today my father would be doing life for child abuse: The way he hit my sister, brother, and me. It's true. But, despite their strictness, my siblings and I loved them unconditionally. And when my father did arrive at the dinner table, we had to say: 'Buon appetito a tutti!' That means good appetite to all. My father would then say: 'Grazie tante!' Then, we could enjoy my mother's wonderful food."

My father may have been strict toward his kids, but everyone in the neighborhood loved him for his generosity and benevolence, a trait many say I've inherited.

During the Great Depression, my father fed the neighborhood. As mentioned earlier, 1448 East Delavan Avenue was a grocery store. However, in the rear of the store was the Salvatore speakeasy. The boxes of bananas, bushels of apples, oranges and vegetables were dispensed freely to the neighborhood poor and hungry. As such, 1448 East Delevan Avenue was a Godsend to many and a successful front for the sale of illegal booze.

My father loved the Arts. He insisted his children take music lessons. Mary studied the piano, Anthony, the banjo, and I studied guitar with the great Tony Militello. Anthony and I were pretty good.

Once, after we performed, I sang East Parade on the WEBR radio program, Uncle Bill's Hour. We won first prize: two, $25 US War Bonds and two pairs of "High-Top shoes" from Liberty Shoe Store. Our victory came as a result of our father's astute business and marketing strategy. He had the bar at Salvatore's Restaurant covered with pads of paper and piles of penny postcards. He had all the bases covered to ensure that his customers voted – and voted often – for us, "The Singing Salvatores" to win first prize. My father mailed every vote to WEBR Radio on North Street. As a result, we not only won but broke the record for the most votes received in Uncle Bill's Hour lengthy history.

My father was not only generous to a fault, but very shrewd. When you came into his saloon, he'd buy you the first and the third drink – all the time. When the customer offered to buy my father a drink, he'd say, "I don't drink but I'll take a cigar." The cigar he put in his pocket cost the customer 15 cents. It cost my father not quite 7 cents to pour that 'free' shot of whiskey. The cost of buying a beer for a customer was about 3 cents. At the end of the night, all those cigars that people bought my father were returned to their rightful box to be re-sold. My father always said, "When I buy someone a shot of whiskey and they buy me a cigar; I'm 8 cents ahead."

In the early 1950s when I was in the U.S. Army and stationed down South, my father always sent care packages: capicola, peperoni, cheese, olives, everything. I fed the entire barracks. After my father died, 1448 East Delavan Avenue was destroyed by fire. We lived across the street. My sister, Mary, recalls that night. She was awakened by the sound of the engines. She looked out the window and saw a big part of her young life go up in flames. She called my brother, Tony: "Tony, Delavan is burning to the ground." She was devastated.

"I began thinking about a tribute to my late father. I went to City Hall. I'd like to put a park on my property at 1448 East Delavan Avenue where my family once had a restaurant. I want a memorial on that land which is now an empty lot." They said, "Fine, put your park there. We'll take it off the tax rolls, but you must maintain it." I said, "OK, and I put a monument with my father's picture in the park. I was happy for a long time after that. But, all of a sudden, a guy who had a business across the street called me to say, 'Mr. Salvatore, I would appreciate it if you took your monument off my property.' I said, What do you mean, your property? The man said, 'I just bought it at a tax auction.'"

Russell continued, "I was furious. He bought all that land for $10,000. I ran to City Hall. They said they forgot to take it off the tax rolls. Sadly, I had to take the monument I built to memorialize my father out of the park. By the time I got around to doing that, the monument was destroyed. My sister, Mary, remembers hollering out the window at kids who were vandalizing my father's monument and throwing rocks and stones at my father's picture."

Good news may be coming. A recent rumor circulated that the City of Buffalo may reinstall and refurbish my beloved park. We'll see right, Papa?

From Skipping Class To First Class

A young Russell Salvatore is pictured here in the late 1940s (Permission from Russell J. Salvatore).

By Joey Giambra,
Well Done: The Life and Times of Russell J. Salvatore (2013)

SCHOOL DAYS

After graduating from BPS 82, Russell Salvatore attended Kensington High School. By his own admission, he was not the best of students. He was convinced the teachers did not like him. "Every time I entered this one classroom the teacher made me turn my desk around and face the wall."

Back then, the Kensington student body was primarily German and Polish with a smattering of Italians in the Bailey-Delavan area. Even now, Russell is convinced that he was singled out because of his Italian ethnicity. That 'dislike' could also be attributed to the long hours that Russell worked in the restaurant after school, hours that took him away from any homework, and street-corner relationships with those his own age.

Salvatore's restaurant opened for business at 8:30 am, and it served food until 2:30 the next morning. Russell recalls:

"People came from the Chevy plant, and from Trico, and we served a square pizza, not a round one. It was my mother's idea. We had lots of customers who loved it. It was topped with grated Romano cheese and pepperoni. It cost 50 cents. We had a gourmet pizza that came with mushrooms for 75 cents. The pizza today with all that junk on it, that's crazy. I love pizza with anchovy. That's how my mother made it for us. Back then, I was skinny; I weighed 135 pounds. My mother, who felt sorry for me, would make me milk shakes with five raw eggs and two scoops of ice cream. She baked bread all the time, and she would fry leftover dough, put sugar on it, and when we came home from School 82 for lunch, that's what we had. Oh, it was so good!"

Though Russell didn't graduate from Kensington High School, he always speaks well of his friend, Frank Ciminelli, who was the graduating class president.

"Frank was smart. He sat in front of me. That was a good thing, because when we had a test, he always let me look over his shoulder. But once, because I put the answers on the wrong line, I failed. I was so bad in school. If I didn't quit, I'd probably still be there today."

Russell was elated when his brother, Tony, went into the Army, saying: "The day I quit school to work full time in the restaurant was the happiest day of my life!"

Reflecting on that time, Russell stated: "Frank Ciminelli was going steady with Rosalie Savarino, a beautiful girl from Harriet Street, who he eventually married. Me? I was going with Barbara Fechter, a really gorgeous German girl. We went together at

School 82 and Kensington. And eventually we married."

At the time, the principal at Kensington High was Mr. Monin, who drove the student body to frenzy whenever he needed support for his athletic programs. Russell Salvatore was never a jock, but he speaks respectfully about Mr. Monin, and the 1948 unbeaten, unscored-against Kensington Knights, the high school football team that went to win the Harvard Cup for three successive years. To get out of going to classes, Russell thought of trying out for the team. But he was too small. So, the next move to escape education was to join the school band. He applied and was given a tuba.

On Friday evening, October 22, 1948, Russell Salvatore, tuba under his arm, wearing his green, gold, and white band uniform, was in Civic Stadium on Jefferson Avenue. The occasion? A first-time ever night football game between two Buffalo high schools, Kensington and Bennett, in which their school bands, resplendent in their uniforms, would play before a record crowd of 51,000.

With the teams settled at the end of the field, Miss Gertrude Lutzi, accompanied by the Bennett and Kensington bands, sang the National Anthem. Her first note sent the enormous crowd into a mystical trance, a silence never before experienced in this concrete cave where the noise of race cars and midget autos was the norm. When Miss Lutzi sang the last note, the cheering throng rose, as if on cue, and the game began.

The Kensington Knights with magical quarterback, Bobby Wilde, halfback Chris Frauenhofer, strong-running fullback Carl Wyles, and Jack Thompson, beat the undefeated Bennett Tigers 28 to 6.

"It was packed. Bedlam," Russell says. "My brother, who went to Kensington before me, was there. I didn't know he was coming. No tickets for this game were sold at the door. It was all advance sales. Tony probably drove a beautiful cheerleader to the game in his purple Cadillac. The crowd! I never saw anything like it in that place before, or after that night. What energy! All you could hear were police sirens, bands, dancers, and screeching singers. There were even some jugglers."

Russell remembers that night vividly: "Every high school band in the city played under the moonlight. With that, and the other lights, the sky was lit up. There were thousands of noisy people, three-deep, circling around the grassy field. After the game, I didn't get on the band bus. I put my tuba in Tony's car, and I went home to change. Later, we went downtown. Tony had lots of money. He was a waiter at the restaurant. Everybody loved Tony, and they tipped him like crazy! That's how he bought the purple Caddy. He went to school with all kinds of girls hanging from the car. My brother was handsome. And he was a sharp dresser. While everybody was having their draped pants made at Charlie Baker's or Seeburg's. We made ours at Chippewa Pants Shop."

Russell reflects on the attire of the young Italian guys in the old neighborhood, "Everybody dressed beautifully," he says.

"You went to the pool room before going to the movies at the Commodore show. We looked terrific, like we stepped out of the movie, Guys and Dolls. Everybody had those crazy, 'zoot-suiters.' I remember Tony Lunghino. When he was older, he owned The Billboard, a strip club on Washington Street, but when he was a kid, he got thrown out of Grover Cleveland High School, and went right away to Kensington. The worst thing I ever did was to make friends with him, because, coming from the West Side, he dressed really bad. His drapes were crazy. Nuts! I never saw anything like it! He must have had a twelve-inch bottom and a forty-inch knee. And he had a big chain that hung from his pocket that you could put under your tires in the winter."

THE BUSINESS OF LIFE

It's 9 am in Russell Salvatore's Grand Hotel on Transit Road in Williamsville, NY. This writer, dressed casually, meets the gracious Russell. He resembles an impeccable Ralph Lauren model, as he greets guests who arrive for one of his wonderful breakfasts. A young man approaches Russell:

"Mr. Salvatore?" "Sir, I am from Columbus, Ohio. I work for a company in Tennessee that sends me all over the world on business. I've stayed in many major hotels; yours is truly one of the best, and so are your employees, and your fabulous food! I was in your dining room last night and I couldn't help overhearing that story about the disagreement with your brother over the water glasses.'" Russell says, "Well, when you're in business, no matter who you're with, everybody's going to have a little scuffle now and then, especially in the restaurant business. A business that I love."

As a youth, Russell Salvatore had no fondness for the restaurant business. He was going to high school. "I am naturally from Italian descent," he says. "And being Italian, you know, you always had to pay attention to your older brother. In the 50s, when brother Tony, who was three years older than me, was drafted, I left high school to help my father run the corner saloon on East Delavan. Well, that was the start of my falling in love with the restaurant business. I ran the place. I didn't have to worry about my big brother knocking me around, hitting me on the head and saying, 'Why are you doing it that way?

Don't do that! Do this!' So anyway, when my brother went into the service, we had the restaurant going on Delavan, which was a very successful business. And I went in there and put in a lot of tables to make it look more like a dining room place instead of a pizza, spaghetti, and meatball joint, you know? I went in and put tablecloths on those tables. And instead of paper napkins, I put linen napkins on them. I figured that if anyone eats pizza, they're gonna use, at least, three paper napkins. That was a penny apiece, so it was three cents. But if you gave them a linen napkin, they only used one, and that was only a penny and a half.

Russell laughs and says, "And that was, you know, a savings. I was a penny and a half to the good. I was always looking at things like that. I used to, you know, watch the ends, I went out and bought beautiful water glasses for the tables, because, if you remember, years ago, you'd go to Deco, you'd go to Your Host, the first thing they'd do is hit you with a glass of water."

Reflecting on those days in the 50s and 60s, Russell said, "I remember when my brother got discharged. He came into the restaurant, and he saw all the changes. Holy cow! I thought a war broke out."

My brother Tony became upset at the changes that were made to the restaurant, questioning the changes: "Who put all this stuff here? What is this? An excited Russell told his brother that he went so far and told his brother that he went as far as to get a Lazy Susan. "Tony, you put the pizza on it and then you put it on a little plate and eat it with a fork and knife. Eating pizza in a classy style! We're the first to do it!"

Tony saw the water-filled glasses, saying: "Why are you putting water on the table? Take the water off the tables. They won't drink beer." Russell responded: "Tony, they will drink beer!" Tony quickly countered: "No they won't!" Russell asserted himself again, saying: "Yes, they will!"

A noisy, physical scuffle ensued. Mr. Salvatore, who was in the kitchen scraping tomato paste from a can, ran out to separate his sons. He sat them down, saying: "Tony, when your brother works, they get water. When you work, they don't get water."

After that, Russell and Tony worked every other night. "There's nothing like being your own boss!" affirmed Russell.

PATRIOTS AND HEROES PARK

We have seen the rise of a pastoral gem in a suburban setting, a slice of soothing parkland in our everyday lives. Across from his Grand Hotel, Russell Salvatore has dedicated his Patriots and Heroes Park to immortalize fallen veterans, first responders, and those who perished on 9-11 and in the ill-fated flight 3407 on February 12, 2009. Eminent sculptor, Donald Parrino, Russell's longtime, visionary friend, will create a stunning fifteen-foot statue of Michael the Archangel, the patron saint of law enforcement. When completed, the work of art will stand between the 9-11 Memorial and that of Flight 3407. Patriots and Heroes Park is a gesture of love and appreciation from Russell Salvatore to the grieving families, and a gift to his beloved community.

Originally, Russell wanted to build a shopping plaza here. He was granted approval by the Lancaster Town Board and secured the financing. Two days later, Russell woke up and a voice asked him, "are you crazy?" "Another business?" He remembered his friend, Charlie Ciotta, suggesting that he should build a park dedicated to the Veterans.

He returned to the Board, and he said he had changed his mind about the plaza and asked for permission to build a park in honor of America's fallen heroes and patriots. The Board said in disbelief, "You want to build a park on one of the most valuable pieces of property on Transit Road?" Russell said, "Yes." Permission was granted. One day, he called the necessary craftsmen, tradesmen, and landscapers and said, "This park is for the people to enjoy and to reflect. I want them to know it will always be there, complete with a 30' X 60' American flag flying above it."

It's snowing lightly on Transit Road. Russell looks out a window and reflects, "Don Parrino designed and made those beautiful statues in my park. The 3407 sculpture was a piece of steel no more than two feet long, and he soldered it together and together and together. What about the 911 Memorial? Don made that by hand. Every statue that's out there, Don Parrino did it. There are little pieces out there that come from Ground Zero. Don is responsible for my Michelangelo. It's wonderful to see how he starts his work. When he gets into a project, there's no stopping him. He works in his garage, you know. You should see him draw. I will never forget the day I hired him. He comes to Salvatore's Gardens, and I say, 'let's do something out here, something unusual' and he says, 'Okay, let's build Rome,' and I said, "what are you talking about? What do you mean, let's build Rome?'"

At the time, Russell was adding another small room where he put an additional eight tables. Instead, he went out 20 feet, and that's when Don Parrino started building Rome.

"There were all these little buildings made from wood. He had St. Peter's Cathedral, the Colosseum…but then, I don't see Don for about a week. I called him, 'Don, where are you? What are you doing? Don laughs, 'I'm building Rome for you.'"

Reflecting on that time, "I went to his home. There he is with a 4 X 8 plywood, and he's soaking it in water to get it so he could bend it into the shape of a dome on Saint Peter's Cathedral. That was the start of my success at Salvatore's Italian Gardens. People were coming in, saying, 'we want to sit in the Roman Gardens.' Others came to take pictures. It was gorgeous. After we built Rome, we put on another addition, and we built the Chariot Room. Later, built a life-size horse – all out of plaster. Then, we added another room and ended up with a museum. I remember other craftsmen that I had hired; I'd say I need a rendering of something. And they'd say, 'I need sixty to ninety days.' Don? You tell him what you want and in one night, he's got it. Because of that talent, that's why Buffalo has this beautiful park."

BUFFALO'S SAM NOTO: A WORLD-CLASS JAZZ TRUMPET VIRTUOSO

Sam Noto is a world-class jazz trumpeter virtuoso that grew up during the Depression on the Lower West Side in Buffalo (Courtesy of jazzbuffalo.org).

By Al Bruno
La Gazzetta Italiana
February 2022

Editor's Note in Italian (italicized):
L'articolo tratta della vita di Sam Noto, un italo-americano famoso per la sua musica jazz. Noto e nato dopo La Grande Depressione negli Stati Uniti. I suoi genitori non lavorano durante la Depressione; dunque, era per lo più povero. Sam voleva suonare la tromba ma non aveva i soldi per comprarla. Con l'aiuto di un professore, lui ha avuto l'opportunità di noleggiare una tromba. E questo era l'inizio del suo successo come musicista jazz. Noto suonava per molte bande a Buffalo, Las Vegas, e Toronto. Aveva ed ancora ha grande fama per il suo talento. Oggi, lui suona ancora in una quintetto a Buffalo. Abita con la sua famiglia in Canada.

ADAPTING AND SURVIVING the unforeseeable trials and tribulations of the Great Depression in the 1930s and early 1940s were painful and disheartening for all that experienced it; in spite of these horrible economic times, Buffalo born-and-bred, first-generation Italian America Sam Noto persevered and never gave up on his dream to become a jazz trumpet player.

Everyone, including his family, thought trumpeting was literally and figuratively "his pipe dream," but Noto's burning desire to succeed motivated him to eventually achieve recognition as a world-class jazz trumpet virtuoso, "bravissimo."

"When it comes to jazz trumpet players, one man's achievements eclipses them all. Like a rare and seldom-seen comet, a jazz trumpet virtuoso like Sam Noto could only burst upon the Buffalo music scene once in a couple of centuries," writes Phil Nyhuis of Jazz Giants. "It's his passion, that unquenchable fire, plus a high level of technical skill and musicality that set Sam apart and can be heard on the many recordings he made over nearly 50 years as one of the world's leading jazz players."

In his biography, Sam Noto: A Life in Jazz, author Joey Giambra assesses the musical passion and contribution of Noto this way: "What Sam Noto has done with his life, and the love he had for what he did, defies description. This was, and still is, a musically philosophical and contemplative artist of the highest order who since his early youth has nourished his soul with his music, and to this, continues to do so."

Remarkably it seems, Noto beat almost insurmountable odds against him, thankfully for him and his family, but there were trying times during the Great Depression that took its toll on Noto and his family; Noto painfully and vividly recalls the effects:

"My father lost his construction job and unable to find another, he couldn't make the car payments and it was repossessed; they came and took it away. That was a sad thing for my father and for us kids, too. My father was unhappy, as were millions of others who couldn't find work. Lacking income, we went on welfare. We couldn't pay the rent, we didn't have food, the whole thing. I knew lots of families from the Lower West Side went through that," writes Noto.

Life during the Great Depression was hard on everyone, no one was exempt. The Notos toted a wagon to the welfare building downtown to get food: chunks of cheese, flour, butter, and all those necessities came from the welfare authorities.

Noto was born on the Lower West Side at 69 Busti Avenue on April 17, 1930; he was the third of five children (three boys, two girls) of Italian immigrants, Louis and Santina Noto from Sutera, Sicily, who originally immigrated to Birmingham, Alabama, in the early 1920s, yearning for a better life in the New World like millions of other Italians looking for the land of opportunity and freedom they heard so much of in sunny Italy.

Louis worked as a coal miner and stocked furnaces at a factory in Birmingham, adapting to a dreadful work life and lamenting: Where was the American Dream they had hoped for before leaving Sicily?

"Those early welfare years on the Lower West Side were rough ones. That's all we knew. We were kids who played in the street and had a good time, but my parents were hurting because they couldn't do right by us. My father was always bugged; angry because of work situation," writes Noto.

The Notos moved to Seventh Street and everyday life was trying and gut-wrenching, a reflection of the desperate economic times, but we certainly know that kids will always be kids, and sometimes that means engaging in expedient things, both misguided and wrongful:

"We'd raid neighborhood fruit trees, and people with shovels would chase us. Then, if the people whose fruit we stole saw us on the street and recognized us, they told our parents. So when we got home, your father would give you a whipping for stealing. But we, me included, we'd never learn. We'd go back and do it again. We lacked material things – bikes, nothing with which to play," recalls Noto. "When the delivery guy brought doughnuts to a store one of us would keep an eye on him, while outside others would raid the truck. Later, we'd eat doughnuts till we were sick to our stomachs."

Noto decided he wanted to play the trumpet, but his parents could not afford the cost of $89 for a brand new trumpet; he was able to rent one from the school for $2 instead. "The whole trumpet thing had to start when I entered Buffalo Public School #76. I was about twelve years old, my first year in the band with Mr. Bish. I did that and practiced and practiced until graduating in 1944," writes Noto.

"Mr. Weis, my high school music teacher, wrote a solo for me. I practiced, practiced, and practiced, and when I played it at the rehearsal I knocked everybody out. Then, I began changing the solo, a little, a little there, putting different notes, creating my own melody, and that's when I began learning about chords, chord symbols, and different scales."

After graduating from School 76, his parents and his older brother, Bill, did not want Sam to pursue his trumpeting. However, Sam wanted to go to Grover Cleveland High School or Hutchinson Technical High School to take advantage of its music program; he was overruled by his family.

"His brother, Bill, decided he should go to a vocational school and study printing, so he would have something to fall back on. Sam told them, 'I want to be a musician, a trumpet player.' His father agreed with Bill. So, Sam went to Burgard Vocational on Kenmore Avenue to take up printing, but he still played his trumpet," writes Giambra. So much so that he was considered a "nerd" by other students because he would play his trumpet on the bus.

Noto started playing locally and at school events, gaining some publicity and momentum. He was given an unexpected opportunity to showcase his trumpeting, and young Noto took it:

"At 16, Sam left the linotype printing program at Burgard High School and went on the road with Allen Craig, a bandleader from Chicago, who fronted a typical commercial dance band. With his mother crying and his Sicilian father scowling, Sam and fellow trumpeter Al Bonati caught a train to Richmond where they joined the band and made $55 a week. The boys had to cover their hotel expenses of $1.50 a night. After the bandleader left with the girl singer and with two weeks of payroll, the stranded lads worked their way back home (Buffalo) to father Noto's 'I told you so,'" writes Nyhuis.

The next couple of years in Noto' life were spent hanging out in Buffalo going to jam sessions, sitting in, and honing his skills at Banny's on Niagara Street and other spots. Sunday afternoons were spent on Broadway and Michigan jamming at the Colored Musicians Local.

"Noto was learning more and more: tunes and chord changes that he'd apply to his playing style. He was happy to hone his skills and played any gig he could get, such as dances and casuals," writes Giambra.

Fast-forwarding to 1952, Noto was gaining artistic momentum in Buffalo: He then began traveling with big bands and playing at gigs and then to large jazz audiences, and ambitiously looking for that big breakthrough opportunity. It happened that year. Noto was invited to play full-time and travel with the Stan Kenton band, providing the long awaited opportunity to be the lead trumpeter and do some memorable soloist performances.

Here is Noto's short biography, his journey to jazz trumpet greatness, courtesy of the Canadian Jazz Archives organization:

"Reputed as an excellent bop soloist, Sam Noto has worked throughout North America with some of the biggest names and best bands in jazz, including Charlie Parker, Dizzy Gillespie, Buddy Rich, Red Rodney, Don Menza, Joe Romano, Larry Cavelli, Louie

Bellson, Kenny Shroyer, Frank Rossolino, Ed Leddy, Archie LeCoQue, Kent Larson, Joe "Red" Kelly, Phil Gilbert, Pearl Bailey, Bob Fitzpatrick, Bill Catalano, Jim Amlotte, Anita O'Day, Lennie Niehaus, Bud Shank, Bill Perkins, Bob McConnell, Mel Lewis, and Richie Kamuca.

"Noto became so proficient he was invited to join Stan Kenton's band as lead trumpet player while still in his early 20s. He played with Kenton full-time until 1958 and again in 1960 after a year-long stint touring Europe with Louie Bellson and Pearl Bailey in 1959. He was a member of the Count Basie Orchestra for two separate periods between 1964 and 1967.

"He worked primarily in Las Vegas after 1969 until relocating to Toronto in 1975. It was while working in Vegas he became acquainted with trumpeter Red Rodney who was influential in Noto's prolific recording career with Xanadu, producing four LP albums from 1975 to 1981 with the Don Schlitten's Xanadu label.

"While in Toronto, Noto quickly became a first-call studio player and was a member of Rob McConnell's 'the Boss Bass' for a number of years in the 80s. He also established his own successful groups including the Sam Noto Quintet, performing frequently on bandstands and concert stages throughout Toronto in the 90s and early 2000s." Noto, indeed, had finally achieved his dream and the overarching American Dream as well, "ancora, ancora."

Noto's connection to Toronto is well documented and he plays with his band in Toronto. Noto has a strong contingency of Buffalo fans, and he continues to play with his Buffalo quintet and rehearse with a big band at the Sportsmen's Tavern on Amherst Street. Nowadays, Noto lives with his family in Fort Erie, Canada, a stone's throw from the streets of Buffalo where he acquired his formative musicianship.

REMEMBERING FRANK A. SEDITA: SOJOURNING FROM "SHOESHINE BOY" TO ATTORNEY TO BUFFALO MAYOR

Former Buffalo Mayor Frank A. Sedita is pictured here in 1965 (Wikimedia.com, Google Art Project).

By Al Bruno
La Gazzetta Italiana,
January 2022

Editor's Note in Italian (italicized):
Frank Sedita fu eletto sindaco della città di Buffalo. Sedita iniziò la sua carriera in politica nel 1950, quando divenne giudice. Durante il suo mandato, il suo principale fu quello di aiutare I poveri a Buffalo. Per questo motivo, decise di ricoprire la carica di sindaco di Buffalo dal 1957 al 1961. Dal 1962 al 1965, non fu più sindaco perché ebbe un lavoro dal governo federale. Sedita, però, volle tornare al lavoro di sindaco. Perciò, fu rieletto sindaco di Buffalo dove mantenne tale posizione per molti anni. Purtroppo, morì nel 1975.

FRANK A. SEDITA was elected mayor of Buffalo for three, four-year terms. Now, five decades later, Sedita is still remembered by most for his openness, compassion, and perseverance.

After graduating from the University of Buffalo Law School during the Depression, Sedita would have many jobs over the next several decades: deputy sheriff, secretary of the division of water, city clerk, and then city court judge. Sedita was elected as a city court judge in 1950, and he saw the plight of the homeless and the alcoholic as he worked with them, assisting them with community resources and in seeking employment opportunities, unlike few before him.

Seven years later, Sedita resigned from his job on the city court bench on September 6, 1957, to pursue his first of three mayoral bids. He ran for mayor, a city with a population of 500,000 in 1957. He won a tough democratic primary and was elected by the slim margin in the mayoral general election over the republican nominee, Chester Kowal, on September 5, 1957, defeating him 72,266 to 72,206 votes, a total of 60 votes; Elmer F. Lux ran as an independent candidate and garnered 45,759 votes. It was only after re-canvassing the voting booths that Sedita was officially declared the winner.

Sedita's bid for re-election in 1961 failed, unfortunately; he lost the democratic primary, running as an independent candidate, and then lost to the republican nominee, Chester Kowal, whom he defeated in the mayoral general election in 1957. Kowal received 74,995 votes and finished well ahead of Sedita, who had 62,196 votes, and Manz had 51,899 votes. Kowal won 13 districts, Sedita 12, and Manz two. Kowal again had overwhelming margins of support in the Polish wards, but he also did better in all other areas of the city than he had done four years earlier.

In 1962, President John F. Kennedy appointed Sedita as the US customs collector for the port of Buffalo, a political appointment that he eventually vacated in 1965 to run for a second term as the Buffalo mayor. Then in 1965, Sedita came back politically with a roar, ran again, and was elected mayor for the second time, winning the democratic nomination and defeating Roland R. Benzow, a republican, in the mayoral general election.

At the 1966 democratic state convention, held In Buffalo's Memorial Auditorium, Sedita was nominated for the office of NYS Attorney General. He was defeated in the general election by Louis J. Lefkowitz. In June 1967, during a memorable Buffalo riot at the Michigan Avenue YMCA, Mayor Sedita faced an angry crowd of young African Americans during an East Side confrontation, and he managed to quell a potentially explosive demonstration.

His popularity ensued, and Sedita was again re-elected for a third, four-year term in 1969, winning by almost 20,000 votes over Alfreda, Slominski, a republican. He ran for Erie County Executive in 1971, but he was defeated by Edward Regan in the general election.

Because of declining health conditions, Sedita submitted a letter of resignation as mayor to the Buffalo Common Council in 1973, ending Sedita's political legacy in Buffalo.

History has assessed Sedita's leadership fairly for his public policies and laudable work while in office: He was a man ahead of his time with a vision for equality and opportunity for all, a courageous advocate for the oppressed. Sedita tackled the unimaginable at the time and dealt with intense racial inequalities that most Americans and politicians of that time would ignore until later times. He gained national notoriety by being the first mayor to endorse Senator Kennedy for president in 1960, a race Kennedy would narrowly win over republican Richard M. Nixon, the standing vice president.

As a promising youngster on Buffalo's Lower West Side, Sedita attended and graduated from Hutchinson Central Technical High School, and then he went on to graduate with a bachelor's degree from Canisius College and a law degree from the University of Buffalo.

Sedita was a first-generation Italian American and was born to Vincent and Josephine Sedita, Italian immigrant parents; he had a total of seven brothers and sisters, and they moved cross-country from New Orleans, Louisiana, when he five years old to Buffalo, the final family destination, where his family would settle and where he would create his opportunities in Buffalo government in the 1950s, 1960s, and early 1970s.

Young Sedita at age 10 was a hustler and an entrepreneur, while garnering good grades and working toward making his parents proud, eventually becoming an attorney in the Buffalo area. Sedita hawked newspapers and worked as a "shoeshine boy," hustling, in downtown Buffalo, a hop-skip-and-jump from his home on the Lower West Side. He would earn fast cash which he would hand over to his parents, and he was somehow able to save a significant amount of cash for himself, aiding him with tuition costs later on at Canisius College and the University of Buffalo.

In the summers between high school and college, he would dutifully sojourn with his family up to pick fruit at the apple and cherry orchards and vineyards in Wilson and Lyndonville, New York, canning fruit in factories, a tradition for Italian immigrants, dating back to their days when they would cultivate and harvest countless rows of vineyards in sunny Italy. Sedita was an ambitious youngster, and he learned the true meaning of hard work, discipline, and the importance of earning money for the family at a young age: That same focus, perseverance, and vision would arm him with a valuable skill set for success as a future, three-term mayor of Buffalo.

Sedita did what a lot of first-generation Italian Americans did to survive in the 1940s, 50s, and 60s: They were disciplined; they did those labor-intensive jobs that few wanted, envisioning a greater end game and working diligently toward those ends like Joe DiMaggio did by hawking newspapers and netting smelly fish and crabs, like Rocky Marciano did by working as a shoemaker in a factory and driving a coal truck, like Yogi Berra did by working in a brick and cement yard, and like Vince Lombardi did as a butcher and hauling 200 lb. slabs of beef in-and-out of refrigerated coolers all day long. They accepted their temporary grueling plight, vocational sojourners-in-action, grinding out those particularly "hard times" like their fathers/papas did and consistently modeled, day-after-day, never missing a day of work.

What they all had in common is that they were hard-working, first-generation Italian Americans, and they learned from their incredibly-focused, work-ready fathers, keeping their end dreams alive in their minds, determined, and persevering when non-Italians, referred to as gli Americani, folded and quit under the grind and duress: They made their Italian immigrant parents proud because they adapted, survived, and succeeded, realizing the American Dream because, above all, they became committed, young Italian leaders, trailblazers, and ambassadors of care for oppressed Italian immigrants, struggling with the intricacies of American culture and language.

They had to succeed and prosper because failure was unacceptable, and therefore, it was never an option for them: Failure meant personal and family disgrace, and they did not ever want to be dubbed, un disgraziato or un schifoso.

Sedita passed away on May 2, 1975; he was 67 years old. Sedita was survived by his widow, the former Sarah Vicanti, a daughter, Mrs. Samuel Campagna, a son, Frank Jr., who was the city's senior corporate counsel and later was a city court judge.

On December 14, 1987, Buffalo Public School #38 was honorably renamed as Frank A. Sedita Community School.

REMEMBERING DR. THOMAS LOMBARDO: BELOVED, BUFFALO WEST SIDE PEDIATRICIAN AND WORLD WAR II HERO

Captain Thomas A. Lombardo is pictured here as the battalion commander and medical chief officer, serving in the Philippines during World War II. (Permission from Dr. Thomas A. Lombardo, Jr.).

By Al Bruno
La Gazzetta Italiana
December 2021

Editor's Note in Italian (italicized):
Il Dott. Thomas A. Lombardo era un pediatra ben conosciuto nella sua comunità. Dopo aver servito durante la Seconda Guerra Mondiale, ha lavorato in Western New York. Giacche parla italiano, poteva comunicare con gli immigrati che abitavano in questa zona. Il Dott. Lombardo aveva un ufficio medico e visitava i suoi pazienti anche a casa. È andata in pensione dopo 36 anni di attività. E morto a 100 anni. L'eredità dell dott. Continuerà ad essere ricordata per lunga perché ha aiutato tante famiglie.

First-generation Italian American Thomas A. Lombardo, Sr., was one of the very best pediatricians, who gloriously returned from World War II as a decorated

Army captain, a Bronze Star hero, and then established a thriving medical practice, serving Buffalo's Lower West Side where he was born-and-bred for eventual leadership and care for others. Dr. Lombardo was beloved and appreciated by his patients; most of his patients in the 1950s, 60s, and 70s were of Italian descent: Italian immigrants, first and second generation Italian Americans, and beyond, and he was truly honored to serve them as their physician.

After his honorable discharge at the end of World War II, Dr. Lombardi completed his pediatric residency at E.J. Meyer Memorial Hospital in 1946, and he began his own practice at 305 Porter Avenue on the Lower West Side, the neighborhood where he grew up in and went to school and church. His practice soon became one of the largest in Western New York. In 1970, Dr. Lombardo moved his practice to Niagara Street, adjacent to Prospect Park, then moving for the last time to Allentown in 1975; Dr. Lombardo retired in 1982.

Dr. Lombardo had a kind demeanor and greeted his patients warmly, saying to mothers in Italian: Per piacere, non ti preoccupare, senora, le cose vanno più bene per tuo figlio/figlia. Dio provvede, which when translated, means: 'please don't worry, mam, everything is going to get better for your son/daughter. God provides.' He possessed a personal touch, an endearing and smiling Italian way about him, and many Italian mothers were certainly comforted with his care. Dr. Lombardo is still remembered for his bedside manner.

After seeing sick children and meeting with mothers all day in his office, he would uncommonly do house calls as well in the early evening; he was tireless, a dedicated caretaker, during the day and a minute man at night. One time, in the cold winter of 1965, he did a home visit to see me at our then address, 513 Prospect Avenue, on the Lower West Side; recalling the visit, Dr. Lombardo took my temperature, I had a fever, and he did an examination; he gave my mother an antibiotic to give me four- times-a-day and assured her and not to worry.

Before leaving, my mother kindly asked Dr. Lombardo to please sit down and enjoy some of her homemade fettuccine with red sauce and meatballs that she prepared for him: It was the gracious Italian way, paisano a paisano, un ringraziamento, which translates as countryman-to-countryman, a thanks or gift, and Dr. Lombardo warmly said, 'no thank you, I have to go.' My mother then began pleading with him in Italian, insisting he sit down, and try her homemade meatballs at least, and Dr. Lombardo relented, calmly sitting down, and he did the gracious Italian thing and ate two of my mother's meatballs, thanked her, and then becoming one of my mother's fondest memories on Prospect Avenue. She would retell the Dr. Lombardo story for years to family and friends, describing what "the Italian way" was like and why it was so endearing (in the mid-1960s) on the Lower West Side.

Importantly, prior to establishing his practice, Dr. Lombardo served in World War II from July 1, 1942, to December 31, 1945. While on active duty, he was called up to replace the medical officer who had been tragically killed by a sniper. Captain Lombardo was ready; he answered the call and dutifully arrived for service at the Pacific Theater of Operations, practicing medicine under the most rudimentary and humanly-trying conditions in the Philippines; he was assigned as battalion commander and medical chief officer in the artillery.

While on active duty, Dr. Lombardo witnessed a historic moment in the Philippines when his battalion landed on Luzon about the same as General Douglas MacArthur did, according to Lombardo's son, Dr. Thomas A. Lombardo, Jr., a physician (orthopedist) as well.

"He climbed down a rope from a large

onto a landing craft. He was standing when General MacArthur landed. The general apparently didn't like his first landing because it wasn't dramatic to be captured on film," retells Dr. Lombardo Jr. "So General MacArthur made them do it all over again. My father saw that."

Dr. Lombardo was the eldest son of Sicilian immigrants, and he was inspired to become a physician from their family physician, recalls Dr. Lombardo Jr.

"He was a family practice doctor who made a house call to my dad's home on School Street on the West Side. He was so impressed with my father's demeanor. The man asked him, 'How are your grades?' my father said: 'My grades are OK.' The doctor then said: 'They can't be OK. They have to be very good. You have to be on the honor roll in every grade, starting right now in grammar school,'" recalls Dr. Lombardo Jr.

That is all the advice that young Lombardo needed to hear, and those words of wisdom ignited not just a fire, rather an inferno, for academic achievement inside of him, bringing out his competitive best, fortunately for him and his family. That physician took a personal interest in him, following young Lombardo through high school and into college, mentoring and encouraging him every step of the way.

Lombardo's new vigor allowed him to graduate from Grover Cleveland High School and then Canisius College with honors; he graduated from Loyola University School of Medicine in 1941 and blossomed into the making of Dr. Lombardo, gracing his Italian immigrant parents and family and making them very proud, retells Dr. Lombardo Jr.

As a nine year old youngster, amazingly, in addition to eventually excelling in academic achievement, young Lombardo was a self-starter, an ambitious entrepreneur, and he earned significant cash by obtaining a paper route with the Buffalo Evening News. He and his younger brother, Phil, later added the Courier Express and the Buffalo Times to their route, which consisted of over 500 customers to whom they delivered the Sunday morning Courier Express. At the time, this was reported to be one of the largest, if not the largest paper route in the country," proudly retells Dr. Lombardo Jr.

"Eventually, he lost the paper route because somebody wrote into Everybody's Column, asking who has the largest paper route in Western New York? The Buffalo News looked it up, and it found out, oh my God, this kid has way too many papers; then, the Courier Express saw the Buffalo Evening News article and said, wait a minute; he works for us, too," jokingly retells Dr. Lombardo Jr.

The entrepreneurial, young Lombardo still managed to keep a very profitable paper route after that negative publicity, and the proceeds certainly helped to supplement the family's income during the Great Depression and helped pay tuition for both brothers to attend Canisius College, as well as aiding young Lombardo with future, medical school costs. True entrepreneurship.

The young Lombardo was certainly remarkable, and he learned the true meaning of hard work, discipline, and the importance of earning money for the family at a young age: That same focus, perseverance, and vision would arm him with a valuable skill set for imminent success as a highly-decorated, WWII Army captain and medical officer and more importantly, in total numbers served, as a beloved, West Side pediatrician who is still remembered today for his care and service for others.

After enjoying 25 years of retirement from medical practice, Dr. Lombardo passed on October 10, 2017; he was 100 years old.

In 1940, he married Lucia Salibene, who died young in 1952. The following year, Dr. Lombardo married Roslyn Viverto-Kaczmarski, with whom he traveled the world, visiting all seven continents together; she died in 2010.

Dr. Lombardo was a member of the Erie County Medical Society, American Medical Association, Buffalo Pediatrics Society, and the American Academy of Pediatrics. He was a certified member of the American Board of Pediatrics, and a staff member of Buffalo's Children's Hospital, Sisters of Charity Hospital, Erie County Medical Center, and Millard Fillmore Hospital.

Dr. Lombardo was the past president of E.J. Meyer Pediatric Alumni Association and was also on the faculty of the State University of New York at Buffalo School of Medicine; he was also a past president of the Romulus Club and the Bacelli Club.

Dr. Lombardo was survived by two daughters, Josephine Arnold and Frances Kraus; a son, Dr. Thomas A. Lombardo, Jr.; a stepson, Joseph P. Kacmarski; a brother, Anthony; seven grandchildren and 12 great grandchildren.

Remembering Mario G. DiCristofaro, Italian-Born Collision Shop Owner Who Could Fix Anything

Mario G. DiCristofaro could phenomenally fix anything mechanical. DiCristofaro came to America in 1960 and lived the American Dream. (Permission from Mario DiCristofaro, Jr.).

By Al Bruno
La Gazzetta Italiana
September 2023

Editor Note in Italian (italicized)
L'articolo descrive la vita di Mario DiCristofaro di Buffalo. DiCristofaro e nato a Pratola Peligna in Abruzzo. Da giovane, DiCristofaro lavora come meccanico di camion in Italia e Venezuela, imparo il mestiere di meccanico di elicotteri. Poco dopo che ritornò in Italia, conobbe sua moglie Rosa Sticca ed emigrano a Buffalo. DiCristofaro era un ottimo meccanico ed ebbe un'officina meccanica che diventò una grande attività. Purtroppo, è morto due anni fa, ma il nome è ricordato oggi per la sua officina ed il suo talent.

Mario G. DiCristofaro, who owned and operated an auto collision shop in Buffalo, died December 12, 2021, at Millard Fillmore Hospital in Amherst from complications due to covid-19. He was 89.

Born in Pratola Peligna in the Abruzzo region of central Italy, DiCristofaro's boyhood memories from World War II included diving into ditches for shelter, as low-flying German airplanes sprayed machine gun rounds and dropped bombs on innocent, hard-working Italian men and women, cultivating the farms and vineyards, heinously motivated, and detested by the Pratolani natives.

The family hid his father, Antonio DiCristofaro, from German troops who were rounding up local men for work camps, coercing them to work hard-labor tasks or face dire consequences of imprisonment, physical torture, and even execution for resisting the German oppressive demands. In fact, as a necessary precautionary measure, town residents would also hide their young daughters in the mountain caves when they learned that the soldiers had infiltrated the town.

After his town of Pratola was liberated, DiCristofaro began working as a mechanic at the age of 12 for his father, who established a trucking business with surplus vehicles he bought from the U.S. Army: an ingenious opportunity to acquire raw materials and spur business growth. Young DiCristofaro was imparted with the business acumen by Antonio, a forward-thinking entrepreneur and visionary in his small town (of Pratola Peligna).

During those early days, Italian fathers led the way with exemplary work habits, modeling vocational readiness and applications, while always striving for perfection; no short-cuts were ever allowed, and they were reminded with a warning: Sempre fai le cose giusti which is translated as: "You don't do things right once-in-a-while. You do things right all-the-time." This was a commonplace mantra articulated in most Italian households by fathers-to-sons on a regular basis. As a positive result, the sons learned all about hard work, toughness, commitment, and perseverance from their fathers. Vocational excellence was always the goal, and DiCristofaro intently absorbed those lessons and achieved an uncanny mechanical expertise, a blessing in effect: The mechanical torch was passed from one generation to the next.

When he was 16, he went to Caracas, Venezuela, with his father and brother Aldo, and stayed there; they returned to Italy a couple of years later. DiCristofaro trained as a helicopter mechanic and was employed by oil companies. He received several awards for his work. DiCristofaro was meticulously imparted specific mechanical skills, developing into a mechanical wizard, "a wiz kid," and delighting his proud father.

"They wouldn't fly a helicopter unless they knew Mario had fixed it," his son-in-law Joseph Ciminelli said.

DiCristofaro returned to his hometown in Italy in 1959 and worked again for his father's trucking company, but he didn't stay for long. A young woman from a neighboring town, Rose Sticca, who was working for New Era Cap in Buffalo, heard about him from her aunts.

"One of her aunts showed her his picture," Ciminelli said. "She went back and they met." It was love at first sight, and it was a match made in Heaven.

They were married in Pratola Peligna. Afterwards, she returned to Buffalo, while DiCristofaro waited in Italy for six months until his American citizenship papers were finalized. When he was able to join her in Buffalo in 1960, Ciminelli said, "There was a big party, a couple hundred people. The aunts did all the cooking."

The Italian aunts prepared a wonderful and abundant assortment of mouth-watering Italian lasagna, homemade meatballs, sausage, peppers and onions, minestrone soup, and tasty Italian pastries (cannoli, chiacchiere, sfogliatelli, and pizzelle) to 200-plus Italian family members and paisani in festive attendance. It was confirmed that the Italian aunts who prepared the delicious Italian meal included the venerable likes of Aunt Maria Buccilli (married to Pietro), Aunt Mary Buccilli (married to Alberto), and Aunt Regatta Buccilli (married to Antonio).

To recognize, Aunt Maria Buccilli wielded a natural flair for leadership in the kitchen and thus assumed the important role of Italian cuisine coordinator for this gala event honoring her beloved favorite nephew, Mario, thereby ensuring fine Italian food with authentic, old-country recipes: She absolutely loved to graciously serve her large Italian family, always smiling, showcasing her delicious Italian meals, and inviting all to eat more to their hearts' content. Aunt Maria Buccilli would repeatedly say: Mangia, mangia. Volete di piu? Translating it as: Eat, eat. Do you want more? There was plenty more that day, simmering on a hot stove, for those with hearty appetites.

DiCristofaro worked for six years for Laura Collision; then, he opened his own shop, Metropolitan Collision Service, located on Military Road near Kenmore Avenue in Buffalo in 1966. He brought his brother, Bruno, over from Italy to assist him and teamed up with his brother-in-law, Frank Sticca, to handle business matters.

Metropolitan Collision was the exclusive repair shop for Budget Car Rental here in Buffalo for 20 years. In fact, what DiCristofaro witnessed was his father's ingenuity during World War II, and he intuitively implemented the same business strategy with Budget Car Rental in Buffalo as his father had done with the surplus U.S. trucks and jeeps left behind by the American troops. Importantly, recognizing a scarcity of places to fix box trucks damaged in accidents, he built an addition to the shop that was tall enough to accommodate them: That structural improvement was key and enabled the American dream to become a reality for DiCristofaro, bettering himself and the future of his family.

"He took us back to Italy in the mid-1990s," Ciminelli said. An old, old man sees him and says, "This guy's a magician. He can fix anything. Somebody would throw out a riding lawnmower, and the next day he'd have it fixed up."

DiCristofaro also bought damaged limousines, Ciminelli added, repaired them and sold them to a local limousine service. He kept one of them, a Mercedes-Benz limousine van he acquired in Las Vegas, and used it to take his extended family on excursions.

"That's when he was happiest," Ciminelli said, "when we would all pile into the van and go out."

His son, Mario Jr., took over the operations in the repair shop after he retired in 1997, but he continued to work there, filling in for a sick employee as recently as last summer.

Dominic Buccilli, Mario's first cousin and an Italian immigrant as well, remembers growing up with the older Mario in their small town of Pratola Peligna in the Abruzzo region during the early 1950s and beyond. "He was always a very active guy, full of energy. Mario was incredibly passionate about his mechanical craft and very much wanted to be a success here (in America). He worked well into his late 80s, but he just wouldn't slow down."

Bruno DiCristofaro, Mario's younger brother who came over from Italy in 1966, praised Mario, saying: "I thank Mario for providing me and my family an opportunity for a better life in America. Mario showed a lot of courage, coming over to America and starting a collision business by himself. He is sorely missed by his family and friends."

DiCristofaro was a member of the Pratola Peligna Italian Club, the Lake Erie Italian Club, and St. Anthony of Padua Catholic Church. He built a bocce ball court behind his home in East Amherst.

In addition to his wife and son, survivors include two daughters, Susan Ciminelli and Lisa Rastelli; a sister, Josephine D'Andrea; his brother, Bruno; three grandchildren and two great-grandchildren.

The Importance of Italian Wine-Making

The beautiful vineyards of the Abruzzi, Italy region are pictured.

By Al Bruno
La Gazzetta Italiana,
June 2020

Editor's Note in Italian (italicized):
Quest'articolo parla dell'arte di fare il vino. L'autore parla della sua famiglia che sta facendo il vino nel XIX secolo in Italia, nella paesino di Pratola Peligna nella regione Abruzzo. Lui dice che non e una sorpresa che l'italia sia conosciuta per I suoi vini perché la nazione ha una una terra buonissima per le uve. Un vino molto famoso in tutto il mondo e Montepulciano d'Abruzzo. Lui quota Jennifer Muhawi, una giornalista che ha scritto del vino italiano. Muhawi dice che il vino era gran parte della vita dei romani antichi. I romani hanno scoperto I metodi per perfezionare il vino, pensando delle uve migliori, la terra giusta, e il processo per stagionare le uve. Adesso, il processo di fare il vino e molto importante per molti italiani. Ci sono tante persone che fanno il vino in casa con la loro famiglia. Attualmente, fare il vino connette le generazioni passate con il presente. Oggigiorno, la Francia riconosce i vini italiani come il vino superior. Questo è giustificato dal fatto che gli italiani sono I pionieri del vino.

The art of Italian wine-making is almost in my DNA, one could easily say. Wine-making dates way back in my Bruno family in sunny Italy in the early 1900s in the small, wine-producing town of Pratola Peligna in the province of L'Aquila in the Abruzzi region.

Their Abruzzi grape produce grew with abundance in, arguably, one of the most fertile valleys in the world, surrounded by the beauty of the hills and mountains; the run-off rain would funnel down into the valleys, moistening the enriched soil, thus sweetening the eventual, luscious grapes into the world's finest wines.

It is no wonder why sunny Italy produces more wine than any other country in the world: The rich, fertile vineyards prove it to be so to this very day. That is why Abruzzi was the homeland to their wine-making industry and way of life, sustaining their century-old tradition.

In fact, Abruzzi's highly-reputed wine, Montelpulciano d'Abruzzo, has earned a reputation as being one of the most widely-exported, classed wines since the late 20th century and presently in this new millennium.

Yes, it is true that the Italians were not the first to invent wine, surprisingly to most. In fact, during the 4000 to 3000 B.C. period, the Greeks brought the art of wine-making to Southern Italy and Sicily (Into Wine, 2007).

"The Romans enhanced the Greek presses used for extracting juices from grapes, increasing the yields, which became especially important as the demand for wine, naturally, as the population expanded," writes Jennifer Muhawi in the article, entitled: "Italian Wine: The Taste of History and Passion" in Into Wine (2007).

"Wine is also a very important part of everyday life, which is why Italians care so much to perfect the production process and quality of taste," writes Muhawi.

She adds, insightfully: "The Romans, with their appreciation for wine, drank it at every meal, experimented with various spices, and created wine with much higher alcohol content than ours today."

The Romans also discovered which grapes were best suited for certain climates (i.e. Chianti's Sangiovese, Barolo's Nebbiolo, Corvina, and Arneis). In fact, the Romans soon realized that aged wines attested better, using wood barrels and glass bottles with corks to store and distribute wine.

"It's not just Italy's history that makes it great, it's the passion they feel every hour of the day – for wine and for life," concludes Muhawi.

Home winemaking revives an Italian tradition. Daniel Pambianchi, writes about Italian winemaking in Accenti, "In years gone by, wine was part of the Italian culture and diet, like bread, pasta and homegrown tomatoes. Lunch simply would not be a meal without wine. Wine was simply part of daily life."

Pambianchi encourages the new breed of winemakers, prompting them to produce: "You can make great wines at home. Learn as much as you can by experimenting. You will be greatly rewarded with the excellent wine you make."

Important to note, within the last 50 years, there has been a surge of quality Italian wine that is considered the best of France, and the reason is due to what we like to call, "I pioneri," the pioneers.

The great Italian winemaking pioneers (and their families) include Antinori, makers of Tignanello; Allegrini, makers of Palazzo della Torre; Lunelli, makers of Prosecco; and Tasca d' Almerita, makers of Regaleali quality wines.

"These are the Italian winemakers, proud of their heritage and proud of their land, who dared to improve the stagnating Italian wine, while never losing their firm commitment to tradition," as quoted in Espresso (2014).

These pioneering winemakers were hugely instrumental in reclaiming Italian winemaking superiority and demand in our wine-loving world.

Winemaking is a Bruno Family Tradition

This is a picture of my papa, Elio Bruno, in 1957, bringing with him from Italy his love for and the Bruno family tradition of Italian winemaking to Buffalo's Lower West Side.

Al Bruno
La Gazzetta Italiana
July 2020

Editor's Note in Italian (italicized):
Il giornalista Al Bruno descrive il orgoglio per la produzione vinicola familiare. La sua famiglia originaria di Pratola Peligna, vicino L'Aquila, in Abruzzo. In questo articolo descrive la famiglia e la parentela. I suoi antenati ebbero le vigne e tutta la famiglia doveva lavorare nei vigneti. Quando il padre venne a Buffalo, New York, port oil talent e l'abilità per fare il vino abruzzese. Al fece il vino con su padre ma con il rimpianto che famiglia Bruno produce più vino.

Dating back to the early 1900s, the Bruno family was primarily concerned with well-maintained vineyards, producing fine wine for sale and for family consumption, subsisting on vegetables like tomatoes, corn, potatoes, onions, and green peppers grown on their other, non-vineyard farmlands.

My grandfather, Loredo Bruno, had five children (all deceased): three daughters, Annuncia, Calarice, and Lucia, and two sons, the older Antonio and the younger Liberato, my grandfather, "Nonno," and he was father to Elio Bruno, my father, "papa." My father had two older brothers, Giovanni (deceased), the eldest of all, and Cosimo (deceased), second son, and two sisters, the older Aquilina (still living) and the younger Silvia (still living); my grandmother, "Nonna," was Anna (deceased). We have numerous cousins living in Italy as well.

My father's family lived in town at 48 Via Pasubio, not more than three blocks from La Madonna Della Libera, the Catholic Church, in town in Pratola Peligna in the province of L'Aquila in the Abruzzi region.

The family home was a small, cement-block unit, with a kitchen and two tiny bedrooms, and connected to a 20-unit, block-long, housing complex, in effect. Furthermore, it was definitely crowded conditions for two parents and five children to endure in that small house, but they managed. The girls slept together and naturally separated them from where the boys slept; it all worked out, miraculously.

The street, Via Pasubio, was not really a street; it was an alleyway that separated these complexes, cement fortresses, on both sides, much like the vivid images portrayed in the Oscar-winning movie, "Godfather II," when Michael Corleone fled the US and was living, for a brief time, in Sicily, strolling through his old neighborhood with cement fortresses around him as well, locating his father's, locked-down home in astonishment.

They were built in the late 1800s, gray

housing monuments built for posterity, and the alleyway was only eight feet in width, barely fitting a small, compact vehicle through the tiny path. Those alleyways were originally built for horses and small carriages, at most, not cars.

The Bruno family home had a small basement, "la cantina," for winemaking and storage. Also, they owned a donkey and would raise a piglet each year for the slaughter and roast, with peppers and onions, for the Easter celebration: This was an annual tradition for the Bruno family.

By the end of October of every October, "Nonno" Bruno would produce an enormous vat of wine, 200 total cubic feet of wine, for sale and sustaining the economic needs of a family of seven in those early days in Italy. Agriculturally, the Bruno family owned four acres of farming land that they utilized for their vineyards, only. They owned a fifth acre that they exclusively designated to grow and harvest their own vegetables for subsistence.

My father would work the farmlands with his papa and two older brothers when it came to stripping old vines, weeding, plowing, and tilling the multitude of rows of vineyards on those four acres. Importantly, they would not forget about the importance of tending to their own acre for their vegetable yields. "Nonno" would deploy his three boys in the early morning on different acres, depending on what work was a priority, and sometimes together, especially at harvest time when they had to work and pick fast, or the produce would go bad and rot.

Winemaking was a community affair from its creation to its enjoyment. The Italian model called for winemaking and fruit production as well and everyone was involved, even the daughters and "Nonna" at harvest time, especially, according to papa.

The winemaking lessons that papa attentively learned in sunny Italy were on display here when he and other immigrant Italians and their first generation, Italian kids strictly maintained and followed the old country ways, adopting and making it part of their new Americana: Italian style.

"From canning garden grown and curing meats to home brewing wine and spirits, the first generation harvested and processed their food in the same manner they would in Italy," writes Melissa E. Marinaro in her article, entitled: "The Tradition of Winemaking in the Italian American Home."

It was a matter of all hands-on-deck as everyone had a role in the wine and fruit production. Marinaro writes: "Each generation of the family helped with food production in some way or another, and homemade wine was no exception." The operation was truly a cultural reflection of winemaking in Italy, and it was automatically established in America; the strength and inputs of Italian clans prompted winemaking in American cities, preserving Italian culture and tradition.

When papa joined mamma and me in May 1957, papa brought with him a bucketful of winemaking and fruit producing schemes and techniques he wanted to establish with Italian family and friends on Buffalo's Lower West Side. Papa discussed it with other Italian family members and other immigrant Italians, looking for the magic to reproduce the robust taste of Abruzzi fine wines in Italy.

There was always a raging debate over the best winemaking techniques and processes, especially in important, wine-drinking sessions, inviting Italian debate, "la ragione," the established truth: There was never a real consensus on wine, inviting more arguing, it seemed.

The winemaking we did was performed at our house at 513 Prospect Avenue on Buffalo's Lower West Side. Papa and I would go to the Clinton Street Market and buy 20 dark red and five white grape cases in late September and October in the early 1960s up and until 1975, when it suddenly ended for me; it was tradition to crush and process the grapes in the basement with mamma's help; sometimes a family relative would help.

The process was work, but it was fun because we were winemaking and the smell of crushed grapes had a pleasant, enticing aroma to me; it was culturally prideful, and it was easy to take it all in and just reflect Italian in everything we did, it seemed. When it came to winemaking, I did it all with papa, including hauling the cases of grape from the car down into the basement; typically, I soon became the primary crusher, and papa would do the grape pressing and funneling the grape juices into wooden barrels.

"Nearly everyone I speak with has a story about wine: loading and unloading boxes of grapes from a vehicle and crushing grapes with "Nonno;" betting glasses of wine on a Bocce game. It's a tradition recalled with fondness," remembers Marinaro. The stories are all different from family to family, but those winemaking times were more special and more memorable than we realized at the time we were winemaking as a family and as Italian people.

What once was an Italian tradition and trademark is no longer for the Bruno winemaking family, regrettably, not here in the US and not in Abruzzi where the winemaking originated and maintained for decades. What motivated me to write these two, related pieces on this great Italian tradition, winemaking?

This reporting insight would not be recorded here and described for posterity, if it weren't for the fact that a family member, living in America, is an already, recognized writer and journalist. Who, then, can certainly retell the family tradition and passion for winemaking than a winemaking relative of a small-time, wine-producing Nonno Liberato Bruno in Abruzzi, Italy – Al Bruno, a grandson, and a teacher, coach, and writer in Buffalo, NY.

The Connecticut Street Italian Festival of the Late 1970s: Cultural Images That no Longer Exist

By Al Bruno
La Gazzetta Italiana
January 2019

Editor's Note in Italian (italicized):
La promozione dei valori italiani del Vecchio Continente fu l'impulso nell'estate del 1976 per portare il Festival italiano su Connecticut Street, nel cuore dell storico quartiere italiano dell'Old West Side di Buffalo. Quattro giorni di celebrazioni prendono il via a luglio con una processione religiosa durante la quale una statua a grandezza naturale di Sant'Antonio con Gesù in braccio veniva trasportata su una piattaforma attraverso le gremite strade del quartiere. Praticamente tutti I venditori erano immigrati italiani o italo americani di prima generazione che vendevano deliziosi piatti italiani o oggetti importati, in clima gioioso creato dalla musica italiana dal vivo eseguita da artisti locali.

Buffalo's old West Side, the 1970s, remains indelibly etched in my childhood memories because it was a simple yet prosperous time in Buffalo's rich, cultural history. It represented a special time when the West Side resonated with an old-country, Italian cultural flavor that was prominent in everything we did in our daily living. Importantly, it was a socially-significant and progressive time when Italian Americans came together, galvanizing, sometimes by necessity, on the West Side to forge a new, American identity while collectively maintaining the proud cultural, vocational, and religious values instilled and experienced in sunny Italy.

Promoting old-country, Italian values was unveiled as the theme and impetus behind relocating the Italian Festival to Connecticut Street on the old West Side in the summer of 1976. Connecticut Street was strategically selected because it was located in the heart of Buffalo's, Italian American community. "We are trying to recapture the old St. Anthony tradition. We are trying to revive the old ways of bringing people together," announced then Chuck Griffasi, the 1976 event chairman. The Connecticut Street site certainly achieved that and much more. The Italian Festival was originally named "La Festa di San Antonio," in honor of Saint Anthony, of Padua, Italy. It was formerly celebrated in downtown Buffalo at St. Anthony's Catholic Church, on Court Street, with the festivities taking place in the Canal District, known as "The Hooks."

The four-day, Italian Festival was kicked off each July with a Catholic procession, elevating the beautifully-decorated, life-size statue of St. Anthony holding the baby, Jesus, on a platform (at shoulder height) on thick, wooden rails and supported by six strong Italian men (three on each side), who were honored to literally shoulder and proudly display San Antonio that day. In the crowd, you could hear the native Italians, repeatedly shouting, "Viva San Antonio," which translates as "Long live Saint Anthony."

The Connecticut Street Italian Festival was a small, quaint, and authentic celebration, and it had a distinct, Italian cultural imprint. Virtually all the vendors were Italian immigrants or first-generation Italian Americans, selling delicious Italian food and imported, Italian memorabilia. The mouth-watering aroma of grilled sausage, onions, and peppers was so inviting and permeated everywhere.

Live Italian music was performed by local artists, like Chuck Cardone, the barber, and ensued all day long, one band after another, it seemed. It featured the Italian dancers, games of chance, children's rides, the Ferris wheel, and much more. Then, the Italian Festival would crown its festival queen, who would graciously address the festival-goers in the Italian language: a cultural tradition that is no longer. The cultural uniqueness of the Italian Festival on Connecticut Street remains a special memory to me.

And I still yearn for that special time when being Italian, Italian pride, meant everything to me. It exuded through me in the way I thought, my family, the friends, the language, the religion, the food, and the music. Sometimes I wish I could go back to 1976 through a time tunnel, and for that one day, experience again those vivid, Italian cultural images proudly on display at the Connecticut Street Italian Festival. Admittedly, I don't think I will ever stop yearning for and reminiscing about that special time, the1970s, when Italian culture and pride was at a zenith and so tightly woven and expressed in our everyday activities and living contexts on the old West Side.

Buffalo's Old West Side of the Mid-1960s

For over 50 years from 1931 to the mid-1980s, Italian-born Emelino and Maria Rico, known affectionately as Papa and Mama Rico, hosted their AM radio show, Casa Rico, presenting the Neapolitan Serenade in Italian from their Seventh Street home on Buffalo's Lower West Side. Casa Rico was broadcasted and warmly received into Italian homes in Buffalo and Niagara Falls (Courtesy of Buffalo Stories archives).

By Al Bruno
La Gazzetta Italiana
November 2018

Editor's Note in Italian (italicized):
Quando I tempi cambiano, i costumi e le tradizioni che contraddistinguono una particolare cultura spessa scompaiono misteriosamente dai quartieri di una città e dalla nostra coscienza sociale. Nonostante ciò, non dovrebbero mai essere dimenticati. Questo e esattamente quello che e successo negli anni '60 nello storico quartiere italiano dell'Old West Side di Buffalo, dove gli ininterrotti eventi culturali hanno dato vita ad un periodo d'oro ed al contempo turbolento, contrassegnato da espressioni culturali, attività e temi memorabilia.

When times change, distinct cultural practices and traditions often mysteriously disappear from city neighborhoods and our social consciousness, but they should never be forgotten. That is exactly what happened here in Buffalo to the omnipresent, Italian cultural fixtures on the Old West Side during the mid-1960s: A golden yet turbulent time defined by memorable expressions, activities, and themes.

Born in Buffalo in 1957, my storied recollections reflect the mid-1960s where I was the only child of Italian immigrant parents from the Abruzzi region in Italy. I spoke Italian before I began to learn and speak English at my first school, Holy Angels, on Porter Avenue.

Here are three vivid images, Italian cultural nuggets from the Old West Side, that I witnessed and would like to share:

Who could ever forget the singing, Italian huckster, a grocer, who came by in the each morning in a box truck, "Amici Italiani, fresco fruita e vegetabli per tutti," shouting and singing loudly and proudly in Italian and marketing his fresh fruit and vegetables as he drove slowly down the street. Within moments, Mama and Zia Marietta would run to the Plymouth Avenue curb hurriedly, in curlers and in full nightgowns, waiting for the Italian huckster.

When he arrived, Mama and Zia Marietta would meticulously inspect and select the fresh produce, negotiating and even arguing in Italian. It was great drama, at times, as Zia Marietta worked her old-country magic to get good produce at a bargain price, "Ho fatto una buona compra oggi (I made a good buy today)," Zia Marietta would proudly say. Then, Mama and Zia Marietta would reach deep into their bras for the necessary greenbacks to complete the transaction. It was a lesson on bartering, the old-fashioned, Italian way.

Prospect Park, located across from Connecticut Street on Buffalo's West Side, was the rallying site for "morra" among the older Italian men. It was a cultural experience in Italian as the men intensely competed to win at the game of morra. Morra is usually played one-on-one or in teams of two and three, displaying fingers and sometimes dueling for hours.

In one instance at Prospect Park, I distinctly recall this large-and-tall, Italian man about 50 in age and balding, who always wore suspenders over his large belly. He had become notorious for his intense exhortations and could be heard from the other side of the park. In a heated and consuming morra contest, this large, Italian man became sweaty and red-faced: His eyeballs were bulging out of his skull, it seemed to me, as he shouted with fierce intensity: "cinque (five), sette (seven), nove (nine)!" until he won or lost. He was committed and fanatical about morra, using a loud, thundering voice, theatrics, and intimidation for pure effect and entertainment for the onlookers; and he hated to lose - you stayed away from him if he lost at morra that day.

On Saturday nights, my parents and I often went to the wrestling matches at Memorial Auditorium. cheering on Illio DiPaolo (from Abruzzo, Italy). We watched him flawlessly execute the airplane spin and pin his opponents to the delights of fans, especially those screaming, "Bravo Illio!" DiPaolo loved his fans, but had a deep love for his paisani, respectfully referring to most of his Italian friends as "compare." He was a gentle giant, an Italian icon locally and regionally, whose cultural identity and wrestling legacy lives on.

These Italian cultural nuggets were real, and they happened. I believe they still proudly resonate and are worth retelling for years to come.

LESSONS LEARNED FROM MAMA BRUNO

Mama Rosina Vittoria Bruno is pictured here with son, little Alberto "Al" Bruno, in 1962 at 116 Plymouth Avenue on Buffalo's Lower West Side.

By Al Bruno
La Gazzetta Italiana
July 2019

Born in Buffalo, NY, on February 15, 1957, my story, Albert Emidio Bruno, begins as the only child of Italian immigrants from the town of Pratola Peligna in the Abruzzo region in Italy, and I naturally spoke Italian before I began to learn and speak English at my first school, Holy Angels Catholic School on Porter Avenue. My early life was "everything Italian" and a very special time for me.

I had Puerto Rican friends who spoke Spanish to me, together with English and Italian, I truly benefited from the great multilingual and multicultural experiences on the West Side: ethnic treasures that I am forever grateful for. Here are several cultural lessons from the mid-1960s that I would like to discuss and share because they were the endearing words of Mama, and those words forever changed the rest of my life:

We lived on Prospect Avenue, next door to D'Youville College on Porter Avenue. I grew up admiring and cheering on Jack Kemp of the Buffalo Bills and Mickey Mantle of the New York Yankees.

Hall of Fame Wrestler Ilio DiPaolo was my local hero, a gentle Italian giant with huge hands and an infectious smile. Papa knew, loved, and exhorted on his famous, Abruzzese paisano on Saturday nights.

The three of us travelled to the old Memorial Auditorium in Buffalo to see DiPaolo outmuscle and outwork his wrestling foes; and for his closing act, he would powerfully hoist wrestlers onto his massive shoulders, whirling them, like a draining washing machine, into an uncontrollable, "airplane spin," his signature move, and then slamming and pinning his opposition for the victory.

The Italian American contingency would roar with delight, and I remember hearing: "Bravo Ilio! Forza a gli Italiani!" All the Italian Americans in attendance passionately identified with DiPaolo: After all, DiPaolo was one of their own and a DiPaolo victory was an Italian victory.

Senator Robert Kennedy seemed like he was everywhere and my Mama, Vittoria Rosina Pizzoferrato Bruno, loved him. My father, Elio Perrino Bruno, was a longtime steel worker for Bethlehem Steel in Lackawanna. Papa and Mama Bruno, a sewing machine operator, were inspirational to me and taught me many important lessons about life.

But one lesson in 1965 at age 8, I will never forget, profoundly affecting me the rest of my life. As a routine, Mama would often give me motherly love and encouragement when we were alone in the kitchen, while Mama stirred the tomato sauce, adding more finely chopped, garlic-and-onions every 15 minutes, it seemed; I would be diligently working on my math and phonics homework at the kitchen table because I still did not have a desk of my own desk yet, and I did not complain; we were poor, but I did not know or feel it.

Mama stressed to me in Italian, "Figlio mio, tu devi sapere che no tutti genti piacciono gli Italiani" which translates as "My son, you need to know that not everybody likes Italian people." Naturally, I was naive and shocked, innocently asking Mama, why are there people out there that do not like Italian people? After all, my life was everything Italian and almost everybody I knew was Italian.

To set the stage and landscape in the mid-1960s, Italians were still being shunned and even discriminated against because of their Italian cultural background; in fact, one of my best friends' last name was Benevenuto, and their grandfather (from Italy) changed their last name to Benton to mask his Italian culture, so he could secure union employment, a common practice back then.

Those first Italians were culturally prideful and absolutely detested not being able to acknowledge who they were, where they were from, and what was their cultural background.

To add further, Mama reassured me not to worry about anything and emphatically stressed to me that all I had to do to succeed in life, in essence, is make sure I go to college, get a degree, and work harder than "gli altri," the other guys. Mama would also say, stressing, "Fa di più di gli altri and fatte vuole bene," translating into the following: 'Albert, do more work (and be more diligent) than the others and make them love you.'

Mama was not well educated, completing only the 8th grade, but she was simple, to the point, profound, and right. Socially and for future, upward successes, Mama would remind me of this: "Vai con chi meglio di tu e fai i spessi," which meant 'befriend those that are better and more accomplished than you and even pay their expenses' to ensure your future successes.

Because of her promising words and vision for me, I was inspired to earn three MS degrees (and a BA degree), becoming a longtime special education and English teacher and published writer. Thank you Mama Bruno for giving me life, most importantly, a personal mantra and inspiration, and the old-country, culturally-instilled perseverance to become a difference-maker in America, forging my path to success.

Sometimes I wish I could go back to 1965 through a time tunnel, and for that one day, experience again those life lessons learned on Buffalo's old West Side. For me, Italian cultural, vocational, and religious traditions and practices guided my ambitious footsteps into a hopeful future. These memorable life lessons were real, they happened; importantly, they must be preserved, or they will be lost forever.

That is why I was inspired to write down my memorable thoughts, preparing my literary version of those old-country, Italian, life lessons that are no longer cited, voiced, and will be forgotten, unfortunately.

These anecdotal accounts refresh us, sometimes amusingly, on those important, Italian mantras: What we were given and prepared with by our Italian parents, using the best of old-country values to interpret, teach, and arm us for success in a progressive and future America. My hope is that these Italian cultural lessons continue to be delightfully revisited, discussed, and retold for years to come.

Immediately Remove Carl Paladino

By Al Bruno,
Artvoice
August 6, 2017

Morally and philosophically speaking, how can Carl Paladino be permitted to continue as a wounded-duck member of the Buffalo Board of Education? Simply explained, Paladino can because he is protected by the first amendment right of free speech, no matter how racially-offensive and warp-minded his toxic, published spew in Art Voice was, shockingly, to virtually all in Western New York.

His unexplainable and disgraceful public utterances are unforgivable for anyone, especially an elected, city official.

His offensive speech clearly violates the decorum that is expected of a city official and to note, a highly-educated, Syracuse law school and St. Bonaventure University graduate, who represents all public school children in Buffalo: A great honor that has been stained irreparably by his arrogance and lack of moral judgment. And now he is running for cover, asking for protection, even forgiveness, for his wrongful, disturbing comments.

It is now a case of too little, too late, Carlo, who is the prize son of hard-working, Italian immigrant parents, bred in South Buffalo's Lovejoy community, and provided with all the Catholic-school training and private opportunities to learn the true meaning of respect, knowing the difference between right from wrong. It is simply inexcusable, given his background, privilege, and substantial resources along-the-way.

The Paladino distractions have annoyed almost all the teachers and even infuriated some. The teachers want him removed immediately, and they have organized and continue to mobilize and demonstrate at rallies at city hall.

We should remember that former BMHA Director Joseph Mascia was charged with a racist tirade, caught on audiotape, and was removed by Mayor Byron Brown. Mayor Brown's ruling is equally applicable to Paladino's case and his fall from grace.

Why then is Paladino protected by the first amendment's right of freedom of speech and Mascia is not? The two cases are really similar, racially-offensive, and politically divisive. They are both city officials and serve the same constituencies, and they have both broken the golden rules of public servitude – decorum and officialdom.

Maybe Mayor Byron Brown needs to intervene here but he cannot. It's technically up to NY Education Commissioner Mary Ellen Elia to do what is right here. She needs to be consistent with Paladino as well and issue an executive order to rid us all of Paladino's antics and tirades like Mascia was by Mayor Brown last month: What is good and right for one city official is also certainly good and right for another city official. It's time to make it two-for-two, and please send Paladino packing permanently, Commissioner Elia.

Let's get focused on the real issues and the business of education like improving existing programs and continuing the notable work in broadening the learning and recreational opportunities for Buffalo students and their families during after-school and on weekends.

FBI Arrests Italian Immigrant Suspect in Extortion Letter to Bruno Family

Rosina Vittoria Bruno and son Albert, age 10 in 1967, were photographed here for a passport. They were escaping Buffalo and planned to hide in the mountains of Abruzzi, Italy, fearing the Mafia threat from the extortion letter. Take notice of the sullen and scared facial expression of Vittoria; she and her family's lives were being threatened and traumatized. For his protection, Albert was never informed of the threat and was only told that the family was going on a short vacation to Italy.

By Al Bruno

La Lettera Estorsione in 1967

A West Side man was arrested Tuesday by the FBI agents and accused of attempting to extort $10,000 from another West Side family by threatening them with the action of the "Black Hand" society.

Arrested at the Bethlehem Steel Corporation Plant in Lackawanna where he works, was Antonio Buccilli, 47, of 92 Plymouth Avenue. Buccilli was charged under the extortion law statute with causing delivery of a letter threatening to kidnap and injure a member of the family of Mr. and Mrs. Elio Bruno, formerly of 513 Prospect Avenue.

The Brunos, distant relatives of Buccillis, have a 10-year old son, Albert. The families frequently interacted together, and Albert was friends with Antonio's younger son, Michael; Albert and Michael would play together all-the-time.

Albert was a fifth grade student at Holy Angels School on Porter Avenue. The principal and teachers were alarmed at the threat on young Albert's life and were instructed by the FBI not to let Albert out of their sight and not to allow anyone but his parents to pick him up from school. Albert was unknowingly and closely followed in his daily walk down Porter Avenue by an assigned, FBI car unit to-and-from Holy Angels School each day, as a precautionary measure by FBI agents.

Large Sum of Money Caused Fierce Jealousy and Family Discord, Targeting Bruno Family

Neil J. Welch, FBI special agent in charge here in Buffalo, said the letter advised Bruno that he was known he had acquired "a large sum of money" recently; that large sum was later specified to be $50,000. Bruno had sold his Prospect Avenue home to D'Youville College, along with other homeowners on Prospect and Fargo Avenues, south of Porter Avenue. Since 1965, D'Youville College has aggressively sought to expand its campus territory on surrounding streets to add more academic centers and dormitories.

The typewritten letter directed Bruno to take $10,000 to LaSalle Park, locating and delivering it to a black-and-white, 1967 Oldsmobile there and instructed in Italian: "Passerai vicino al caro butterai la busta con dieci mila dolari e sarai al sicuro," Translated into English, it means: "Place the envelope with $10,000 into the car and that should be a certainty."

And further, it warns in Italian that on September 18, 1967: "Si no abbiamo trovate niente nel caro, qualcuno della famiglia scoprirà. Visequiremo dove andate." Translating it, it means: "If we don't find the envelope in the car, one of the family will perish. We are watching wherever you go." The letter was signed "The Mafia" and contained a representation of a hand formed out of typewritten capital letters.

What an evil and threatening letter the Bruno family had to unfortunately experience because they legitimately found "una fortuna" in America. Antonio Buccilli's nervous unrest with jealousy and pride, two of the seven deadly sins, succumbed him to do something evil and illegal to Elio Bruno, the Catholic confirmation sponsor, "compare," to Antonio's oldest son, Rocco, irreparably tearing apart the two families forever. Unspeakable trauma.

Recalling the incident, Welch said the FBI tactical team met at the Bruno's apartment on Busti Avenue to go over the details of the LaSalle Park meeting that most dangerous night, Monday, September 18, 1967, with Elio and Rosina Vittoria Bruno; Albert was taken to a relative's home and was never informed of anything regarding the extortion threat, again as directed by the FBI. "I never seen so many guns and rifles in my life (on my kitchen table). I was really scared for my husband, Elio," painfully remembered Rosina Vittoria Bruno.

Welch said the meeting in the park was supposed to have taken place Monday night, but that it did not actually take place. Bruno nervously circled the entire, oval-shaped, entrance and exit roads of LaSalle Park twice in his white, two-door, 1963 Chevrolet Belair with a sealed, white envelope containing counterfeit cash. He was accompanied by armed FBI agents, out-of-sight, hiding and curling under a blanket on the backseat floor, side-by-side, tightly-positioned, with a transmitting radio, communicating with other FBI tactical teammates, identifying themselves as "blanket" to others during the frequent radio operations that night.

They failed to locate the 1967 Oldsmobile they were instructed to look for, according to the letter details. Afterward, it was reported by Bruno's, West Side friend, Albert Scialfo, an established West Side attorney handling the case, that approximately 30 to 40 FBI agents were in plainclothes at LaSalle Park that dreadful night, anticipating armed conflict; fortunately for all, it never happened.

It was discovered, Welch said, that Buccilli was arrested the very next day, September 19, on the basis of some fingerprints discovered on the letter; Buccilli's fingerprints were on file with the U.S. Immigration Service; they were accessed, and it was confirmed. Importantly, it was investigated and later revealed that Buccilli had absolutely no connection with organized crime, acted alone, and admitted that he extorted Bruno and when asked why, bluntly saying in court, "I did it as a joke," With no prior arrests and a clean record, Buccilli was given probation at sentencing by the judge.

The Bruno family was up-in-arms after learning of the sentencing, given the emotional turmoil they had painfully suffered through, believing the Mafia was truly after them, living in constant fear. The Brunos recently applied for their passports and were planning to "escape back to Abruzzi, Italy, and hide in the caves of the mountains," Elio Bruno would later say. "We did not know what else to do. The Mafia does what it says it will do, I know that growing up in Italy. That's no joke, like Antonio Buccilli said to the judge."

Sadly, to make matters worse for the Bruno family, Rosina Vittoria Bruno was three months pregnant and had suffered through a miscarriage as a result of the trauma on her and her family. Her West Side physician, Dr. Joseph Ricotta, reported in a letter, dated October 10, 1967, to the court, "When examined by me on September 25, 1967, the patient had been in a state of extreme anxiety for approximately three to four weeks relative to a personal problem regarding an extortion attempt that had been made upon her family."

The "Black Hand" was a secret organization which preyed on newly-arrived immigrants to the United States in the earlier part of this century. Native Italians shared a grave fear of the "Black Hand," and in Italian, "La Mano Nera." Today, it is generally regarded as the Mafia or Cosa Nostra.

Assisting in the investigation and arrest was Sergeant Louis V. Tedesco of the Buffalo Police Special Fraud Squad. Welch said the offense carries a possible 10-year prison term and a fine of $5,000 as well, as appearing on the front page of the Buffalo Courier Express, a daily newspaper published in the AM, on September 20, 1967, under the headline, "FBI Grabs Suspect in Threat Try." Buccilli is pictured in handcuffs with the caption reading, "Antonio Buccilli…nabbed by the FBI."

Extremely Painful, Life-Threatening Experience for the Bruno Family

WKBW –TV, channel 7 in Buffalo, aired the story with videotape of the arrest, making it the lead story on the 6 pm news that evening with the venerable Irv Weinstein reporting the FBI arrest at Buccilli's workplace, the Bethlehem Steel Corporation. This was a day of huge relief for the Bruno family, and then sadness and tears ensued in total disbelief and wonderment.

"Dio mio, lui ha fatto per la gelosia," cried out Rosina Vittoria Bruno, translating it, it means: "My Lord, he did it out of jealousy." Her nephew, Dominic Buccilli, the son of Buccilli's older brother, Pietro, was physically overtaken with writhing pain and horror, uncontrollably contorting, collapsing-and-fainting twice from his chair onto the kitchen floor at his 116 Plymouth Avenue home, upon shockingly learning about the arrest of his endeared uncle, Zio Antonio.

For the chronicle and posterity, it was an extremely painful, life-threatening experience for the Bruno family that is still felt today: For justice and eternal truth, the Buccilli family has an enormity to account for to God for their evil and harmful, traumatizing deeds on earth. As a result of the trauma, the Bruno family irreparably lost a future son or daughter by miscarriage.

This heinous act will never be forgotten by the unfortunate souls who were preyed upon intentionally, forever innocent, and still alive, Elio and Albert Bruno, father-and-son, to retell the horror and unpunished oppression; sadly, before being deceased in 2009, Rosina Vittoria Bruno often lamented and was brought to agonizing tears, knowing she lost a very much wanted and beautiful child. Thankfully and in praise, the glory of God knows the truth about everyone and everything, as the Holy Bible clearly emphasizes to all. "Dio vede e provvede."Amen.

Al Bruno and Danielle Bruno experience elation after Danielle's law school graduation ceremony from Florida Coastal Law School on May 14, 2016.

About the Author

Al Bruno is a retired teacher and writer from the Buffalo, New York area. To summarize, Al has worked a total of 34 years in education: 25 in public education, four in higher education, and five in adult education. In addition to these teaching experiences, Al has experience as a head football and basketball coach for the Buffalo Public Schools.

Al has written and published numerous sets of articles on education, culture, and sports. In June 2020, Al published his first book in 2020 and revised it in 2021, entitled: *Buffalo Sports Headliners and Insights*. In addition to keen interest in sports reporting and publishing, Al has published scholarly articles about special education law, educational leadership, and adult learning workshops, focusing on parental participation and activism.

Born in Buffalo in 1957, Al is a first-generation, Italian American, whose parents are immigrant Italians from Abruzzi, Italy, grew up on the Lower West Side of Buffalo, and clearly has a strong interest in Italian language, history, and immigration, publishing articles in those areas and has published articles and features about the Italian sporting greats like Coach Vince Lombardi, Joe DiMaggio, Rocky Marciano, and Yogi Berra and many more. These published articles spurred the publication of Al's third Italian book, entitled: *17 Italian Greats in Sports and Italian Insights* in 2022, revising it last in 2023. In 2021, Al published his third book, *Education News, Research & Cultural Insights*.

Al is a retired, special education and English teacher for the Buffalo Public Schools. Academically, he has earned three MS degrees in student personnel administration, multidisciplinary studies, and educational administration and a BA in communications. He holds four NYS teaching certifications in special education, English, Spanish, and elementary education.

www.ingramcontent.com/pod-product-compliance
Lightning Source LLC
Chambersburg PA
CBHW080458110426
42742CB00017B/2923